Patriotism Against a Globalist Agenda

A CHANGING WORLD

To George & Paula
enjoy this knowledge

Love
Caroline

CÉSAR VIDAL

Original title: *Un mundo que cambia*

The Agustin Agency is a division of The Agustin Agency Services, LLC, and is a registered trademark.
www.theagustinagency.com

This book can be ordered in high volume as gifts, for fundraising events or for ministry or business training by writing to Sales@TheAgustinAgency.com.

For wholesale sales to bookstores, distributors or to resell, please contact the distributor Anchor Distributors at 1-800-444-4484.

Scripture quotations marked NKJV are from the New King James Version of the Bible, public domain.

Translation: TLM Editorial Services, Inc.
Interior Design: Deditorial.com
Photograph: Betty Graham
Cover Design: Chris Ward

ISBN: 978-1-950604-06-7 (Paper)
ISBN: 978-1-950604-07-4 (Ebook)

Printed in the United States of America.

20 21 22 23 BETHANY PRESS 9 8 7 6 5 4 3 2 1

CONTENTS

INTRODUCTION

On December 26, 1991, an event of extraordinary importance in universal history took place. It involved the dissolution of the Soviet Union, an event of enormous repercussions that almost no one had anticipated. In fact, only the historian Andrei Amalrik[1] and Nobel laureate and writer Alexander Solzhenitsyn,[2] two Russian dissidents, had enough courage and vision to forecast that such a seismic event would take place. To be honest, the reality is that the vast majority of analysts did not expect such an outcome. Professor Javier Tusell—in one of the most ludicrous records of Spanish academic history ever recorded—wrote just a few days before the collapse of the USSR that it would continue to be a reality during the next millennium and that even Communist Germany would surpass the West in a few years. It was an outlandish absurdity, but it certainly was not an isolated incidence. In fact, none of the intelligence agencies of the Western powers foresaw the collapse of the USSR...which does not say much about their effectiveness.

It was true that the repressive character of the Soviet model was already impossible to conceal. For example, the time had already passed when the existence of the network of concentration camps could

1. A. Amalrik, *Prosushchestvuyet li Sovietskii Soyuz do 1984 goda?* (Amsterdam, 1970).
2. A. Solzhenitsyn, *Pismó Vozhdyam sovietskogo soyuza* (París, 1974).

be blatantly denied. It was an obvious reality since 1917,[3] but it had exploded in the West's face with the publication *Gulag Archipelago* by Alexander Solzhenitsyn[4] in the early seventies of the twentieth century. No less obvious was the oligarchic character of its social structures, which not only did not especially favor workers and peasants—to quote a famous Soviet slogan—but, in fact, favored those whom the Russian Voslensky called the *Nomenklatura*, that is, an entire caste of privileged.[5] However, despite the network of concentration camps, the absence of freedoms, the injustice of a ruling class of party officials, and the comparative backwardness in economic terms, no one expected the demise of the Soviet dictatorship, and in a special way included the socialists as well as the communists from the left-wing worldwide.

The unexpected triumph of the Cold War—the United States and its allies really had not defeated the USSR; however, the USSR had undeniably lost—triggered a wave of extraordinary optimism. What had been longed for, but not predicted, had now become a rapid, accelerated, and bloodless reality. It is not surprising that Francis Fukuyama[6] set out to announce the end of history, an end that also implied the recognition, at the same time, of the capitalist system and democracy. After the demise of the USSR, one could only hope that the whole planet would accept both aspects in a way that was impossible to avoid. As the one who writes these lines, the reality, however, is that history did not come to an end. It did not come to pass because history never ends, but rather continues to march on. Other empires succeed others, some powers replace others, some cultures prevail

3. In this regard, the bibliography is very extensive, and we have included it in C. Vidal, *La revolución rusa. Un balance a cien años de distancia* (Buenos Aires, 2017). Of particular interest, in order to show that it was not a phenomenon known after the fact, see J. Baynac, *El terror bajo Lenin* (Barcelona, 1978) and G. Legget, *The Cheka. Lenin's Political Police* (New York, 1986), updated edition. A first literary approach to Soviet repression (1924) is found in Vladimir Zazubrin's *Su trilogía siberiana* (Madrid, 2015), a compiled collection of his novels *La astilla*, *La verdad pálida*, and *Vida en común*, which are mandatory reading.

4. There are different translations, not always complete, in different languages. We have used *Arjipielag GULAG* by Solzhenitsy (Moscow, 2015), the latest version of the great work revised by the author himself.

5. M. Voslensky, *La Nomenklatura* (Barcelona, 1981).

6. F. Fukuyama, *The End of History and the Last Man* (New York, 1992). In 2006, Fukuyama published a new edition with an additional epilogue, where he intended—with rather little success in our view—to try to continue defending his thesis almost a decade and a half later.

over others, but history continues its course and predictably will continue to do so until, in fact, the end of the ages.

In a repetition of the errors contained in the analysis of former times, although it is indisputable that the Cold War had come to an end, there are more than a few who intend to continue analyzing the current global situation from the perspective of a historical period that, indeed, already ended four decades ago. Claiming to understand the present with the paradigms of the Cold War—even to a large extent with those of the Left and Right—is a very serious mistake with consequences that are extremely harmful. History has continued to move forward, and just as it would have been foolish to claim to understand Europe at the end of the nineteenth century on the basis of what life was like for Napoleon, who was finally dethroned in 1815; it is absurd, and even ridiculous, to try to understand our world on the basis of what the Cold War entailed.

Our world has continued to change since 1991, and what is even more important is that this combination of changes is constant and involves colossal challenges that the human race has never had to face before. Far from democracy and freedom being two realities that seem to come about almost naturally, the fact is that they are more threatened than ever. And this threat is not only external but, to a large extent, also internal.

In the first part of the present work, we will take into account the analysis of democracy as a recent and often failed system, as well as consider the dangers that now threaten its very survival. The second part is devoted to the globalist agenda, which constitutes a real threat that seeks to destroy national sovereignty, the power of the States, and the democratic system itself. Finally, the third paints a global picture of how reactions are already perceived in light of this globalist agenda, although not all of them lead to a future of freedom, and, certainly, the human race runs a true and real risk of being subjected to totalitarian systems of various kinds.

Without the slightest desire to embrace an alarmist catastrophism, the author is convinced that we live in a decisive time in history, and not only because technological advances or population displacements have no parallel in the future of humanity. It is also because what is at stake is not only the expansion of the democratic system, but its consolidation in a generous number of nations and even its survival in others, including even the United States itself. This last circumstance is of enormous relevance worldwide, but it is also personal for the author of this work.

Seven years ago, I was forced to exile myself from my home country because I was informed that my life was in danger of being the target of a bomb attack. Although I had the possibility of going to different nations, and some of them even offered to grant me citizenship immediately, I never doubted that the right choice was the United States. I did so because I was totally convinced that it is a land historically characterized for basing itself on freedom, and because I strongly believe in the definition that Lincoln gave of it as "the last best hope of earth." Time has passed since then, and the one who now writes these lines is already a citizen of that great nation and feels deeply proud and grateful for it. Even more: in his heart he holds the conviction that the United States continues to be, today, the last best hope on earth, and that is why he has written this book. As long as the United States remains faithful to the worldview that laid its foundations even before its birth as a nation, there will be hope for freedom and prosperity for the rest of the globe. If, on the contrary, the battle for freedom is lost on American soil, the future of the planet will inevitably be tragic. The one to judge the validity of this assertion, and other theses, will, as always, be the reader.

Miami — Washington — Miami, winter of 2019-2020

PART I

THE UNCERTAIN FUTURE OF DEMOCRACY

CHAPTER I

DEMOCRACY, A NEW ARRIVAL IN HISTORY (I): The First Democratic Experience

Democracy, a New Arrival

Today, the idea of democracy is hardly discussed or opposed in most parts of the world. Although it remains a minority phenomenon, the fact remains that even dictatorships are eager to present themselves as democracies. There are exceptions, of course, such as China, North Korea, Cuba, or Saudi Arabia that do not even pretend to fake it, maintaining totalitarian structures with a certain degree of some freedom; however, generally speaking, discussing democracy is not considered acceptable. In the Islamic dictatorship of Iran, elections are held, and although these are limited by the Qur'an, which is saying a lot, they insist on pointing out the democratic character of the governments that have emerged from the ballot box. The situation can be even worse in nations in Asia, Africa, and America, where official democratic structures barely conceal dictatorial systems.

Even in the theoretical field, few authors dare to challenge democracy head-on.[1]

For many, this situation is considered even in a positive way. In light of this point of view, democracy would be a reality so indisputable and so irreversible that even dictatorships pay tribute to it and, sooner or later, will give way to its establishment in their respective countries. This analysis is understandable, but the reality is that it is profoundly mistaken. First, as we will see in this chapter, democracy is never irreversible nor established permanently. On the contrary, history tells us that between the first democracy, which failed, and the second one more than two millennia passed, a circumstance that should cause us to reflect upon. Secondly, the reasons for the disappearance of the first democracy do not establish the circumstances of the past but, in fact, continue to persist today and in a distressingly real way. Thirdly, democracy is a very recent phenomenon that has appeared in our history. Of course, it can be said that since the American Revolution of 1776, a multitude of nations have opted for democracy, but that statement simply does not correspond to reality. In fact, democracy has been greatly absent in the Islamic world, the Buddhist world, the animist world, and the Catholic world until just a few years ago. Even during the twenties and thirties of the twentieth century, the Vatican preferred an alliance with Mussolini's fascism and abandoned an incipient form of Catholic Christian democracy.[2] In fact, even decades after the Second Vatican Council, democracy has been a fragile and minority phenomenon in nations that are sociologically Catholic. On this basis, it is not surprising that democracy has been an exceptional phenomenon until very recently in most of Europe and Latin America, and virtually all of Africa and Asia. Finally, it should be noted that democracy has historically been linked to a very concrete worldview to which we will refer in the book as a whole. When that worldview does not exist or disappears, democracy easily becomes a dying phenomenon. However,

1. An exception would be Jason Brennan, *Against Democracy* (Princeton, 2016), which opposes the criterion of the effectiveness of democracy, something, by the way, that is very similar to what the Chinese government maintains.

2. In this regard, see: M. Gallo, *Mussolini's Italy* (New York, 1973), pp. 142ff.; pp. 179-80.

for now we are going to pause and take into account the first democracy in history and the reasons for its disappearance.

The Failure of the First Democracy in History

It is generally known that the first democracy in history emerged in Greece. To tell the truth, the same term comes from the Greek word, where *demos* means "people," and *kratia* means "power." Democracy would therefore be the form of government in which the people are the ones who hold the power and who are therefore opposed to the monarchy, the government of one, or to the oligarchy, the government of a few. Democracy was not, however, a reality throughout Greece. In fact, it was limited to Athens, a *polis*, or city-state, and did not even span its entire history.[3]

Athenian democracy began its journey in the fifth century BC and ended in the fourth century BC. In total, it did not even survive for two centuries, and, curiously, its end was predicted many years in advance by some of the most eminent minds in Greece. Why did Athenian democracy end? Why did it not return? Why did the judgment pronounced upon it continue to be negative among the most illustrious minds in Greece?

The reasons for the end of democracy are diverse and began to be described when democracy was still a reality. The first cause was what was called "popular blindness," which was caused by ignorance. As the great poet Pindar[4] pointed out: "The bigger the crowd, the more blind they are in their heart. The historian Plutarch, with a hint of bitterness, pointed out that in democracy, "although those who spoke

3. There are various analyses of the development and end of Greek democracy. Of particular interest are C. M. Bowra, *Periclean Athens* (London, 1971); C. Farrar, *The Origins of Democratic Thinking* (Cambridge, 1988); D. Kagan, *Pericles of Athens and the Birth of Democracy* (New York, 1991); L. M. Maciá Aparicio, *El estado ateniense como medelo clásico de la democracia* (Madrid, 1993); R. Osborne, *Demos: the Discovery of Classical Attica* (Cambridge, 1985); F. Rodríguez Adrados, *La democracia ateniense* (Madrid, 1998); *Idem*, *Historia de la democracia* (Madrid, 1997); J. de Romilly, *Problémes de la democratie grecque* (Paris, 1975).

4. Nemeas VII, 24.

were the most skilled, those who made the decisions were the ignorant."[5] Xenophon, or whoever went by that name, painfully affirmed in his *Constitution of the Athenians* that, in the end, those who held decisive power were not the best and most educated, but the most stupid and ignorant.[6]

That ignorance, if not stupidity, of the people made them an easy tool in the hands of unscrupulous politicians. The great Aristophanes, who had an ability to find humor in the most terrible of situations, demonstrated in his comedy *The Knights*[7] that, in the end, whoever led the people was not a person of decent morals or education, but rather a scoundrel for the simple reason that he was the most suitable person.

Euripides mentioned the ignorance of the people in his tragedy *The Suppliants*[8] as one of the reasons why the democratic system could not work. It was clearly absurd for ignorant people to make decisions on issues of enormous importance.

The second cause for the failure of democracy lay in the fact that the ignorance of the people was compounded by the ease with which they could be manipulated, a vulnerability that stemmed from their own desires. The way in which the Greek authors defined those negative desires varies, but it is always very significant. For example, Plutarch calls it *eros*,[9] the term from which we derive our word *eroticism*. In other words, it was as if saying that the people, far from controlling their passions, were dragged along by them like a sexual urge. As individuals, citizens might possess a certain degree of good judgment, but when taken as a whole, from the multitude, they possessed, according to Solon, "an empty mind,"[10] or, according to Aristophanes, they were "gaping like [they were] chewing dried figs."[11] With a society

5. Solón 5, 6.
6. *Constitution of the Athenians*, 1, 5.
7. *The Knights*, 178-93.
8. *The Suppliants*, 417-22.
9. *Pericles*, 20, 4; *Alcibiades*, 17, 2.
10. *Fragment*, 11, 5
11. *The Knights*, 751-55.

like that, who were ignorant and carried away by passions, Euripides stated that "you will be able to obtain what you wanted from them without any difficulty...for those who keep an eye out for opportunity cannot achieve a more valuable commodity."[12]

That kind of follow-up from sycophantic and promise-making politicians aimed at flattering the people would serve to greatly weaken freedom in Athens. At the end of the day, as the great speaker Demosthenes would point out, truthful speech was not tolerated, and freedom of speech was expelled from the arena of political debate.[13]

Of course, there were politicians—like Pericles—who had managed to guide the people and keep them on the path of wisdom and common good,[14] but that had not been the usual development of politics. To tell the truth, the politicians were looking to gain and maintain power on the basis of popular vote, and in order to achieve it, they did not seek to attain the common good for all, but to simply flatter the masses. It never ceases to seem strange that a character like the demagogue Cleonte took advantage of the anger—*orge*—of citizens,[15] and that made him the politician most listened to by the people.

Ignorance, vulgar passions, and demagogy all blended together so that the wishes of the citizens increased more and more.[16] What they expected from the elected rulers was not that they would rule well for the benefit of the community, but that they would be given more and more, they would be flattered more, and that their desires would be fulfilled more. After all was said and done, public offices were not occupied by the best candidates, but by those who had the most insolence to flatter the people and offer to satisfy their cravings. The result could not be good. As Euripides[17] pointed out, politicians, when addressing the people, "extolled and flattered them, and pulled them in every direction for their own interests. Today, they cause about

12. *Orestes*, 696-703.
13. *Demosthenes, Philippics III*, 4;1, 40.
14. *Peloponnesian War II*, 65, 9.
15. *Peloponnesian War III*, 36, 2.
16. *Peloponnesian War IV*, 17, 4; IV, 65, 4; VI, 11, 5.
17. *The Suppliants*, 411ff.

the people's delights, but tomorrow, they will cause their misfortune. Then, to hide their mistake, they would constantly slander, thus escaping any punishment."

Of course, the people were convinced that they were the ones who held the reins of politics, since they were being given what they wanted. A very different reality was captured by the comic playwright Aristophanes.[18] "Oh, people, how beautiful your government is. Everyone fears you like a tyrant. However, it is not difficult to lead you where you want to go. You like to be flattered and deceived. You are always listening to the charlatans who stand with their mouths open, and your spirit travels far without leaving home."

Other evils were added to the internal corruption into which the democratic system had fallen. The first was the intervention in the politics of other city states. Athens claimed the right to interfere in the progress of other political entities allegedly as a guarantor of democracy. That imperial impact caused the second evil: a growing military spending.[19] The feasibility that this was not sustainable was obvious to anyone who examined reality without prejudice, but, again, the demagogy of the rulers and the passions of the people combined so that war began to be considered as a profitable business by many Athenians. For those directly involved in the war, it became a source of significant economic benefits derived from the city states' budgets as well as the plundering of the attacked nations. But there were also sections of the population who received subsidies from the Athenian government related to military operations who saw it as a lucrative business. Few wanted to face the fact that the war entailed a huge cost to the system and that the bill, in the end, would have to be paid.

The picture of Athenian democracy is easy to imagine. Politicians had concluded that it was relatively easy to achieve and maintain power. All it took was to replace truth with flattery, competence with electoral promises, and good government with lies. The people,

18. *The Knights*, 1114-1120.
19. *Peloponnesian War* VI, 24, 3.

whose individual traits could be more or less sensible, reacted much less shrewdly on a mass scale by eagerly following the politicians who fawned over them. Of course, they did not think about the cost of fulfilling those electoral promises. They even foolishly supported the wars they had been convinced of by the moral superiority of Athens, wars from which they thought they could only derive benefits.

This combination of factors ended the Athenian democracy in the course of its confrontation with Sparta, another Greek state, which was not democratic but rather one of a totalitarian nature. In 399 BC, democracy had returned, but grounded on even weaker foundations. In fact, that same year, the Greek philosopher Socrates—the most decent man in Athens—was sentenced to death by a people's court. For his disciples Jenofonte[20] and Plato,[21] such an act proved to what extent democracy had proven to be an unfair and even foolish system. Socrates was ultimately executed because democracy was not willing to allow him to speak freely[22] as the *Criton* would point out in the dialogue that bears his name: "The majority is able to produce not the smallest evils, but precisely the greatest, if someone has incurred their hatred."[23] Certainly, the "politically correct view" was not a creation of the twentieth century.

If democracy considered true and honest men a threat, if it limited freedom of expression, if it was, in all reality, an exchange of interests between masses without moral principles who only were eager to receive power, and politicians dedicated to demagogy, it could not last much longer. In fact, well-known people such as Xenophon, Plato, and Aristotle considered its demise the best that could happen to it, because it was no more than another form of tyranny. The fifth century BC had not come to an end yet when the system disappeared, not to reemerge for centuries.

20. Xenophon would record his version of the condemnation and execution of Socrates in his *Apology of Socrates* and *Memoirs of Socrates*.

21. Plato recounts the episode in his *Apology* and in the *Criton*.

22. R. Waterfield, *Why Socrates Died* (New York, 2010), points out this aspect to the point of presenting Socrates as a scapegoat. Depending on the meaning given at the end, its assessment can be considered correct.

23. *Criton*, 44.

CHAPTER II

DEMOCRACY, A NEW ARRIVAL IN HISTORY (II): The Foundations of Modern Democracy

The Roots of Modern Democracy (I): The Reformation and the Supremacy of the Law

Democracy disappeared from Athens and, incidentally, disappeared from the world. Rome admired the brilliant Greece, but never had the slightest intention of imitating its democratic system. First, it was a monarchy. From there it became an oligarchy, called *res publica*, that is, a public institution, and finally, it went from a supposedly republican military dictatorship to an empire. The collapse of that empire, brought down by the inability to defend its borders and contain barbaric migrations, did not usher in democracy either. The West was filled with monarchies fighting each other and resisting successive invasions, of which the most dangerous were those driven by belief in Islam. In 1188, the first Parliamentary focus emerged in Spain, more specifically in the kingdom of León, thanks to the Magna Carta Leonesa. However, it was short-lived and cannot be described as democratic. Neither was the later English Magna Carta of 1215, which restricted the monarch's power to the nobles. The centuries of the Middle Ages were totally contrary to a democratic vision, in part, by the influence of a Hellenic philosophy—especially, Plato and Aristotle—which was contrary to democracy and, in part, by the total influence of the Roman Catholic Church, which for centuries had legitimized the absolute power of both the pope and the king, as long as the king submitted to the dictates of the Holy See. That view would be decisively broken—there were precedents throughout the Middle Ages—by the Protestant Reformation of the sixteenth century.

At the end of the fifteenth century, the need for reform within the Catholic-Roman church was indisputable for anyone with a minimum of spiritual sensitivity.[1] In the previous decades, in the first place, the papacy had practically become the ministry of religious affairs of the French monarchy by moving its headquarters from Rome to the city of Avignon. Then came a schism that confronted two popes for decades, who excommunicated each other. At one point there were four.[2] The fact that a council finally accepted the existence of a single pope and condemned the others solved the problems of the papal chain of command, but the immense spiritual corruption that had accumulated for centuries remained unscathed. Far from resembling early Christianity, the Roman Catholic Church was a mixture of Greek philosophy, Roman law, and pagan spirituality. On the contrary, the Reformation, which began at the first part of the sixteenth century in different parts of Europe, sought to return to original Christianity on the basis of the oldest historical sources, those contained in the Bible.

The purpose of the Reformation was merely spiritual and did not take long to focus on the assertion that the only source of revelation lay in the Bible (*Sola Scriptura*): that only Christ was Savior and Mediator (*Solo Christo*), and that salvation was not the fruit of human merit, but of God's undeserved grace or favor, a favor that could only

1. On the origins of the Reformation, see: C. Vidal, *El legado de la Reforma* (2016), pp. 15-58.

2. On the subject, see: O. Prerovsky, *L'elezione di Urbano VI* and *l'insorgere dello scismo d'Occidente* (Rome, 1960); M. Seidlmayer, *Die Anfänge des grossen abendländischen Schismas* (Münster, 1940); W. Ullmann, *The Origins of the Great Schism* (London, 1948).

be received through faith, but never bought or acquired (*Sola Gratia, Sola Fide*). That these conclusions meant the end of the spiritual corruption of the Middle Ages and with it those of the Roman Catholic Church was obvious, but this is a subject on which we will not dwell at this time. On the contrary, we must point out that the recovery of the text of the Bible, and of the values contained within it, provoked a real revolution that affected aspects such as economy, art, education, science, and politics among others.[3] In fact, the work of the Reformers as expositors of the Bible was to lay the foundations for the reappearance of modern democracy. The reason for this gigantic leap in the history of mankind was born directly from the recovery of a series of values contained in the Bible, which, on the contrary, were rejected and even persecuted by a Roman-Catholic Europe.

The first of these values was the recovery of the proposition that the law is one and the same for all. Or, if one prefers to put it another way, that the law has supremacy that is exercised without exception. In the Middle Ages, the Roman Catholic Church had systematically and consciously crushed such an idea. The law not only was not the same for everyone, but it also contained express privileges for the pope, bishops, and clergy as well as emperors, kings, and nobles. On the contrary, these privileges were not available to the vast majority of the population. Furthermore, the same misdeeds were not punished in the same way, depending on who committed the crime.

The Reformers soon discovered that such an idea—justified again and again by popes and kings—collided head-on with the examples contained in the Scriptures. The examples were undoubtedly abundant. Let us remember, for example, how the prophet Nathan had rebuked King David despite being the hero of Israel and had announced to him a punishment for breaking the law that was tragically fulfilled (2 Samuel 12). Similarly, Elijah had publicly accused Ahaz and Jezebel, the king and queen of Israel, precisely for breaking the law, even though, in appearance, they had met all formal requirements

3. On the subject, see: C. Vidal, *El legado de la Reforma* (Tyler, 2016), pp. 257-344.

(1 Kings 21). Such a view had been violated throughout the Middle Ages, but it was recovered by the return to the Scriptures and brought about practical consequences quickly. That knowledge of the Bible soon produced practical consequences. We are going to pause on one of those examples derived from reflecting on the Bible.

In 1538, the French Reformer John Calvin and some of his collaborators were expelled from the city of Geneva by the authorities. Certainly, the rulers of Geneva were in favor of the Reformation and did not believe that the Roman Catholic Church taught the truth, but they felt that Calvin held too strict views. Consequently, Calvin was not arrested, tortured, or executed, as was the general rule in Roman Catholic Europe, but he was asked to leave the city. That moment was used by Cardinal Sadoleto to send a letter to the public authorities of the city, urging them to reject the Reformation unequivocally and to return to obedience to the Roman Catholic Church. Cardinal Sadoleto's letter was well written, but the truth is that he did not have to convince the Genevans, since they had already requested in 1539 that Calvin (who was still banished) respond to Sadoleto with a letter. Calvin wrote his reply to Cardinal Sadoleto in just six days, and thus a text was born that became a classic in the history of theology. It is beyond the scope of this chapter to go into depth regarding the booklet, but it is necessary to mention it because in it you can see two views of the law that differentiated—like so many other things!—the nations in which the Reformation triumphed from those in which this did not happen, which, respectively, either paved or blocked the path to democracy.

The question that arose was whether the criterion of conduct should be defined by submission to the law or, on the contrary, by the institution that established without superior control what is meant by a law that one must submit to. Cardinal Sadoleto defended the second criterion, while Calvin supported the first. For Calvin, it was obvious that the law (in this case, the Bible) held supremacy and, therefore, if a person or institution departed from it, it lacked legitimacy. Cardinal Sadoleto, on the other hand, argued that it was the institution that decided how that law was applied, and that departing from obedience to the institution constituted an extraordinarily serious act. The Reformation opted for the first view, while in nations, such as Spain, where the Counter-Reformation was established, a different principle was maintained, which established not only that everyone was not equal before the law, but that, in addition, there were social sectors not subject to it. Hence, it created—rather it strengthened—a culture of justified legal exception.

The examples of this difference have continued until today, as we will have the opportunity to see. Even if we ignore the violations of the law perpetrated by certain sovereigns such as Felipe II, who ordered a state crime, such as the murder of Escobedo,[4] or who violated the Aragonese code of laws in persecuting Antonio Pérez,[5] the truth is that the problem, unfortunately, goes much further than the illegalities that have occurred in the most diverse regimes and times. It is more about the fact that it was accepted without question that important sectors of the population—basically, the Roman Catholic Church and the monarchy—were not subject to the rule of law.

On the contrary, in reformed Europe, the law was placed above people and institutions. It could not be otherwise if, by taking into account God's law contained in the Bible, the institution that, by definition, was most sacred, the papacy, had been called into question, thereby reaching the conclusion that it had been delegitimized because of its conduct. The fact that the nations in which the Reformation triumphed admitted almost immediately the supremacy of the law over individuals and institutions had impressive results.

Tragically, however, the primacy of the law was to be ruled out from Roman-Catholic nations such as Spain, France, or, subsequently, the Latin American republics. Incidentally, to conclude the account of the theological confrontation between Calvin and Cardinal Sadoleto, it should be pointed out that the Genevan authorities, showing remarkable intelligence, examined both positions, rejected Cardinal

4. Geoffrey Parker, *Felipe II* (Barcelona, 2010), pp. 659ff.
5. *Idem*, *Ibidem*, pp. 864.ff.

Sadoleto's proposal, and called on Calvin to return to Geneva. Such a decision was going to bring about positive consequences.

The Roots of Modern Democracy (II): The Reformation and Limited Power

The Reformation not only brought with it the idea of the supremacy of the law, but it also, in a very special way, influenced the development of important essential tools for the defense of freedoms, for the proper functioning of the State, and for the establishment of a democratic system such as the concept of public service and limited power, the election of magistrates, and the separation of powers.

This view—typical of the Reformation and so different from those that existed in the scope of the Counter-Reformation—also had its roots in Scripture. Precisely in a preaching on 1 Samuel 8[6]—the episode in which Samuel responds to Israel's desire to have a king, warning them of the dangers—Calvin pointed out two aspects of enormous relevance. The first was the need for government to be limited in order to avoid its dangers, and the second was that the king was also subject to a higher sovereignty. According to Calvin, "there are limits prescribed by God for the power (of kings), within which they must feel satisfied: specifically, to work for the common good and to rule and lead the people in true fairness and justice; not to swell up with their own importance, but to remember that they too are subjects of God." Calvin claimed that God had established the magistrates "for the benefit of the people and the benefit of the republic." In fact, kings had authority only to the extent that they fulfilled the conditions of the covenant. Of course, subjects had to submit to the authority of kings, "but at the same time kings have to take care of the public welfare so that they can fulfill the duties prescribed to them by God with good counsel and mature deliberation." It is more than obvious that

6. The text can be found in Charles Raynal and John Leith (eds), *Calvin Studies Colloquium* (Davidson, 1982).

such a view of government was totally different from that of Roman Catholic nations such as Spain or France.

Calvin, in addition, went further in pointing out the limits of power or the service character of the rulers. Thus, and this was an extremely important step, he pointed out the biblical basis for the popular election of public office. Commenting on the passage in Deuteronomy 1:14-16 on the election of the judges, Calvin wrote: "Here it appears very clearly that those who were to preside over the trial were not appointed only by the will of Moses, but were elected by the people's votes." And this is the most desirable kind of freedom, that we should not be compelled to obey every person who can be tyrannically placed to rule over us, but rather the one who is voted in by an election, so that no one should rule unless they are approved by us. This is also confirmed in the next verse where Moses relates that he expected the consent of the people and that nothing was attempted that was not agreeable to all. This republican ideal defended by Calvin on the basis of the Scriptures also implied denouncing that oppressive behavior of the magistrates "who take part in plundering to enrich themselves at the expense of the poor."

Certainly, the defense of the supremacy of the law, the limitation of political power, and the representation of the rulers implied indispensable steps in the advance towards democracy. However, the anthropology of the Reformation, an anthropology derived directly from the Scriptures, was not so naive as to think that human beings tended toward good or that certain limits would be accepted willingly. That is how a political idea as fruitful and beneficial as the division of powers would emerge from it.

The Roots of Modern Democracy (III): The Reformation and the Separation of Powers

Far from encouraging an optimistic view of human beings, the Reformers were more than aware that, both individually and collectively, we are a fallen species tending towards evil. Precisely because of this, an absolute power could never lead to happiness but would very easily lead to tyranny. In fact, the papacy was an indisputable example of that reality. A bishop of Rome who had no constraints over his power had for centuries been abandoning the humility of the manger of Bethlehem or that of the Cross of Calvary in order to build the very expensive Basilica of St Peter in Rome, which was certainly extraordinary from an artistic point of view, yet built with funds of moral origin more than questionable. It was not an isolated episode, but the continuation of what they considered a degenerative process. Hadn't the popes moved the court from Rome to Avignon for purely political reasons (1309-1376)? During the fourteenth century hadn't the Catholic-Roman church not suffered a schism that resulted in the creation of two popes—at one point there were up to four—who were excommunicated reciprocally (1378-1417)? Had not the warrior popes of the Renaissance—great patrons and even gifted politicians—become famous basically for not focusing on godliness as their first task (1417-1534)? Well, if that happened with people who, by definition, were supposed to be exemplary and pretended to be the successors of the apostle Peter, what could be expected of political power? If one wished to respond to such an anthropological challenge, it only made sense to not only subject power to the rule of law, but also to divide it and make it impossible to harm basic freedoms beginning with that of conscience.

In just a few decades, this view—certainly novel and, of course, radically opposed to that of the Europe of the Roman-Catholic Counter-Reformation—was articulating a series of constraints against absolutism in the nations where the Reformation had triumphed. In the Netherlands, a republic with freedom of worship was quickly established, where, for example, asylum was granted to the Jews who had been expelled from Spain in 1492. The family of the philosopher Spinoza was an example of so many who found a place where they could prosper freely. The Scandinavian nations witnessed the birth of a growing Parliamentarism. In England, in the first half of the seventeenth century, a Parliamentarian army, made up mainly of Puritans, rose up against Charles I. Its intention was not a revolution that would introduce a utopia, but that it would foster respect for rights such as freedom of worship, expression, representation, and private property. Thus, in 1642, the same year that the heroic Spanish infantry regiments (Tercios españoles) were on their way to their last and useless bloodletting for the greater glory of the Austrians and the Roman Catholic Church, the soldiers of the English Parliament carried with them a Soldier's Bible that had been printed by order of Cromwell. The text, which included an anthology of biblical texts, began by pointing out the illegality of the plundering and continued to demonstrate, biblically, the justification for the cause of freedom. In a very significant way, the English Protestants achieved the victory of Parliament against the monarchical despotism, while the Spanish Roman Catholics—despite having been the first nation to know an embryo of Parliamentarism with the medieval courts—saw how their hegemony was lost thanks to the chain of absolute kings bent on being the sword of the Counter-Reformation. The events in history, with all due respect, do not happen by themselves.

When the victory of the English Parliamentarians took place, the number of Protestant treaties laying the foundations for future democracy were already quite numerous. In fact, Theodore Beza, Calvin's successor in the Geneva pastorate, had previously written *The Right of the Magistrates*, a work that justified armed resistance against tyrants. Around 1550, John Ponet, a bishop of the Anglican Church, wrote *A Short Treatise of Political Power*, justifying resistance against tyrants by appealing to the Bible. In 1579, the *Vindiciae Contra Tyrannos* (*Claims Against Tyrants*) was published, where the idea of the social contract essential for the development of later liberalism was formulated, stating that "there is always and everywhere a mutual and reciprocal obligation between the people and the prince.... If the prince fails to keep his promise, the people are exempt from obedience, the contract is nullified, and the rights of obligation are without force." In other words, the legitimacy of a ruler is not derived from a divine right backed by the Roman Catholic Church, but from a social contract existing between him and those he rules over. When this covenant was not fulfilled, as in the case of Solomon's son, the people had a right to resist. In a very significant way, the Jesuits had begun to defend the legitimacy of murdering a king, but only if he was a heretic. In fact, various terrorist commandos organized by the Jesuits attempted to assassinate Elizabeth I of England. On the contrary, the Reformers did not intend to maintain ecclesial privileges but rather defend freedoms.

The Protestants, certainly, could live under a ruler who espoused another religion and serve him with loyalty, but they saw no legitimacy in someone who suppressed the rights of their subjects and oppressed them. It cannot, therefore, come as a surprise—in fact, it was totally logical—that political liberalism had been devised by John Locke, the son of a Puritan who had fought against Charles I of England. During the final part of his life, Locke—who was greatly influenced by the Westminster Confession and other Puritan documents—was convinced that his most important writings were his comments on the New Testament, but posterity has not viewed him that way. When Lord Shaftesbury was ordered to write a constitution for the Carolina colony, he asked for Locke's assistance. In the text, which he wrote at the request of Lord Shaftesbury, Locke insisted on the granting of freedom of conscience not only to Christians of any denomination but also to Jews, Indians, "pagans and other dissidents." It was a point of view that was a natural derivation of the Reformation, but which had to reach the second half of the twentieth century so that it could also be accepted, at least theoretically, by the Roman Catholic Church.

Locke was a very persuaded Protestant; perhaps some would call him fundamentalist today, and that is precisely why he believed that only those religions that are false need to rely on "the use of force and help from men." Of course, as a good Protestant, he was also aware that human nature has an undeniable tendency towards evil, and that is why the "powers" had to be separated to avoid tyranny.

Such a liberal view, in the historical sense of the term and not the one that it has acquired in recent decades, fit perfectly within the nations where the Reformation had triumphed. It was, however, unacceptable in those nations, such as Spain or France, where the Roman-Catholic Counter-Reformation had prevailed. For the former, there was no institution—including the ecclesiastic one—that had not been tainted by this evil human tendency. Curiously, the rules of procedure of some denominations of the time, such as the Presbyterians, managed to instigate a division of powers that amazes anyone who reads their documents today. For the latter, it was obvious that there were sacred institutions that could not be limited nor subjugated by the rule of law. With that history behind us, it should come as no surprise that the idea of separation of powers in Roman Catholic nations would be limited to a few educated and, generally, liberal minds. Both the Left and the Right would historically prefer that the separation of powers did not exist. That is because in some instances it would have affected sacred institutions such as the Catholic Church or the monarchy. In others, such as the Spanish Franco regime or the Argentinian Peronism, it was because a different principle was forged that was based on a supposed coordination of powers that diametrically opposed the separation advocated by the liberals. In many cases, without knowing it, they were only affirming the validity of a Protestant formula, which insists that the concentration of powers can only degenerate into tyranny and must therefore be separated. However, the restoration of democracy in a way that remains exemplary would not take place in Europe, but rather on another continent across the ocean.

CHAPTER III

DEMOCRACY, A NEW ARRIVAL IN HISTORY (IIII): Modern Democracy Takes Root in America

The Puritan Origin of American Democracy (I): The Bill of Rights and the Declaration of Independence

In the previous chapter, we pointed out how that while Catholic-Roman Europe was sinking more and more into an absolutist view of power, both political and religious, Reformed Europe was advancing on the path that would eventually lead to democracy. The greatest advance took place in England, and that progress was directly due to the influence of the Puritans. These Puritans would sail to the West Indies in search of greater freedom of conscience, would become the backbone of Parliamentary resistance against Charles I's totalitarianism and, finally, they would permanently lay the foundations for the triumph of Parliamentarism before the end of the seventeenth century. While a considerable sector of the Anglican church felt comfortable with a very moderate form of Protestantism that, historically, would be consolidated as the closest Protestant confession to Rome, another very relevant faction advocated for deepening this reform by adapting the existing ecclesial reality to the model contained in the New Testament. The supporters for this position received various names: Puritans, because they pursued an ideal of biblical purity; Presbyterians, because their churches were governed by elected priests instead of following an episcopal system like the Roman Catholic or the Anglican system; and also Calvinists, because their theology was strongly inspired by the works of the French Reformer John Calvin. This last aspect had enormous consequences in many areas. As we will point out, these included not only the consolidation of the Parliamentary system, as we will see, but also a remarkable economic and social development in England.

The victory of Cromwell and the Puritans in the civil war (1642-49) led to a victory crowned with the trial and beheading of King Charles I. In fact, those steps were taken with such extraordinary legal accuracy that, over the centuries, they would lay the foundations for international law against war crimes in the twentieth century.[1] However, that important triumph did not establish Parliamentarism. In 1660, the Restoration began, which brought Charles II, the son of the executed monarch, to the English throne. From that time until his death in 1685, Charles II—a remarkably immoral king in his private life—not only persecuted Parliamentarians but also conspired against the popular will to submit England to the rule of the Roman Catholic Church. The objective pursued by Charles II was also pursued by his son James II.

Seen in this perspective, it is unsettling to think what might have become of England—and freedom in the world—if James II had achieved his goal. Determined on dragging England into submission to the Roman Catholic Church, James II removed the Bishop of London and got rid of Protestant professors from Magdalen College at Oxford and replaced them with Roman Catholics. In the meantime, James II created a standing army and placed Catholics in command positions while purging the English army in Ireland of Protestants. Not

1. In this regard, see Geoffrey Robertson's magnificent book, *The Tyrannicide Brief. The Story of the Man Who Sent Charles I to the Scaffold* (New York, 2005).

content with trying to control the university education and the armed forces, James II extended Parliament's power illegally, tried to create a monarchical party that would counteract conservatives (Tories) and liberals (Whigs), and even ordered the arrest of William Sancroft, the archbishop of Canterbury, and six other bishops. The king's despotic action was annulled by the courts, and the seven bishops were declared innocent amidst the cheers of the people.

The tension between the supporters of freedom and King James II came to a real crisis when he had a son who was expected to complete the task of subjecting England to royal despotism and the Roman Catholic Church. Up until that time, the hope of the English Parliamentarians had been for Mary, the king's daughter, to reign, who was a Protestant, which would mean the salvation of Parliamentarism and religious freedom. Now, in the face of what could become a real national disgrace, Tories and Whigs decided to defend England's freedom. In 1688, Mary, her husband, the Dutch State Governor William of Orange, and Parliament initiated a revolution that would go down in history with the nickname of Glorious, because it took place without any bloodshed.

In a very significant way, William was lauded when the people saw the slogan "I will uphold the liberties of England and the Protestant religion" appearing on their banners. Even Princess Anne, the daughter of James II, converted to Protestantism. James II could have accepted the help of Louis XIV, the absolute monarch of France, but he understood that he had no guarantee of winning a civil war.[2] Captured while attempting to flee the country, from which the Queen and the Prince of Wales had already escaped, James tried to remain on the throne, but he understood that such a possibility was not an option. Later, he tried to return to power by relying on the Roman Catholic population of Ireland, but he was defeated, and in 1691 the victory of Parliamentarianism was achieved.

2. It is revealing that Pope Innocent XI decided to help William of Orange financially because he considered it more important to curb the power of Louis XIV of France, an ally of James II, than to submit England to the Holy See. As on so many other occasions in history, before and after, mere politics weighed more heavily on the papal decision than the principles it supposedly defended.

The Glorious Revolution held extraordinary importance in the history of democracy. The Bill of Rights that was born from it completely eliminated the possibility of an absolute Catholic-Roman monarchy. Parliament essentially limited royal power by preventing it from arbitrarily suspending laws, imposing taxes, or maintaining a standing army in peacetime. Since 1689, the English regime has been, without interruption, a Parliamentary monarchy in which, moreover, the Parliament elected by the people has not ceased to increase its power in parallel with the loss of the same by the king. The influence of the Puritans had consolidated a Parliamentary system that would eventually become a democracy, but their greatest achievement would be achieved less than a century later and across the Atlantic.

It is common knowledge that in 1776, settlers from a territory that is now a part of the United States rebelled against the English monarchy by declaring themselves independent. Such a fact, enormously relevant to universal history, is usually explained today as an offshoot of the European Enlightenment and carried out by a group of politicians mostly theistic or unbelieving. The view has been able to advance itself considerably, but, plain and simple, it does not correspond to reality. Truth be told, the American Revolution ended up leading to the establishment of a democracy based on "the will of the people" and a worldview that was fundamentally Puritan. Without these two central circumstances, the revolution would never have led to the creation of the first democracy in contemporary history and, above all, would never have enjoyed the success it has achieved, uninterruptedly, for more than two centuries.

From the beginning, it must be clearly established that the basis of the American Revolution was NOT the Enlightenment. Contrary to what is often claimed, the Enlightenment did not hold to a democratic view, but rather a despotic and oligarchic vision of political power. Their goal was not that political power should lie in the hands of the people, but that royal absolutism should be "enlightened" by the advice of "*philosophes*." The German philosopher Immanuel Kant maintained that the enlightened prince was the one who allowed religious freedom, no doubt, an essential issue for the Founding Fathers, but not an adequate one.[3] Figures like Voltaire wanted—and, certainly made efforts in this regard—kings like Frederick II of Prussia or Catherine the Great to allow themselves to be inspired by them, but not relinquish, even in part, any power to the people.[4] On the contrary, the motto of "Enlightened Despotism," was "all for the people, but without the people." Of course, those who were "enlightened" could share definite goals with the Puritans, such as the need for fair trials, religious freedom, or the abolition of torture, but their worldview differed much more significantly. The Enlightenment worldview was certainly not the one held by the American patriots, and to insist on identifying them with each other is a serious mistake.

Secondly, it should be pointed out that the population of what would become the United States was largely Puritan. This aspect carried with it immense relevance for a century and a half. We must now pause and consider its influence on the politics of the American patriots.

During the seventeenth century, the Puritans, eager to experience a greater freedom than that which they enjoyed in England, opted primarily for two paths. Those who remained in England formed the essential core of the Parliamentary party—sometimes even Republican—that went to war against Charles I, defeated him, and, through various changes, was essential for the formation of a representative system in England. But there were quite a few who decided to emigrate to Holland, where the Calvinists had established a peculiar system of freedoms that provided refuge to Jews and followers of various faiths, or to leave for the English colonies of North America. In fact, the famous and often quoted Pilgrim Fathers of the Mayflower ship were nothing more than a group of Puritans.

Beyond the Thanksgiving celebrated by them for the first time, the arrival of the Puritans to what was to become the United States was one of the most important events in all of history. The Puritans included John Endicott, first governor of Massachusetts; John Winthrop, second governor of the colony; Thomas Hooker, founder

3. Immanuel Kant, *Contestación a la pregunta ¿Qué es la Ilustración?* (Madrid, 2012).
4. J. I. Israel, *Democratic Enlightment* (Oxford, 2013), pp. 110ff.

of Connecticut; John Davenport, founder of New Haven; and Roger Williams, founder of Rhode Island. Even a Quaker like William Penn, founder of Pennsylvania and the city of Philadelphia, had Puritan influence, as he had been educated by teachers with this theological affinity. Of course, the educational influence was essential, for it was not in vain that Harvard—as well as later Yale and Princeton—was a university founded in 1636 by the Puritans.

When the American Revolution broke out at the end of the eighteenth century, the demographic weight of the Puritans in the English colonies of North America was enormous. Of the approximately three million Americans living at that time in that territory, 900,000 were Puritans of Scottish origin, 600,000 were English Puritans, and another 500,000 were Calvinists of Dutch, German, or French background; that is, their worldview was similar to that of the Puritans. Their influence did not end there. In fact, the Anglicans, like George Washington, who lived in the Colonies, were largely of Puritan persuasion, since they were governed by the Thirty-nine Articles, a doctrinal document that espoused this position. Thus, at least two-thirds of the inhabitants of the future United States were Calvinists or, if you prefer, Puritan-inspired Reformers, and the other third mostly identified with groups of dissidents such as Quakers or Baptists. On the contrary, the presence of Roman-Catholics was almost negligible, and the Methodists had not yet made an appearance with the force they would later have in the United States.

Such a circumstance was not overlooked by the English authorities. In fact, the spiritual landscape in the insurgent colonies was so obvious that in England the United States War of Independence was called "the Presbyterian Rebellion,"[5] and a supporter of King George III

5. In this regard, see Kevin Phillips, *The Cousins' Wars: Religion, Politics and the Triumph of Anglo-America* (New York: Basic Books, 1999), 92, 177. In a similar sense: Henry Ippel, "British Sermons and the American Revolution," *Journal of Religious History* (1982), vol. 12, 193; James Graham Leyburn, *The Scotch-Irish: A Social History* (Chapel Hill: University of North Carolina Press, 1962), 305; *The Journal of Presbyterian History* 54, no. 1 (1976); David Calhoun, *Princeton Seminary* (Edinburgh: Banner of Truth, 1994), vol. 1, 15; H.M.J. Klein, ed., *Lancaster County, Pennsylvania: A History* (New York and Chicago: Lewis Historical Publishing Co., 1924), vol. 1, 86; Paul Johnson, "God and the Americans," *Gilder Lehrman Institute Lectures in American History*, Oct. 1999; John A. Mackay, "Witherspoon of Paisley and Princeton," *Theology Today*, January 1962, vol. 18, No. 4.

said: "I fix all the blame for these extraordinary proceedings upon the Presbyterians." As for the British Prime Minister Horace Walpole, he summed up the events before Parliament, stating that "Cousin America has run off with a Presbyterian parson." They were not mistaken and, to cite a significant example, when Cornwallis was forced to retreat and later capitulate at Yorktown, all the colonels of the American army except one were priests from Presbyterian churches. As for the soldiers and officers of the entire army, just over half also belonged to this religious movement. Of course, the English knew perfectly well who they were up against in America. As George Trevelyan, a British historian specializing in the American Revolution, pointed out, King George III's supporters argued that "political agitation against the Royal Government had been deliberately planned by Presbyterians...it was fostered and abetted by Presbyterians in every colony.[6] Similarly, John C. Miller pointed out: "In the end, the Churchmen believed that the Revolution was a Presbyterian-Congregationalist plot).[7]

This overwhelming demographic majority of Reformers influenced, of course, the configuration of a new system, which was already democratic in nature. As the English statesman Sir James Stephen would point out, political Calvinism was summed up in four points: (1) the popular will was a legitimate source of power of the rulers; (2) that power could be delegated to representatives through an elective system; (3) in the ecclesiastic system clerics and laity should enjoy equal but coordinated authority; and (4) there should be no alliance or mutual dependence between Church and State. These were, of course, principles that are now widely recognized in the West, but which were far from being widely accepted in the sixteenth century.

This worldview would be reflected from the very beginning in the legal declarations of the American patriots beginning with the Declaration of Independence. In fact, the first American pro-independence text was not, as is generally thought, the Declaration of Independence drafted by Thomas Jefferson, but the text on which

6. Sir George Otto Trevelyan, *The American Revolution* (New York, 1915), vol. III, pp. 311-312.
7. John C. Miller, *Origins of the American Revolution* (Boston), 1943, p. 186.

the future US president was inspired. This was none other than the Mecklenburg Declaration, a document signed by Presbyterians of Scottish and Irish origin in North Carolina on May 20, 1775.[8] The Mecklenburg Declaration contained all the points from which Jefferson, a year later, would develop his views on national sovereignty, the struggle against tyranny, the elective nature of political power, and the division of powers. In addition, it was approved by an assembly of twenty-seven deputies, all of whom were Puritans, of which one-third of them were priests of the Presbyterian Church, including its president and secretary.

The Declaration of Independence not only moves one because of the beauty of its words, but also because of the depth and realism of its concepts. Suffice it to recall the parts that perhaps make up the heart of it: "We hold that these truths are self-evident, that all men are created equal, that they are endowed by their Creator with certain inalienable Rights, that among them are Life, Freedom and the pursuit of Happiness.... That to secure these rights, Governments are instituted among Men, deriving their just Powers from the consent of the governed, ... That whenever any Form of Government becomes destructive of these ends, it is the Right of the People to alter or to abolish it, and to institute new Government, laying its foundation on such principles and organizing its Powers in such form, as to them shall seem most likely to affect their Safety and Happiness." In other words, the Declaration affirmed the equality of human beings, the fact that they were endowed with inalienable rights that came from the Creator, that among them were life, freedom, and the pursuit of happiness, and that governments, derived from the will of the people, were intended to ensure those rights, by guaranteeing that the form of government could be altered or replaced when it did not fulfill that duty.

All these aspects are extremely important. Let us look, for example, at the wording of rights in the Declaration of Independence.[9]

8. The authenticity of the Mecklenburg Declaration has been debated. To read a favorable view of it, see: http://charlottemuseum.org/the-evidence-in-favor-of-the-mecklenburg-declaration/.
9. Of particular relevance, see: G. T. Amos, *Defending the Declaration. How the Bible and Christianity Influenced the Writing of the Declaration of Independence* (Charlottesville, 1994).

Far from claiming that their authority derived from themselves, the American patriots appealed to the laws of nature and of nature's God. In other words, they believed that there were natural laws, and that those natural laws came from the same God, and that it was the English king, and not them, who was breaking them. Therefore, the cause for independence was a legal and noble cause born not only of human will, but out of respect and love for laws derived from God himself. This view was alien to the Enlightenment, but it fully harmonized with the view of the Puritans. The rights of citizens are not the result of human whim but emanate from God himself and are above other considerations.

Previously, in 1764, twelve years before the Declaration of Independence, James Otis had already appealed to these God-given natural rights to oppose the legality of the Stamp and Sugar Acts that tried to impose new and unjust taxes on the Americans. The following year, in 1765, Massachusetts asserted that "there are certain essential rights of the British constitution and government which are founded in the law of God and nature, and are the common rights of mankind. He then indicated that "the inhabitants of this province are unalienably entitled to those essential rights, in common with all men; and that no law of society can, consistent with the law of God and nature, divest them of those rights."[10] These statements are extremely important because the rights recognized in England and, therefore, also in the English colonies were not the result of mere human will or the gracious concession of the king. They merely recognized the existence of rights common to all human beings, not only to the English or to the subjects of those nations that recognized them in their legislation, but rights that possessed an innate natural basis and were derived from God. This idea originated with the Puritans, but they, in turn, did not attribute its conception to themselves, but rather pointed out that its origin lay in the Bible

10. Alden Bradford (ed.), *Speeches of the Governors of Massachusetts, From 1765 to 1775; and the Answers of the House of Representatives to the Same; With Their Resolutions and Addresses for That Period* (Boston, 1818), text-fiche, 50, LAC 15249.

and, especially, in the second chapter of Paul's letter to the Romans. This was pointed out, for example, by Sir Edward Coke in 1610 in his *Calvin's Case*, but Coke simply repeated what had been written two generations earlier by the French Reformer.[11] Therefore, unlike what Roman Catholic theologians affirmed, rights did not derive from their acceptance and legitimization by the ecclesiastical authorities, who, supposedly, represented God, nor from royal benevolence, but rather a higher law from God.

Both John Adams[12] and Thomas Jefferson,[13] the authors of the Declaration of Independence, were deeply steeped in Edward Coke's thoughts and clearly left them reflected in the text. A similar conclusion had also been reached by the Puritan John Locke, who not only maintained that the Bible was "infallibly true"[14] but also maintained a deeply biblical theology in his heart. Thus, he came to affirm truths such as "Scripture alone" or "justification by faith." Regarding the first truth, he wrote: "The holy Scripture is to me, and always will be, the constant guide of my assent; and I shall always hearken to it, as containing infallible truth relating to things of the highest concernment... where I want the evidence of things, there yet is ground enough for me to believe, because God has said it: and I shall immediately condemn and quit any opinion of mine, as soon as I am shown that it is contrary to any revelation in the holy scripture.[15]

Similarly, on justification by faith, Locke, who is often accused of being a simple deist, stated: "All being sinners and transgressors of the law, and therefore unrighteous, are all liable to condemnation, unless they believe, and, in this way, through grace are justified by God by this faith, which shall be accounted to them for righteousness."[16] Far from being a deist, Locke appears as a more than convinced Puritan, which is logical, on the other hand, since, for

11. *Institutes of the Christian Religion*, Book IV, chapter 20, section 16.

12. Louis Wright, *Magna Carta and the Tradition of Liberty* (Washington, 1976), p. 45.

13. Daniel J. Boorstin, *Hidden History* (New York, 1987), p. 103.

14. John Locke, *An Essay Concerning Human Understanding* (New York, 1959), vol. 2, p. 120.

15. Locke, *Essay*, vol. 1, prologue at 1.

16. John Locke, *The Reasonableness of Christianity with a Discourse on Miracles and part of A Third Letter Concerning Toleration* (Stanford, 1958), 52, sec. 227.

example, that was the faith that had been passed down to him by his father, a Protestant minister, and the fact that he often quoted *The Laws of Ecclesiastical Polity* by the Puritan theologian Richard Hooker (1554-1600).[17]

This view of the rights common to the human race—rights such as life, freedom, and the pursuit of happiness—were part of truths that did not arise from the human heart, but were "self-evident," a term taken directly from Paul's statements in Romans 1:19-20. As the Declaration pointed out, "We hold these truths to be self-evident, that all men are created equal, that they are endowed by their Creator with certain unalienable rights, that among these are life, liberty and the pursuit of happiness. That to secure these rights, governments are instituted among men." The list of rights itself could not be any clearer. Far from promising happiness to all citizens, he pointed out that government existed to guarantee life, freedom, and that people could seek happiness because—what sensible person can doubt that?—there is no human authority that can guarantee happiness to anyone.

The Founding Fathers, of course, were versed in the "*philosophes*" of the Enlightenment and, likewise, exhibited no small knowledge of the Greek and Roman classics.[18] However, the real and indisputable basis of their political view came from the biblical worldview of the Puritans, thus shaping a view of political rights that was based on a series of authors that began in the pages of the Bible and, through Calvin and various lawyers and Protestant theologians, were passed down to Locke and Coke. However, it would not only be a question of the view of rights and the legitimization of independence, but it would also profoundly inspire the first democratic constitution in contemporary history—the Constitution of the United States of America.

17. Regarding this, see W. von Leyden (ed.), in John Locke, *Essays on the Law of Nature* (Oxford, 1954), 17, 67.

18. In this regard, see: Carl J. Richard, *Greeks and Romans Bearing Gifts. How the Ancients Inspired the Founding Fathers* (New York, 2009), and *Idem*, *The Founders and the Classics. Greece, Rome, and the American Enlightenment* (Cambridge, MA, 1995).

The Puritan Origin of American Democracy (II): The Constitution[19]

If the influence of the Puritan worldview was especially decisive in the drafting of the Declaration of Independence, and dates back to a form of thought that Calvin and Paul of Tarsus had reached, this influence can also be seen in the Constitution of the United States. Certainly, the four political principles of Calvinism outlined above were essential in shaping it, but another absolutely essential element was added to them, which, in and of itself, serves to explain the very different development followed by democracy in the Anglo-Saxon world and the rest of the West. The Bible—and the confessions arising from the Reformation were very insistent regarding this—teaches that the human race is a species deeply affected by the fall of Adam. Of course, human beings can do good deeds and perform actions that show that, although tainted, they carry in themselves the image and likeness of God. However, the tendency toward evil is undeniable and must be carefully guarded against. For this reason, political power must be divided, so that that it does not become concentrated in the "hands" of a few, which will always lead to corruption and tyranny, and equally must be controlled. This "pessimistic," or simply realistic, view of human nature had already led the Puritans during the sixteenth century to develop a form of ecclesial government that, unlike the Catholic or Anglican episcopalism, divided it into several levels that stopped and counterbalanced each other, thus avoiding corruption.

19. The bibliography on the true origins of the United States' Constitution is abundant, though, paradoxically, not well known. We have addressed the issue in a specific chapter of *Nuevos enigmas históricos al descubierto* (Barcelona, 2003, in press). A very interesting study of its origins in seventeenth-century colonial thought can be found in P. Miller, *The New England Mind. The 17th Century* (Harvard, 1967). The relationship between reformed thought and democracy can be examined in R. B. Perry, *Puritanism and Democracy* (New York, 1944); and, more specifically, in D. F. Kelly, *The Emergence of Liberty in the Modern World. The Influence of Calvin on Five Governments from the 16th Through 18th Centuries* (Phillipsburg, 1992); and J. J. Hernández Alonso, *Puritanismo y tolerancia en el período colonial americano* (Salamanca, 1999). Approaches from a "direct" or "indirect" theological perspective are indispensable for analyzing this topic. They can be found more or less specifically in J. A. Froude, *Calvinism* (London, 1871), and L. Boettner, *The Reformed Doctrine of Predestination* (Phillisburg, 1932). Finally, I must mention a remarkable essay written by J. Budziszewski, *The Revenge of Conscience. Politics and the Fall of Man* (Dallas, 1999), in which some of the most relevant aspects of the political analysis of the Puritans are taken up from a philosophical perspective.

In this regard, the Founding Fathers were expressly transparent. One of the most quoted biblical passages in their debates, writings, and correspondence is the one contained in Jeremiah 17:9, where it clearly points out that the heart of man is deceitful, i.e., he is deceived and deceives; above all ese, he is perverse, which poses serious problems in understanding it. Given that human inclination toward evil, it is unacceptable to run the risk of concentrating power in the hands of a few. The testimonies of the founding Fathers in this regard are extremely relevant. Thus, John Adams, quoting Jeremiah, said: "Let me conclude by advising all men to look into their own hearts, which they will find to be 'deceitful above all things and desperately wicked.'"[20] The fact that Adams did not believe—unlike the *philosophes*—in an innate goodness in human beings was something he repeated on many occasions, basing his view on the text of the Bible. Thus, in his Sixth Letter on *The Right Constitution of a Commonwealth Examined*[21] Adams stated: "To expect self-denial from men when they have a majority in their favor, and consequently power to gratify themselves, is to disbelieve all history and universal experience—it is to disbelieve revelation and the Word of God, which informs us 'the heart is deceitful above all things and desperately wicked'" (Jeremiah 17:9). There is no man so blind as not to see that to talk of founding a government upon a supposition that nations and great bodies of men left to themselves will practice a course of self-denial is either to babble like a newborn infant or to deceive like an unprincipled impostor." Adams not only relied on that which was reflected in the Bible, but he also made it clear that not to assume that view implied a dangerous foolishness.

No less convincing would be George Washington himself, who pointed out to the American people: "A just estimate of that love of power and proneness to abuse it which predominates in the human heart is sufficient to satisfy us of the truth of this position. The necessity

20. John Adams, *On Private Revenge* III, published on September 5, 1763, in the *Boston Gazette*, reproduced in *The Works of John Adams* (Boston, 1851), vol. III, p. 443.

21. Taken from *A Defense of the Constitutions of Government of the United States of America* (London, 1794), vol. III, p. 289.

of reciprocal checks in the exercise of political power by dividing and distributing it into different depositories...has been evinced by experiments ancient and modern, some of them in our country and under our own eyes."[22] Once again a less than optimistic, but a healthy and realistic, view of human beings and politics became evident.

In light of the deep distrust of human nature, which was more than justified, the Founding Fathers added an understanding of the political system that the Puritans had already started in England, but that would reach its consummation in the United States. We refer to the assertion of separation of powers, an assertion that emerged directly from the Bible. Power, whose model was God, should be divided into judicial, legislative, and executive branches, as indicated in the passage of Isaiah 33:22. God could certainly consolidate those three powers without them degenerating into tyrannical behavior. Men, however, definitely could not do it. And precisely for that reason, these powers should be separated and exercised within certain limits. As Samuel Adams so clearly pointed out, he stated: "In all Good governments, the Legislative, Executive and Judiciary Powers are confined within the limits of their respective departments."[23]

In 1785, James Madison stated exactly the same view: "The preservation of a free government requires not merely that the metes and bounds which separate each department of power be universally maintained but more especially that neither of them be suffered to overleap the great barrier which defends the rights of the people. The rulers who are guilty of such an encroachment exceed the commission from which they derive their authority and are tyrants."[24] The Constitution of the United States not only stemmed from a realistic analysis of the human condition, but in addition, it also influenced

22. *Address of George Washington, President of the United States, and Late Commander in Chief of the American Army to the People of the United States, Preparatory to His Declination* (Baltimore, 1796), p. 13.

23. Words addressed to the Massachusetts legislature on January 19, 1796. See Samuel Adams, *The Writings of Samuel Adams* (New York, 1908), vol. IV, pp. 388-389.

24. James Madison, *A Memorial and Remonstrance Presented to the General Assembly of the State of Virginia at Their Session in 1785 in Consequence of a Bill Brought into That Assembly for the Establishment of Religion* (Massachusetts, 1786), pp. 4-5.

ideas such as limited power and the separation of powers, powers that had to be restrained and counterbalanced so as not to degenerate into tyranny. This division even made it possible to overcome one of the defects of the English Parliamentary system, which was the submission of the executive to a Parliament from which it was born. However, the Declaration of Independence and the Constitution of the United States were not the only contributions of the Puritans to the shaping of American democracy. They were joined by the Bill of Rights.

The Puritan Origin of American Democracy (III): The Bill of Rights

After the signing of the Constitution at the Philadelphia convention on September 17, 1787, it was mandatory that the text be ratified by nine of the thirteen states in order to become legal. Delaware, Pennsylvania, New Jersey, Georgia, and Connecticut ratified it quickly, but suddenly the procedure stopped when Massachusetts insisted that the Constitution should have a Bill of Rights. That position had a clear resonance in the state conventions of New Hampshire, Virginia, and New York, which became a threat that the Constitution would not be ratified. The threat became more than tangible when, in August 1788, North Carolina declared that it would not ratify the Constitution until it included the Bill of Rights. Only the Federalists' promise—as those who defended the Constitution were called—that the Bill of Rights would be added at the first meeting of Congress after ratification led the thirteen states to ratify the Constitution on September 13, 1788.

The Bill of Rights is essentially a collection of ten amendments drafted by James Madison[25]—a firm Protestant believer—that were

25. James Madison is one of the most extraordinary characters of the more than remarkable group of Founding Fathers. Of particular interest is the recent study by Rodney K. Smith, *James Madison. The Father of Religious Liberty* (Springville, 2019). Also of relevance are: Randolph Ketcham, James Madison, Charlottesville, 1990; William C. Rives, *History of the Life and Times of James Madison* (Boston, 1859); Michael Signer, *Becoming Madison* (New York, 2015).

added to the Constitution. Its importance for the history of the United States is absolutely essential. It is no less so for democracy because it involved the consummation of a development whose closest antecedent was the English Bill of Rights of 1689.

Significantly, the first right recognized was that of religious freedom, an absolutely impossible extreme in the Catholic-Roman, Muslim, or Buddhist nations of the time. As Madison himself would point out: "The Religion...of every man must be left to the conviction and conscience of every man; and it is the right of every man to exercise it as these may indicate. This right in its nature is an unalienable right. It is unalienable; because the opinions of men...cannot follow the dictates of other men: It is unalienable also; because what is here a right towards men, is a duty towards the Creator... This duty is precedent both in order of time and degrees of obligation, to the claims of the Civil Society."

From this "freedom of conscience," which was impossible in Roman-Catholic or Islamic societies, the Bill of Rights gave rise to four other freedoms indispensable for a democratic society: "Congress shall make no law...abridging the freedom of speech or of the press; or the right of the people peacefully to assemble, and to petition the government for a redress of grievances."

The second amendment, which is so controversial today, established the right "to keep and bear arms." The third, fourth and, in part, fifth amendments were designed to protect the private property of citizens. The rest of the fifth and sixth amendments related to the due process of citizens, something unthinkable in Catholic nations, but whose origin can be found in the limits established in the Bible for judiciary power, even in cases of particularly horrible crimes (Deuteronomy 17:2-7). The same can be said in the case of the sixth and seventh amendments, where the jury—again, something unknown in the Roman Catholic nations—has its roots in Numbers 35:24-5, where judgment is determined by the congregation, or the eighth amendment drafted against excessive bail and fines, and against cruel and unusual punishment, both circumstances that were common in some Catholic nations where the Inquisition continued to use torture to extract confessions from prisoners, where witch burning remained common, and where the executions of heretics continued well into the nineteenth century.

The ninth amendment is also of particular relevance because it states that rights do not originate from the Constitution but predate it, in accordance to the Protestant interpretation of the present rights, for example, in the Declaration of Independence. Finally, the tenth underscores the limitation of governmental power by stating that "the powers not delegated to the United States by the Constitution, nor prohibited by it to the States, are reserved to the States and the People." Unlike political conceptions that would take root in other nations, the Bill of Rights made it clear that the people did not just vote, thus transferring sovereignty to institutions. On the contrary, it remained sovereign.

It is significant that on the same day that the first Federal Congress approved the Bill of Rights, on September 25, 1789, it also promoted a resolution that stated: "That a joint committee of both Houses be directed to wait upon the President of the United States to request that he would recommend to the people of the United States a day of public thanksgiving and prayer, to be observed by acknowledging with grateful hearts the many signal favors of Almighty God..." Such an initiative by the legislature was an unquestionable tribute to the Puritans, who had celebrated the first Thanksgiving in 1621. It is not surprising that Mr. Roger Sherman justified this day of thanksgiving by appealing to precedents contained in the Bible and, in a very special way, to those contained in 2 Chronicles 5-7 and 1 Kings 7-8. The recommendation that was given to George Washington resulted in the first federal proclamation of a Day of Prayer and Thanksgiving. In it, the president proclaimed:

> "Whereas it is the duty of all nations to acknowledge the providence of Almighty God, to obey His will, to be grateful for His benefits, and humbly to implore His protection and favor...

> Now, therefore, I do recommend...that we may then all unite in rendering unto Him our sincere and humble thanks for His kind care and protection of the people of this country... And also that we may then unite in most humbly offering our prayers and supplications to the great Lord and Ruler of Nations, and beseech Him to pardon our national and other transgressions... to promote the knowledge and practice of true religion and virtue.[26]

By their actions, the Founding Fathers had accomplished a line of restoration of democracy that had taken its first steps with the Protestant Reformation of the sixteenth century, which had won resounding victories with the Puritan revolutions of the seventeenth century, and along with the work of authors like Locke and Coke, it had crystallized into a concrete political system, a truly exceptional system. It was an exception in its time, but it was an exception that had to endure through the ages.

26. *The Providence Gazette and Country Journal* of October 17, 1789, p. 1. George Washington, "A Proclamation," October 3, 1789, date of observance November 26, 1789.

CHAPTER IV

DEMOCRACY, A NEW ARRIVAL IN HISTORY (IV): The Exceptionality of American Democracy

The American Exceptionality

It is very common to refer to American exceptionality. All questions aside, these references are correct. In a very real sense, American democracy was exceptional. This circumstance explains its success, sheds light on the reasons for the failures of democracies in other nations, and allows us to identify the risks that threaten it today.

American exceptionality was explicitly recognized by the French liberal Alexis de Tocqueville, who stated in his work *Democracy in America*: "The position of the Americans is therefore quite exceptional, and it may be believed that no democratic people will ever be placed in a similar one."[1] This circumstance was undeniably derived from the Puritan heritage and from a series of obvious characteristics that were derived from it. First of all, as we have observed, it implied the recognition of the role of God in the history of humanity, a God

1. Alexis de Tocqueville, *Democracy in America* (New York, 1840), vol. II, pp. 36-37.

to whom we must publicly acknowledge and thank for His goodness. Secondly, it affirmed a set of inalienable rights that did not originate from men but from that God, and included, among others, life, freedom, and the pursuit of happiness. When it comes to the fulfillment of these rights, religious freedom comes first. This does not imply submission to a particular religious faith, but precisely the opposite, that is, the freedom of every human being to worship God in accordance with his own convictions. Third, government is limited and aimed at protecting inalienable rights and not at granting or controlling them. This form of government exists by the consent of the governed and their submission to that set of rights. Finally, given the sinful human nature, the powers of the State must be divided and separated, restraining and counterbalancing each other in order to avoid spiraling down into tyranny.

These characteristics, which were doubtlessly exceptional in the eighteenth century, but not so common today, explain the success of American democracy, and also the repeated failures of other attempts to implement it. They also point to red flags that, if not heeded, could place the survival of democracy in a dangerous situation.

The Limitations of Other Democracies

The next attempt to create a democratic system took place in France before the end of the eighteenth century. Dale K. Van Kley made it clear in his day that the origins of the struggle for freedom in France *also* existed in Calvinism[2] and, in fact, preceded the Enlightenment by almost two centuries. However, there was a fundamental difference. While the vast majority of the population held a Puritan worldview in the United States, that worldview did not even remotely occur in France. Very likely, that aspect was due in large part to the fact that the French Revolution overlooked the lessons of American democracy.

2. D. K. Van Kley, *The Religious Origins of the French Revolution. From Calvin to Civil Constitution, 1560-1791* (New Haven, 1996).

Certainly, it opened the way for freedom of conscience by recognizing, for the first time in French history, the religious freedom of Protestants and Jews. However, this idea of freedom, which originated within a Catholic-Roman society, neither knew nor wanted to avoid an indoctrinating tone derived from power itself. The government did not recognize rights, whose origins traced back to God—as Thomas Jefferson or James Madison had asserted—but rather imposed them. It's more than that. The government intended to lead the people toward happiness regardless of what the people might think. It is hardly surprising that the constitutional monarchy was transformed into a regicidal republic and that that regicidal republic gave birth to the Reign of Terror, the only way to enforce the rights of man. Rousseau and other *philosophes* might have believed in the natural goodness of man, but the reality is that, in the end, in order to enforce happiness, they resorted to spilling rivers of blood. Not surprisingly, the French Revolution halted the Reign of Terror by an oligarchic coup during the month of Thermidor (the second month of the summer quarter) and eventually led to the military dictatorship of Napoleon Bonaparte in control of an empire.

Certainly, the French Revolution was not unfruitful. It achieved some conquests, such as freeing itself from the yoke of the Roman Catholic Church, recognizing religious freedom, and opening up education and administration of the State to everyone. However, the reality is that not only did it not implant democracy in France, but it placed the nation on a path of ups and downs between reaction and liberalism that were repeated throughout the nineteenth century. In no small measure, such terrifying results were a result from the influences that shaped the revolution, which went far beyond Calvinism and included the French Enlightenment and Freemasonry. Moreover, the population, who were mostly Roman Catholic, had not been shaped by these principles.

The situation with Spain fared no better. In 1808 the nation was invaded by Napoleon's troops. The Spanish armies were not worthy adversaries against the French weapons and, defeated time and time again, the resistance was reduced to guerrillas forces and, later, a small English contingent that landed on the Iberian Peninsula. One after another, the Spanish cities capitulated, with the exception of Cadiz in the south. The Spanish Parliament, equivalent to the English Parliament, would meet at this location, and it was where the first Spanish Constitution was drafted. The most diverse judgments have been made about it, but what is undeniable is that the 1812 Constitution failed. At the end of the day, the liberal revolution was nipped in the bud by King Ferdinand VII, and the Spanish nineteenth century became a continuous confrontation between those who believed in the modernization of a shattered Spain and those who, on the contrary, thought that clinging to the old regime would lead the nation to a happy utopia, which, incidentally, never came to pass for the simple reason that it had never existed. The reality is that, at least in theory, the 1812 Constitution could have triumphed in its noble endeavor; but the faults that condemned it to failure had already been pointed out at the time by José María Blanco White, and ignoring such a voice had brought about dire consequences.

José María Blanco White is one of the most extraordinary figures of the Spanish nineteenth century, although his heterodox status has determined his ignorance—provoked from above—by the vast majority of Spaniards. A Catholic-Roman cleric, of Sevillian origin, who ended up embracing Protestantism in one of the most interesting spiritual journeys of his century, and an outstanding representative of the so-called 1808 generation and a convinced liberal, he was thirty-five years old when the courts met on the island of León to fulfill their legislative duty. As editor of the political section of the *Semanario Patriótico*, since 1808, he championed the need to draft a liberal constitution while becoming one of its propagandists of the need to create a favorable public opinion.

In 1810, when Seville fell into the hands of the French, Blanco moved to England, where he continued writing from the fortress that his newspaper, *El Español*, had become. A liberal and patriotic publication, *El Español* is one of the indispensable sources for understanding the history of Spain as well as the progress of the liberals. Through thousands of pages, Blanco became an exceptional witness to the constitutional process, but also one of its most lucid critics, fundamentally because he knew how to foresee that the process begun with the meeting of the courts would end tragically.

Blanco's background was rooted in the Enlightenment. As early as 1796—when he was only twenty-one years old and was an irreproachable priest—Blanco had read in the Academy of Human Letters an epistle to Don Juan Pablo Forner in which some of his essential topics already appear, such as the defense of science—nicknamed by some ecclesiastics as "insufficient"—, the resistance against the "oppressive tyrant," which could be religion and fanaticism as an enemy of the Truth. During the years 1803-1808, his writings praising the British model of society and education appeared in *El Correo de Sevilla*. At the time, he not only devoted himself to learning languages, but also devoted himself to the reading of forbidden books, not infrequently lent to him by the learned Forner.

In 1805, Blanco moved to Madrid, where, in addition to his activities at the Pestalozziano Institute, a true educational revolution founded by a central European protestant,[3] he frequently attended the social gatherings of other Spanish intellectuals such as Quintana, Juan Nicasio Gallego, or Campmany. He remained in the capital of Spain until the arrival of the French invaders, when he decided to return to Seville. The journey—detailed in his *Letters*, of which one of the readings is absolutely mandatory in order to know and understand the Spanish nineteenth century—showed him a Spain far removed from the ideals of Enlightenment and liberalism in which the people were prey to social and economic backwardness and religious fanaticism. Dismayed, Blanco White realized, under the guise of patriotism, how only terrible outbreaks of violence and bloodshed were taking place in many towns. Once in Seville, Blanco gave himself over to the cause of freedom, but without deluding himself. He was painfully aware that "the popular cry,

3. In this regard, see: J. M. Quero Moreno, *Enseñar para la vida. El Protestantismo en Pestalozzi y en el krausismo español* (Madrid, 2015).

even if it expresses the sentiment of a majority, does not deserve the name of public opinion, just as the unanimous claims of an act of faith do not deserve it," and it was not because "dissent is the great characteristic of freedom." There could hardly be dissent in a Spain marked by the activity of the Inquisition, by the prohibition of lectures, and by a narrow-minded Roman-Catholic religious monolithism.

During those years in Seville, Blanco—who was in contact with characters such as Saavedra, Jovellanos, Garay or Quintana—became a paradigm for the defense of the drafting of a constitution, precisely when the idea was extremely foreign to the vast majority of Spaniards. It is no surprise that Quintana, the founder of the *Semanario Patriótico*, would entrust his friend Isidoro Antillón with the History section, but the Politics section was given to Blanco. The motto of the publication was obvious: "Defending above all, the emerging Spanish freedom." For this reason, the *Semanario* would last "as long as the simple truth breathed in it, as long as flattery did not come and stain it; as long as the hatred of tyranny communicated its fire, while patriotism gave it its haughty boldness."

Blanco launched his proposals in favor of a constitution from the *Semanario*: a call for a meeting with national representation, called courts; the independence of millions of Spaniards in the face of "the capricious whims of one"; and that "each citizen would come to feel their own strength in the political machine." If, on the one hand, he cried out against the invader; on the other, he raised his voice for the freedom of the people. On December 7, 1809, Blanco concluded his *Dictamen sobre el modo de reunir las Cortes en España* (His opinion on how to bring together the courts in Spain). In it he pointed out that there was no point in insisting on the historical precedents of the courts, insofar as, except for some scholars, nobody knew them. On the contrary, the essential thing was to bring them together as a matter of urgency in order to avoid the ambitions of those who had already conceived hopes of leadership and to get them to give it "not to a class of men, but to the homeland, not to a corporation, but to the entire nation."

From London, Blanco was already enthusiastically applauding the successive successes of the courts, such as the approval of freedom of the press or the declaration of sovereignty of the nation. It is no less true that he soon regretted other aspects. For example, the regulation of freedom of the press in Spain promulgated by the courts displeased Blanco because it was very restrictive and thus eliminated the possibility that a despotic action by the courts could be restrained by public opinion. In the same way, Blanco realized that the Regency continued to exercise considerable power over the courts, when, in his opinion, the courts should separate themselves from the government. As he pointed out: "Put, for example, an Argüelles in the State Ministry, a Torreros in the Grace and Justice Ministry, a Gonzalez in the War Ministry, and you will see how activity grows and how the two powers communicate strength."

Between 1810 and 1814, the publication directed by Blanco published the instructions given by the Boards to the deputies, Jovellanos' dictamen before the Central Council, the *Reflections on the Spanish Revolution* by Martínez de la Rosa, and the full text of the Constitution of 1812, but, above all, he analyzed the texts with a rigor that is astonishing for its clarity. In a very special way, Blanco wrote a set of writings known as the *Letters of Juan Sintierra* where he pointed out the problems he saw in the activity of the courts and in the possibilities of the constitution having a happy future.

Blanco complained, for example, that many issues were not resolved in the courts in an open forum, but in the hallways and secret meetings, or that the deputies seemed to be spending more of their time in social gatherings rather than in the service of the nation. Also, in trying to show off, those in government overestimated themselves and lost contact with reality. On top of that, the courts suffered from flaws that did not escape White. Thus, he mentioned how the Americas, part of Spain at the time, were not sufficiently and legitimately represented; and how members of the Parliament were not employed by the State, and, above all, how it was a great mistake that the courts were not the ones who decided the regulation of taxes. However, where Blanco was most accurate was in the flaws of the constitution.

First, the constitution lacked realism in addressing the relationship between the courts and the crown. For the time being, the deputies might have thought that the legislative branch would have no problem with the executive branch given the provisional government's minor influence, but "when a real person comes to the throne, they will see how futile their victory has been in the absence of a ruler." The constitution, according to Blanco, "hardly even took into consideration its precautions against royal power," which could end up having a tragic end. Second, the constitution denied a principle as important as that of religious liberty in order to please the Catholic Church. That circumstance pained Blanco to the point of regretting the religious intolerance "that darkened the first page of the constitution that wants to defend the rights of men." In fact, the courts, "converted into a council, not only declare what is the religion of Spain (to which they have an undeniable right), but they condemn all other non-Catholic nations. In other words, "the Spaniards must be free in everything except their consciences," as is clear from Article 12, which says, "A cloud that darkens the dawn of freedom is rising in Spain." Blanco did not intend for a secularist system like the one established in France during the Revolution to be established, and he even insisted on being very careful in dealing with the aristocracy and the Catholic Church. However, he was convinced that such prudence could not imply the elimination of religious freedom, since, if that fact were to be admitted, an absolutely essential right such as freedom of conscience would be violated, and if freedom of conscience were to remain in the hands of an institution such as the Roman Catholic Church, which used the Inquisition, what other freedoms, in practice, were going to be left to the Spanish people?

In 1814, Blanco White pointed out that "very serious mistakes have been made by the leaders of the courts, but they are errors that originated from a very noble principle." However, it was made clear why the 1812 Constitution was doomed to failure. The reasons would be none other than the lack of Parliamentary check-and-balance controls over the king and the absence of religious freedom, which, by impeding freedom of conscience, would end up invalidating other rights, such as freedom of expression. To make matters worse, the way in which the Hispanic-American representation had been approached was wrong and led to foreseeing future conflicts.

The failure of the Cadiz Constitution was a tragedy for freedom, but there can be no doubt that Blanco White was right in all his precautions, in all his warnings, and in all his predictions. At the outset, the return of Fernando VII immediately resulted in the suppression of the constitution and in an absurd but determined attempt to return to the Old Regime. Blanco had pointed it out. The arrival of a king unwilling to capitulate would nullify the work of the courts.

Immediately afterwards, the upholding of the privileges enjoyed by the Roman Catholic Church had a disastrous effect on the development of Spanish constitutionalism. Still in the third decade of the nineteenth century, the Spanish Inquisition executed a heretic—the Protestant Cayetano Ripoll[4]—whose horrendous crime had been not to pray the Hail Mary in class. To tell the truth, in no small measure, the Spanish nineteenth century was characterized by the attempts of the liberals, who were Roman-Catholic, to create a modern state and those of the Roman Catholic Church by preventing it, who were convinced that such a step would bring with it the end of its privileges and, sooner or later, the freedom of conscience.[5] The fact that such a circumstance was masked in a succession of dynastic wars does not negate its terrible reality—if anything, it accentuates it—nor that, unfortunately, its ramifications would extend out even further.

The Constitution of 1812, which was one of the noblest achievements in the history of Spain, ended up failing not because of the lack of patriotism or the brilliance of its editors but, basically, because of the way in which they let themselves be carried away—an opinion espoused by Blanco White—by an idealism that blinded them to the reaction that the great beneficiaries of the Old Regime—the absolute monarchy and the Catholic Church—would have against the improvements of the constitution. Throughout the nineteenth century, the

4. On the same note, see: C. Vidal, *El 'ultimo ajusticiado* (Barcelona, 1996).
5. In this regard, see: *Historia secreta de la iglesia católica en España*, pp. 419-423; 453ff.; 473ff.

Spanish Parliamentarism's complete inability to create a democratic State became readily apparent, a State that the Roman Catholic church always opposed, and one that the majority of the population did not support. Unlike what happened in the United States, there was no worldview to support such a system. In 1931, the proclamation of the Second Republic opened the way to a democracy, but it was submerged in a confrontation of revolution and counter-revolution that led to a civil war and a military dictatorship that lasted for almost four decades. A democratic constitution was adopted in 1978, but today the system is in deep crisis and the nation is facing an uncertain future.[6]

The situation was no better in those nations that emerged at the end of the Spanish empire. In them, the main reference was—which is logical—the more than imperfect Cadiz Constitution where neither the right to freedom of conscience nor the separation of powers existed.[7] After the restoration of absolutism was carried out in Spain—as Blanco White had foretold—the independence fighters of New Spain proclaimed the Constitution of Apatzingán on October 20 of that same year. Blanco's inspiration in the Cádiz Constitution was obvious and was not unique. Truth be told, it was the interim solution adopted in many places[8] while waiting for a new constitution. As Mario Rodríguez pointed out, "The Spanish liberalism that was forged in Cadiz provided key ideological lines for a program of modernization and independent existence."[9] The most remarkable influence of the Constitution of Cadiz is seen in the Uruguayan Constitution of 1830,[10] in the Chilean Constitution of 1822,[11] in the Argentinian

6. Regarding this subject, see the Stella Maris prize-winning essay: César Vidal, *El traje del emperador* (Barcelona, 2015).

7. For an overview of these influences, see: Alberto Ramos Santana (coord.), *La Constitución de Cádiz y su huella en América 2011*.

8. Demetrio Ramos, *América en las Cortes de Cádiz, como recurso y esperanza* (1987), pp. 116-117.

9. Mario Rodríguez, *El experimento de Cádiz en Centroamérica 1808-1826* (1984), p. 108. On the influence of Cádiz in Central America, see: Jorge Mario García Laguardia, *Centroamérica en las Cortes de Cádiz* (1994).

10. In this regard, see: Héctor Gros Espiel, *La Constitución de Cádiz de 1812, la Constitución del Reino de Portugal de 1822, la Constitución del Imperio de Brasil y la Constitución de Argentina de 1826 como precedentes de la Constitución uruguaya de 1830 (2004)*; Ana Frega Novales, *Ecos del constitucionalismo gaditano en la Banda Oriental de Uruguay* (2011).

11. Cristián E. Guerrero Lira, *La Constitución de Cádiz y Chile* (2011).

Constitutions of 1819 and 1826, in the Bolivian Constitution of 1826,[12] or in the Peruvian Constitutions of the first third of the nineteenth century.[13] In fact, the influence of the Constitution of Cadiz went beyond the strictly Spanish sphere to influence constitutions such as the Portuguese of 1822, the Brazilian of 1824, and, in general, the development of Brazilian constitutionalism.[14] Overall, the texts—which were totally different from the Constitution of the United States—did not recognize the principle of freedom of conscience and maintained a rather deficient separation of powers. It is not surprising that the constitutional history of all of Latin America has been a virtual ups and downs in which coups, revolutions, and dictatorships—military or left-wing—have taken up far more space than even the appearances of a democratic system. Ultimately, the Puritan tradition, absolutely essential for the formation of American democracy, was absent and was replaced by a liberalism mortally wounded by the Roman Catholic Church, a bitter enemy of freedom of conscience and of education. Added to these factors, which are sufficient to explain the failure of democracy in Latin America, was another of no small significance. We refer to the influence of Freemasonry.

The beginning of the independence struggle in Spanish America against Spain took place at dawn on September 16, 1810, in Mexico, and its main protagonist in this attempt was a freemason named Miguel Hidalgo and Costilla Gallaga. Freemasonry had been introduced in Mexico just four years earlier. In January 1809, a French agent named Octaviano d'Alvimar contacted Hidalgo with the intention of offering him help for anti-Spanish subversion. It was not long before Hidalgo did indeed rise up in arms against Spain, and he certainly knew how to act with remarkable skill because the uprising placed him under the banner of Our Lady of Guadalupe, and the cause of independence linked her with promises to divest the rich to give to the

12. See: F. Javier Limpias, *¡Viva la Pepa!* (2011).
13. Teodoro Hampe Martínez, *Sobre la Constitución de 1812: las Cortes gaditanas y su impacto en Perú* (2011).
14. See: Vicente de Paulo Barreto, *A Constituiçao de Cádiz e as origens do constitucionalismo brasileiro*, 2004; Andrea Slemian y João Paulo G. Pimenta, *Cádiz y los imperios portugués y brasileño* (2011).

poor and take revenge against the Spanish. The difference with the process of independence of the United States is obvious.

The severity of the uprising was extraordinary. Priest Hidalgo murdered, for example, all the Creoles when he took the city of Guanajuato, and his enemy, General Calleja, when he recovered it, ordered the prisoners' throats be slit so as not to waste ammunition by shooting them. Finally, after half a year of fighting, Hidalgo was captured and shot. For the moment, the danger of independence was averted. It wasn't going to be for long, and in a very significant way, freemasonry was going to have an extraordinary role in the later history of Mexico.

Possibly, the most impressive character of the process of independence of Latin America is not Simón Bolívar, as is often said, but José de San Martín.[15] The figure of Saint Martin is not usually analyzed in depth often, and even when its study is addressed, it usually falls back into other topics and avoids compromising data such as that of his membership in Freemasonry, which is a hard pill to swallow for many Roman Catholic Argentinians. San Martín was a Mason, as he admitted it in several of his letters, and his career in Freemasonry is more than documented. As if that were not enough, his political career would be totally incomprehensible—perhaps it would not even have taken place—without Freemasonry.

It is known that the departure of San Martín from Spain in 1811 was directly related to the idea of reaching Latin America and unleashing a revolution against Spain there, a revolution that the invaded metropolis was not going to be able to repel. It is less known that San Martín left Spain with the support of the French occupation authorities and the support of Freemasonry. In fact, the researcher José Pacífico Otero discovered in the Segovia military archive an authorization dated September 6, 1811, which allowed San Martín to go to Lima.

15. On the Argentinian emancipator, see: J. L. Busaniche, *San Martín visto por sus contemporáneos* (Buenos Aires, 1942); E. Fontaneda Pérez, *Raíces castellanas de José de San Martín* (Madrid, 1980); J. Lynch, *San Martín. Argentine Soldier, American Hero* (New Haven, 2009); B. Mitre, *Historia de San Martín y de la emancipación sudamericana*, 3 vols. (Buenos Aires, 1950); P. Pasqual, *San Martín: La fuerza de la misión y la soledad de la gloria* (Buenos Aires, 1999).

On the fourteenth of the same month, San Martín left Spain accompanied by some friends, all of them Freemasons. As he has made clear, Enrique Gandía and those with him all set off with French funds to unleash subversion on the other side of the Atlantic. However, before leaving for the American continent, St. Martin landed in London, where he met with members of another Masonic lodge, the Great American Meeting, inspired by the Venezuelan Freemason Francisco de Miranda—who already in 1806 had tried to carry out an uprising against Spain—and in which San Martín had been initiated up to the fifth degree. It was on board an English frigate, the *George Canning*, that the Masonic conspirators arrived in Río de la Plata in 1812, a very convenient circumstance, since the nationality of the ship concealed the origin of the undertaking.

Were Saint Martin and his companions mere agents of Napoleonic Masonry? It is difficult to answer this question in a categorical manner because of the absence of sources. Surely, one could rather speak of a confluence of interests between Napoleon and the insurgents. It is more relevant to point out that in order to advance his objectives, San Martín, together with Carlos María de Alvear and José Matías Zapiola, created an organization that would be called the Lautaro Lodge, taking its name from a Mapuche Indian who had faced the Spanish in Chile and who had finally been defeated and killed by Juan Jufré's troops. Some authors such as Jesuit Ferrer Benimeli, who has even denied that San Martín was a Mason, have wanted to ignore the masonic character of the Lautaro Lodge, but the truth is that it is indisputable and there are numerous documents. The letter sent in 1812 to Juan Martín de Pueyrredón, also a Mason, in which San Martín uses the Masonic rubric of three points is well known. As well as the testimony of the son-in-law of the Liberator, Mariano Balcarce, when, at the request of Benjamin Vicuña Mackenna, he replied: "Following faithfully the ideas of my revered father-politician, who in life did not want to speak of his connection with Freemasonry and other secret societies, I believe I should refrain from making use of the documents I possess in this regard." In fact, the view of God that Saint Martin had was not the Catholic one that would have been expected—there are inflammatory anticlericalism texts, on the other hand—but that of the Creator, which is very much in harmony with the Masonic tradition. Also, in line with this, it clearly set out his final wish: "I forbid any kind of funeral, and from the place where I die, I am to be taken directly to the cemetery, without any accompaniment, but I would like my heart to be buried in the cemetery in Buenos Aires." In 1824, Saint Martin retired to France, whose Freemasonry had played such an important role in the emancipation process. He died on August 17, 1850, in a house in Boulogne sur-Mer., but it wasn't until three decades later that his remains would be sent to Buenos Aires.

However, it is not just about the Masonic affiliation of Saint Martin. The articles of the Lautaro Lodge[16] are very explicit and form the embodiment of one of the foundational dreams of Freemasonry, which is bringing about political change not at the urging of the people, but by the means of an enlightened minority also destined to govern the new society. The text quoted is, of course, the exposing of a real plan to first gain and then monopolize the power in the new American society born from the emancipation movement. This circumstance explains that, as stated in its Article 5: "No Spaniard, no foreigner, nor no more than one clergyman, one who is considered more important because of his influence and relationships," can be accepted into the Lodge. Or even more important, according to Article 11, the members of the lodge will agree that "no one will be employed in any important position of influence in the government, neither in the capital, nor outside it, without the approval of the Lodge, meaning domestic and foreign envoys, provincial governors, generals in charge of armies, members of the superior courts of justice, prominent ecclesiastical positions, leaders of line regiments and militia corps and others of this kind."

Naturally, the members and founders of the Lautaro Lodge were aware that in a postcolonial society where press censorship would

16. Reproduced in B. Vicuña Mackenna, *El ostracism del general O'Higgins* (Valparaiso, 1860).

disappear, even in part, and where there would be, at least formally, a certain weight of public opinion, control over it would be essential, and thus its Article 13 states: "Starting from the principle that the Lodge, in order to consider any employment for one of its members, must take into consideration and respect public opinion, the members who are about to accept any position must work on acquiring it."

This concern for public opinion should include, for example, supporting the brothers of the lodge at all times, but with discretion. In this regard, Article 14 states: "It will be one of the first obligations of the brothers, by virtue of the purpose of the institution, to help and protect themselves in any conflict of civil life and to support each others' opinions; but, when the latter opposes the public, they must at least observe silence."

Of course, a plan for the conquest of power of these dimensions could not admit leaks, and the General Constitution of the Lautaro Lodge included a set of criminal laws, of which the second stated: "Every brother who reveals the secret of the existence of the lodge by word or sign shall be put to death, by whatever means is appropriate."

The lodge founded in 1812 in Buenos Aires achieved each and every one of its objectives. Not only did it provoke and secure South American independence, but it also overthrew the so-called second Argentinian triumvirate and put in its place another formed by members of the lodge. In 1816, despite internal differences, San Martín presided over the Lautaro Lodge, which had branches in Mendoza, Santiago de Chile, and Lima, and was preparing to create the Army of the Andes, a formidable military machine that was to expel the Spaniards from the continent and reach Peru. San Martín, as a good Mason, was obsessed with the symbolism of the sun, which he included in the Argentine flag, and accepted with immense pleasure the cries of tribute they paid to him as the son of that sun when he triumphantly entered Lima. On July 26, 1822, San Martín met with Simón Bolívar in Guayaquil to plan for the future of Latin America.

However, Saint Martin was not the only major Mason in the emancipation movement.[17] Bernardo O'Higgins, the emancipator of Chile; and Simón Bolívar, who was an essential instrument in the independence of nations such as present-day Colombia, Venezuela, and Panama were also Freemasons. So was Admiral William Brown,[18] an Irishman who was possibly instrumental in the cause of independence, or Peter I of Brazil, who was the driving force behind the emancipation of that Portuguese colony.

It is significant that Simón Bolívar, the other great protagonist of emancipation along with San Martín, despite his status as a Mason, ended his days hating secret societies. On November 8, 1828, when it became obvious that the great dream of freedom controlled by the Masons was to become an unmanageable nightmare, Bolívar issued a decree banning "all secret societies or confraternities, whatever they were called." The reason for taking such a step could not be more explicit in the legal text mentioned: "Having experience, both in Colombia and in other nations, that secret societies mainly serve to foster political upheavals, disturb public peace and order; and by concealing all their operations in a veil of mystery makes one presume fundamentally that they are not good, nor useful to society, and that therefore they arouse suspicion and alarm all those who ignore the objectives that secret societies are involved in..." Bolívar—no doubt—knew what he was talking about.

There can be little doubt about the failure of democratic regimes to this day in Latin America. However, it should not surprise us. Their foundation was not a worldview like the Puritan one that was based on the Bible, and, hence, was inclusive of realities such as insistence on freedom of conscience, the divine origin of human rights, or the anthropological pessimism that gave rise to the limitation of political power or the separation of powers. On the contrary, the constituent processes were the result of the dialectic between a Roman Catholic

17. Seal-Coon, "Spanish-American Revolutionary Masonry" in AQC, 94, 98-103.
18. On Brown, see: Levi-Castillo, "Admiral William Brown" in AQC, 102, 16-24 and, especially, H. R. Ratto, *Almirante Guillermo Brown* (Buenos Aires, 1961).

Church fiercely opposed to freedom of conscience, among others, and a Freemasonry that dreamed of manipulating the population and ruling from the shadows. On that basis—which was so different from the United States—is it surprising that attempts at democracy failed? There's more. Is it surprising that democracy failed in Roman-Catholic nations such as Spain, Portugal, and Italy well into the twentieth century, and even then leading to clearly flawed systems? Let's take it a step further: is it surprising that if it has had painful results in Roman Catholic nations, it has been worse in the Islamic or Buddhist nations?

Far from being a mere system of periodic elections, seeming freedom of expression and the press, or a plurality of parties, democracy goes far beyond what the American system has demonstrated since its inception. It also implies moral support without which democracy cannot survive. John Adams, the second president of the United States (1797-1801), in a letter addressed in October 1798 to the militia of Massachusetts, stated categorically: "We have no government armed with power capable of contending with human passions unbridled by morality and religion. Avarice, ambition, revenge, or gallantry would break the strongest cords of our Constitution as a whale goes through a net. Our Constitution was made only for a moral and religious people. It is wholly inadequate to the government of any other." However, not any morality or any religion fit the constitutional mold. On June 28, 1813, John Adams pointed out in a letter to Thomas Jefferson[19] that "the general principles on which the fathers achieved Independence were... the general principles of Christianity... Now I will avow that I then believed (and now believe) that those general principles of Christianity are as eternal and immutable as the existence and attributes of God."

The Founding Fathers had solved the great underlying problem that destroyed Greek democracy. On the basis of a people ascribing to the worldview of the Puritans, it was possible to create a system where anthropological pessimism limited power and divided it, where

19. *The Works of John Adams* (Boston, 1850), vol. X, pp. 45-46.

freedom of conscience and religion were considered the first rights, where the exercise of rights was granted to anyone, even to those who belonged to an entity such as the Roman Catholic Church, which persecuted that worldview fiercely, and where a politician's actions could not be based on flattering the people and buying them electorally, because the government was committed to defending certain rights—like life, freedom, and the pursuit of happiness—which were not concessions of power but originated in God Himself, something that was a self-evident truth. The inescapable question is whether democracy can survive when it is not based on similar foundations. To answer that question we will dedicate the following pages.

PART II

THE DANGERS THAT ARE STALKING DEMOCRACY

CHAPTER V

THE GROWING STATE INTERVENTION (I): The Interventionist State

Pikketty and the Fallacy of Equality

In recent times, a French economist named Thomas Piketty has acquired remarkable popularity. Director of Studies at the School for Advanced Studies in Social Sciences, Associate Professor at the Paris School of Economics, and Centennial Professor at the International Inequalities Institute, which is part of the London School of Economics, Piketty is a staunch supporter of the theses that defend a growing interventionism of the State. In 2013 Piketty published *Capital in the Twenty-First Century*, a work in which he argued that the rate of return on capital is higher in developed countries than the rate of economic growth. This circumstance will cause an inequality of wealth that will not stop growing and that will have to be combated through a growing tax that will lead to its redistribution. Piketty's theses fit perfectly with the Left, but they have had repercussions in Right-wing forces as well. In no small measure, they are the consummation of a whole historical trajectory that began with his parents—who were

Trotskyists and participated in May '68 Movement—and which continued on with Piketty himself, who taught at the Massachusetts Institute of Technology (1993-35), and after teaching at different educational institutions, he joined the scientific orientation board of the think tank *À gauche*, founded in Europe by Michel Rocard and Dominique Strauss-Kahn. In 2006, Piketty became the first president of the Paris School of Economics, where he worked only a few months before leaving this position to serve as economic advisor to the socialist candidate Ségolène Royal. Royal failed and, in 2007, Piketty returned to teaching. In 2009, Piketty was implicated in a domestic violence complaint by his girlfriend Aurélie Filippetti. From such a delicate situation, Piketty emerged recognizing the truth of the accusations and apologized. In 2013, Piketty won the Yrjö Jahnsson Award for economists under forty-five. Two years later, Piketty not only allowed himself to reject the Legion of Honor but was appointed economic adviser to the British Labour Party.

Piketty has not had the slightest success in terms of the results of the politicians he has advised, but he has become an icon of Western economy. Based on the thesis that the first purpose of democracy must be to end inequality, Piketty maintains that the goal will be achieved by depriving citizens of their property through taxation and then proceeding to distribute it. In this way, the State would take care of citizens from the cradle to the grave, covering needs such as education, health care, and even the receipt of a minimum social income. Almost all the fruits of their labors would be returned for anyone in need of services, which would eventually achieve equality. It is not surprising that such a view has had repercussions, because in different countries democratic systems have been following a development similar to that seen in Ancient Athens, where the catering to the desires of the citizens became the driving force of politics. First of all, however, it is debatable that the aim of the State—especially the democratic one—is to achieve equality for all citizens, and that even certain ends that we could call social have to be achieved through increased taxes and the dispossession of people's fruits of labor.

Let us first focus on equality as a value. I think one example will make clear what I want to communicate. Let us think of two societies. Let's imagine that everyone who lives in society A earns twenty units of value. All are equal and the supposedly desired goal of equality has been achieved. Now imagine another society we will call B. In it, the differences in income are considerable, even astronomical. The person who earns the most can earn a thousand or even ten thousand units of value, but those on the lower tier earn only fifty. Now let us reflect a little. Is it preferable to live in an egalitarian society where everyone earns the same even if it is a small amount, or would it be better to live in a society where there is inequality, but where one earns two, four, ten times more? To give an example, would the reader prefer to ride a bicycle in a society where people can only buy a bicycle, or would he prefer to own a car even if that car is worse than that of the wealthiest? Let us continue with more examples. Would you prefer to live in a 325-square-foot house like the rest of the citizens, or would you prefer to live in a 1,075 one, even though there are people who live in huge mansions? To summarize the thesis, do you prefer to live in equality, even if that equality implies misery, or do you prefer to live well, very well, even if there are people who still live better?

The reality is that the battle for equality contains a huge fallacy, and it is that of thinking that equality is the highest good when the truth is that it is not. Not only that. In fact, it is a great evil and an immense injustice. To think that those who work harder, who are more talented, who try harder, who sacrifice more professionally have to receive the same reward as the lazy, the stupid, or the uneducated is an attack not only on justice, but against common sense itself. Justice is not equality, but rather giving everyone what they deserve. That is true when the result of that equality that they claim to impose is injustice, dispossession of the property of those who have earned more, loss of freedom and creation of a State that can present itself as democratic, but that, in reality, only increases its intervention to become a dangerous enemy of freedom, property, and even life itself. Perhaps if we examine the origin of this contemporary quest for equality, we can understand the reality that hides behind this cause.

The Origin of the Interventionist State (I): Marx and Engels[1]

The revolutionary processes in which the nineteenth century was so plentiful, the belief in a supposedly scientific evolution of Humanity, the faith in utopias, and the detachment from any norm of moral character gave rise, among other fruits, to the birth of socialism. Its influence in the twentieth century was going to be extraordinary, and considering that communism alone resulted in the death of more than a hundred million people by repression or hunger, it is difficult to believe that the balance was positive. However, nothing that had taken place should have caused any surprise. Marx had announced it point by point in his most widely read work: *The Communist Manifesto*. It is significant that socialism, in just the course of a few years, was almost uniquely connected with the names of Marx and Engels, and that, as with no one else, they both grasped and expressed the essence of that political doctrine.

The years from 1844 to 1846 were of extraordinary importance to Marx and Engels. It was precisely on the first time they met in 1844 that they discovered that they had reached a complete agreement on the theoretical aspects. The two of them met again in the spring of 1845 and, according to Engels, by that time Marx had finished outlining his materialistic conception of history, and both began to elaborate on that result in more detail. According to Engels himself, Marx's theory was in fact a "*discovery*" that "*would revolutionize the science of history.*" In other words, Marx's conception was more of a scientific

1. The bibliography on Marx and Engels is vast. Among the latest studies, we highlight M. Gabriel, *Love and Capital. Karl and Jenny Marx and the Birth of the Revolution* (New York, 2011); S-E Liedman, *A World to Win. The Life and Works of Karl Marx* (London, 2018); G. Stedman Jones, *Karl Marx. Greatness and Illusion* (Cambridge, MA, 2016). For the analysis of the *Communist Manifesto*, we have followed César Vidal, *Camino a la cultura* (Barcelona, 2005).

finding than a philosophical concoction. Precisely for this reason, Engels thought that henceforth it was necessary not only to "*reason scientifically*" his views, but also to do everything possible to "*win the European proletariat*" over to the new "*doctrine*."

Marx and Engels were certainly about to begin a fruitful collaboration, and that took place during those first years precisely over those two premises, primarily indicated by the second one. In the first place, they tried to give a more finished form to what, quite pretentiously, they considered a scientific discovery from which would emerge works such as *Theses on Feuerbach*, *The German Ideology*, and *The Poverty of Philosophy*. Secondly, they took some more practical steps, such as joining the League of the Just that, since the workers' congress of June 1847, became the Communist League. It was precisely this entity that, at its congress during November-December 1847, entrusted them both with the drafting of a programmatic document that would become known as the *Communist Manifesto*. The moment seemed the most suitable for maintaining optimism. Germany especially seemed ripe for revolution. In the summer of 1844, there had been an insurrection of weavers in Silesia. That same year began the bad harvests that lasted until 1845. During 1845 and 1846, a plague struck that affected especially the potato, the basic food of the workers. In August 1846, the population of Cologne clashed with the garrison. In 1847, hunger riots erupted in Berlin, Ulm, and Stuttgart.

The heated German situation had its parallel in other nations. In France, the government of King Louis-Philippe was faced with hunger riots and a *petite bourgeoisie* that wanted the electoral census to be expanded, which could easily lead to the proclamation of the Republic. In the summer of 1847, various Italian states started rising up against Austrian rule. In October-November of the same year, Switzerland was torn apart by a civil war.

Marx and Engels argued in their writings that the world revolution, a revolution that would impose a proletariat dictatorship, was about to happen imminently. Engels referred, for example, to the "short time" left to the bourgeoisie, and in his *Principles of Communism*, written in the autumn of 1847, he stated that "*according to all indications, the proletariat revolution is soon approaching.*" In the midst of this spirited, almost feverish atmosphere, Marx and Engels wrote their most widely read work, the so-called *Communist Manifesto*.

The very beginning of the *Manifesto* is masterful. In fact, from the first lines it tries to grant an importance, which does not correspond to reality, to the communist movement and, at the same time, to establish it as the possessor of a redemptive message that will be heard internationally:

> *A spectre is haunting Europe – the spectre of communism. All the powers of old Europe have entered into a holy alliance to exorcise this spectre: Pope and Tsar, Metternich and Guizot, French Radicals and German police-spies.*
>
> *Where is the party in opposition that has not been decried as communistic by its opponents in power? Where is the opposition that has not hurled back the branding reproach of communism, against the more advanced opposition parties, as well as against its reactionary adversaries?*
>
> *Two things result from this fact:*
>
> *I. Communism is already acknowledged by all European powers to be itself a power.*
>
> *II. It is high time that Communists should openly, in the face of the whole world, publish their views, their aims, their tendencies, and meet this nursery tale of the Spectre of Communism with a manifesto of the party itself.*
>
> *To this end, Communists of various nationalities have assembled in London and sketched the following manifesto, to be published in the English, French, German, Italian, Flemish and Danish languages.*

We are not going to dwell on a detailed analysis of the Manifesto, but we are going to dwell on some of the measures that

Marx and Engels advocated in order to implement the communist dictatorship.

After a first part of his exposition in which they indicated that the class struggle is inevitable and that the proletariat must annihilate the bourgeoisie in order to free itself, Marx introduces the subject of the Communist Party and its role in this historical process:

> *In what relation do the Communists stand to the proletarians as a whole?*
>
> *The Communists do not form a separate party opposed to the other working-class parties.*
>
> *They have no interests separate and apart from those of the proletariat as a whole.*
>
> *The immediate aim of the Communists is the same as that of all other proletarian parties: formation of the proletariat into a class, overthrow of the bourgeois supremacy, conquest of political power by the proletariat.*

Right at this point in the discourse, Marx introduces the criticism that the communists make of culture, law, the family, or the homeland according to the bourgeois model. From their point of view, these are nothing but concepts that seek only to perpetuate the power of the bourgeoisie and the exploitation of the proletariat:

> *Your very ideas are but the outgrowth of the conditions of your bourgeois production and bourgeois property, just as your jurisprudence is but the will of your class made into a law for all...*
>
> *On what foundation is the present family, the bourgeois family, based? On capital, on private gain. In its completely developed form, this family exists only among the bourgeoisie. But this state of things finds its complement in the practical absence of the family among the proletarians, and in public prostitution.*

> *The bourgeois family will vanish as a matter of course when its complement vanishes, and both will vanish with the vanishing of capital.*
>
> *... The working men have no country. We cannot take from them what they have not got.*
>
> *... The Communist revolution is the most radical rupture with traditional property relations; no wonder that its development involved the most radical rupture with traditional ideas.*

The final goal of the proletariat is, therefore, to seize political power and from it carry out "a despotic violation of the right of ownership," which in the most advanced countries will be embodied in very concrete measures:

> 1. *Abolition of property in land and application of all rents of land to public purposes.*
> 2. *A heavy progressive or graduated income tax.*
> 3. *Abolition of all rights of inheritance.*
> 4. *Confiscation of the property of all emigrants and rebels.*
> 5. *Centralization of credit in the hands of the State, by means of a national bank with State capital and an exclusive monopoly.*
> 6. *Centralization of the means of communication and transport in the hands of the State.*
> 7. *Extension of factories and instruments of production owned by the State; the bringing into cultivation of waste-lands, and the improvement of the soil generally in accordance with a common plan.*
> 8. *Equal liability of all to work. Establishment of industrial armies, especially for agriculture.*
> 9. *Combination of agriculture with manufacturing industries; gradual abolition of all the distinction between*

town and country by a more equable distribution of the populace over the country.

10. *Free education for all children in public schools. Abolition of child factory labor in its present form. Combination of education with industrial production, etc.*

Marx' and Engels' words are certainly a disturbing description of what has been the evolution of democracies in recent decades. In a systematic way, an attempt would be made to advance toward a socialist society through increased State interventionism. Such interventionism would deprive citizens of their property, deprive them of the right to educate their children, erode the family, which is seen as an enemy to be destroyed, and control the economy from above. It is enormously interesting to see that Marx and Engels did not think that such measures would be taken following the conquest of power—as has happened in nations such as Russia, China, or Cuba—but before, in order to facilitate the conquest of power by the communists. To achieve this, communists would support any movement that would create tensions within the society:

> *In short, the Communists everywhere support every revolutionary movement against the existing social and political order of things.*
>
> *In all these movements, they bring to the front, as the leading question in each, the property question, no matter what its degree of development at the time.*
>
> *Finally, they labor everywhere for the union and agreement of the democratic parties of all countries.*
>
> *The Communists disdain to conceal their views and aims. They openly declare that their ends can be attained only by the forcible overthrow of all existing social conditions. Let the ruling classes tremble at a Communistic revolution. The proletarians have nothing to lose but their chains. They have a world to win.*
>
> *Working Men of All Countries, Unite!*

The revolution hoped for by Marx and Engels broke out in 1848, but contrary to what both had advocated, it did not lead to the victory of the proletariat and the annihilation of the bourgeoisie, but had very different results. Between 1848 and 1852, not only were the revolutions stifled, but Louis Bonaparte also staged a coup d'état in France, initiating the Second Empire, and the dissolution of the League of Communists took place. As a forecast of the immediate future, the lines written by Marx and Engels could not have been more unsuccessful.

In the longer term, the same thing happened with the *scientific* view that Marx and Engels claimed to have discovered. Over the decades, the more advanced capitalist countries not only drove away the specter of a crisis that would bring about the collapse of the system, they eradicated child labor for the first time in history; and not only did the middle classes not become proletarian, but the proletariats became the middle class. On the other hand, the countries that had adopted Marxist principles as authentic dogma of faith ended up, one after the other, at the bottom of the system. In the end, its workers had been suffering a much lower standard of living than those who found themselves in capitalist countries.

However, the theses of State interventionism did not disappear with the collapse of the USSR. On the contrary, decades before that event occurred, they found an extraordinarily important manifestation in fascism.

The Origin of the Interventionist State (II): Fascism[2]

Unfortunately, the word "fascism" is not understood by the majority of the world's population. The Left turned it into a scathing term

2. On fascism, see: J. P. Diggins, *Mussolini and Fascism: The View from America* (Princeton, 1972); R. Eatwell, *Fascism: A History* (New York, 1995); A. J. Gregor, *The Ideology of Fascism: The Rationale of Totalitarianism* (New York, 1969); R. O. Paxton, *The Anatomy of Fascism* (New York, 2004); W. Schivelbusch, *Three New Deals: Reflections on Roosevelt's America, Mussolini's Italy and Hitler's Germany 1933-1939* (New York, 2006); Z. Sternhell, *The Birth of Fascist Ideology* (Princeton, 1994).

that served to denigrate Ronald Reagan and Margaret Thatcher as well as conservative or classically liberal policies. Labeling someone a fascist means stigmatizing and denigrating them, removing them from the social debate and condemning them in the same way that the fascist regimes were condemned by their defeat in the Second World War. This behavior may have an advantage in the propaganda realm and the political struggle, but it becomes a major disadvantage by failing to see to what extent many of the policies pursued within democracies, especially by the Left, are openly fascist. Once again, the knowledge of history sheds no small light on what we are living in today.

At the outset, it must be stressed that fascism is only a form of socialism that had huge fans in its day. Winston Churchill went so far as to say in relation to Mussolini: "If I had been an Italian, I am sure I should have been whole-heartedly with you from the start to finish in your triumphant struggle against the bestial appetites and passions of Leninism."[3] Gandhi visited Mussolini in the 1920s, delighted to meet a politician of his rank, and left a graphic testimony of the event.[4] In 1934, even Cole Porter wrote of Mussolini in a song, saying, "You're the Top" in the world...although he finally had to change the lyrics of the song. All this was happening while fascist Italy was the most interventionist State on the planet, with the sole exception of the Soviet Union. To understand this circumstance, we must examine history.

Mussolini was born in 1883, and in 1900, while still a minor, he joined the Italian Socialist Party (PSI). After obtaining the title of schoolteacher in 1902, he took refuge in Switzerland, where he developed revolutionary socialist activities and began writing in the media. After an amnesty, he returned to Italy in 1904. In 1910 he was appointed secretary of the provincial socialist federation of Forli and soon after became editor of *La Lotta di Classe* (The Class Struggle), the socialist weekly magazine of this region, and increased its sales. The victory of the hard socialist wing at the Congress of Reggio Emilia,

3. M. Gilbert. *Winston S. Churchill. V: Prophet of Truth, 1922-1939*, p. 226.
4. https://www.youtube.com/watch?v=ZcUPkbYuhok.

held in 1912, gave him enormous importance, since he defended the expulsion of the reformist socialists. During that time, he took over the leadership of *Avanti*, the main Milanese socialist newspaper, the official party publication, while at the same time directing *Utopia*, his own journal in which he defended the socialist revolution, where ideological debates were expressed and there was ample room for revolutionary unionism with its advocates.

The break with the PSI occurred at the outbreak of the First World War. Mussolini was not a supporter of the neutrality defended by the PSI, and in 1915 he founded the newspaper *Il Popolo d'Italia*, which he named the proletarian newspaper. From it he defended intervention in the conflict alongside the Allies and against Germany. In August 1915, he volunteered to go to the front, where he was seriously wounded in 1917, thus becoming a war hero. In 1919, Mussolini created in Italy the Fasci italiani di combattimento, which would become the National Fascist Party in 1920. Mussolini himself would explain that fascism was a type of socialism, but not an internationalist Marxist type, but rather nationalist.

On May 25, 1922, he organized his assault for power through the so-called March on Rome. When Mussolini and his fascists marched in mass to Rome to take power, King Victor Manuel III refused to sign the State Siege Decree proposed by Ivanoe Bonomi, the head of the government, thus making any armed opposition by the army impossible. It's not only that. On October 30, 1922, the king also commissioned Mussolini to form a new government, despite the fact he did not have a majority in Parliament. What followed was an increasing State intervention in the lives of citizens still living under the guise of Parliament.

Mussolini reached an agreement with the Roman Catholic Church that is still in force today: the Lateran Pacts. In addition, he undertook an ambitious program of State works, boosted the state economy and private control, and enacted labor legislation, which met with applause from the ILO (International Labor Organization), which stated that Italy had the best social system in the world, supported by structures such as *dopolaboro* (after work) and trade unions. Jonah Goldberg has supported the thesis, advanced by other authors, that Roosevelt's New Deal incorporated Mussolini's interventionism.[5] Parallels exist, even if, quite possibly, Roosevelt was inspired more by legislations such as those of the Prussian chancellor Bismarck.

After an undeniable electoral victory, Mussolini maintained the monarchy, but he dismantled the Parliamentary system by establishing a dictatorship that suppressed political parties, freedoms, and any trace of a representative system. However, there was very little political opposition to the extent that Mussolini did not have to resort to extreme repressive measures for years and confined himself to imprisoning or banishing a few hundred opponents. The Roman Catholic Church and the monarchy supported him, but, above all, Mussolini was supported by large masses of people who had had no problem exchanging their freedom for the enjoyment of socialist laws.

If Mussolini had merely maintained the socialist regime—fascism—in Italy, it is possible that he would have retained power indefinitely with growing international applause. Only his desire to create an Italian empire by invading Ethiopia in 1935—a move that was heartily backed by the Italian bishops—turned a part of the international community against him. It was this repudiation that impelled Mussolini to ally himself with a man he despised: Adolf Hitler. The founder of German National Socialism, a Germanic version of fascism, Hitler had also come to power democratically and had begun a government of State interventionism that eventually became a dictatorship. In the end, Hitler's defeat in World War II would also provoke Mussolini's defeat and his death in 1945. The military failure, anti-Semitism—initially absent from Italian fascism with which many Jews were affiliated—and, above all, the horrible war crimes brought Mussolini into disrepute and led to the forgetting of his policy of State interventionism and, above all, the extent to which he would

5. Jonah Goldberg, *Liberal Fascism. The Secret History of the American Left from Mussolini to the Politics of Meaning* (New York, 2007).

inspire and does inspire many of today's policies in dictatorial systems as well as democratic ones.

As in Ancient Greece, the creation of favored masses by so-called social benefits ended up in eliminating Parliamentary and democratic systems by instituting dictatorships. It was a step that Marx and Engels had foreseen and that Mussolini and Hitler had taken advantage of to establish their systems of nationalist socialism. That danger persists to this day.

The growing State interventionism—supposedly provoked by the pursuit of equality and social justice—erodes the foundations of democracy by opening the way for certain determined politicians to seize power on the basis of flattered patrons whose approval is sought. The large subsidized masses in Latin America and the immigrants—often illegal—of Hispanic origin in the United States and of Muslim origin in the European Union are the sectors of population, often ethnic, whose recipients of social aid can tilt their vote towards certain political choices that have become the battering rams, often unaware, that are launched against the democratic system with the aim of collapsing it in the same way as it happened in ancient Athens.

However, these political forces do not, by themselves, have the economic power to carry out such programs. How, then, do they pay for them? We will approach that question in the next chapter.

CHAPTER VI

THE GROWING STATE INTERVENTION (III): Increasing Taxes

Other Times, Other Places

As we saw in the previous chapter, Marx and Engels saw with great clarity that the road to the conquest of power and the establishment of the dictatorship of the proletariat necessarily involved a fierce attack on private property. One of the extraordinary means for achieving that goal was the progressive raising of taxes, the growing dispossession of inheritances, and the launching of programs that we could call social. If, on the one hand, the first two measures would create a growing impoverishment of the middle classes and their proletarianization; on the other, these new masses who were thrust into impoverishment would become favored sectors that would support the communists in their assault on power. Fascism did not carry out these confiscatory measures, but it did know how to use social measures to win over a huge social base, which, helped by State aid, watched passively and even complacently as the Parliamentary regimes disappeared. In today's democracies, the banner of equality and social justice is being raised in a similar way to impoverish and proletarianize even the middle classes while creating a huge clientele that will eventually bring to power parties that promote socialist measures, leading these democratic systems to their demise. Not all parties have to assume theories like those of Piketty that would imply depriving the middle classes of almost all of their profits in exchange for a supposed equality. However, the strategy is the same, and it is the same because it is a privileged way of turning citizens into mere subjects subjected to the State. Such an idea has numerous supporters even in parties to the right of the political map. So much so that these tax increases are supported even by sectors of the population that are totally harmed by these measures, but they are unable to see it because of political and media propaganda. However, that concept has not always been the case and, to tell the truth, it clashes with the very path of democracies. An example of this can be found in the history of the United States itself.

As we indicated in the first part of the book, American democracy was shaped by the Puritan worldview. The approach that it gave to taxes was not, in this respect, an exception. In the Bible, there are references to taxes that are worthy of consideration. For example, the Torah envisioned a fixed tax of one tenth of the profit earned (Deuteronomy 26). Significantly, that tithe was paid annually, but it was divided into three-year periods. One year, the money was collected, but the Israelite did not turn it in, but spent it on himself and on his family so that he was aware that what he received came from God's generosity and that God wanted him to enjoy the fruit of his work with his family. Another year, that tithe was given to the people who served in the temple, as they had no other income, since the tribe of Levi had been excluded from the division of the land. Finally, in the third year, the tithe was intended for the truly unprotected of society, such as widows and orphans. Significantly, this tithe tax was not increased because the person had more income, but it was imposed equally to everyone on the understanding that the tithe of the rich person would always be greater than that of the poor person. It was, therefore, the tax that is usually called head tax (poll tax); that is, each person paid the same proportion of their income even if the amount varied in the end.

Of course, the Old Testament did not overlook the fact that there would be rulers who would try to raise taxes above that level, but, in a very significant way, that practice was not presented as a good one, but was pointed out as part of the abuse of power. Thus, in pointing out the risks of having "a king like the nations," the prophet Samuel was concerned enough to remind them that, among them, not only would there be the creation of a bureaucracy that the Israelites would have to maintain (1 Samuel 8:11-13), but also attendants (v. 14), as well as an additional tithe (v. 15 and 17) that, logically, would end up making the people unhappy (v. 18). Regrettably, Israel did not heed the wise counsel of Samuel but were bent on being like other nations (vv. 19-20). The figures given are nevertheless significant. The maximum amount of taxes would reach 20% of each person's income. The idea of the redistribution of wealth, in addition, appeared quite alien to the teaching of Moses and the prophets.

The way in which the subject of taxes is approached by the apostle Paul, precisely in relation to a description of the purposes of the State, is extremely striking. The text in question is found in Romans 13:3-6 and reads as follows:

> For rulers are not a terror to good works, but to evil. Do you want to be unafraid of the authority? Do what is good, and you will have praise from the same. For he is God's minister to you for good. But if you do evil, be afraid; for he does not bear the sword in vain; for he is God's minister, an avenger to execute wrath on him who practices evil. Therefore, you must be subject, not only because of wrath but also for conscience' sake. For because of this you also pay taxes, for they are God's ministers attending continually to this very thing (NKJV).

Paul's words are worthy of reflection. The apostle was not an anarchist, nor did he think that State power was illegitimate. On the contrary, the apostle affirmed that State order is indispensable in a fallen world. Hence, God points out its need. Now then, its purpose is none other than to maintain order and to punish those who break the law. Precisely because of this, it holds in its hands the power of the sword. This defense of the security and integrity of citizens is what justifies its existence and also legitimizes that it can collect taxes.

The apostle's teaching is more than interesting because it gives a description of what some today would call a State minimum. The purpose of the State is not to flood citizens with services, much less to force equality, but simply to maintain security and order by punishing those who break it. Such a principle is generally applicable and does not differentiate between democratic and nondemocratic governments. In addition, it points out that this is the purpose of taxes.

Not surprisingly, these views were reflected in the work of the Founding Fathers. Already before the revolution, Benjamin Franklin would write in 1758 in the *Poor Richard's Almanac* that "it would be a hard government that should tax its people one-tenth part of their income." It is even more significant that Article I, Section 9 of the United States Constitution states that "no capitation, or other direct, tax shall be laid, unless in proportion to the census or enumeration herein before directed to be taken." In other words, for the Founding Fathers—who had risen up against English dominance precisely when it discharged new taxes on the Americans—capitation was, as in the Bible, the tax model even if one accepts the possibility of some other direct tax. All in all, those taxes "shall be UNIFORM throughout the United States (Art. I, Sec. 8)."

Such a view—with deep Biblical and Puritan roots—only began to break down in the late nineteenth century as a result of ideologies such as Progressivism and Poststructuralism, which meant not seeing citizens as part of the nation, but as part of specific social groups. Such a view has, among other negative consequences, that of setting some sectors of the population againt others. Under this approach, which clashed head-on with the thinking of the Founding Fathers, in 1894, Congress passed a law that differentiated the treatment between the rich and the poor. The senator, and former congressman, Justin Morrill (1810-1898) perfectly captured some of the dangers inherent in that measure by stating: "In this country, we neither create nor tolerate any distinction of rank, race, or color, and should not tolerate anything else than entire equality in our taxation." Morrill was by no means insensitive to the needs of society. Founder of the Republican Party, to him is owed the Morrill Land-Grant Acts, which established federal funding for the creation of public colleges and universities. That is how as many as one hundred and six colleges were founded, including state universities, polytechnic colleges, and agricultural and mechanical colleges. He was also responsible not only for the current Library of Congress, but also for the creation of several colleges and universities for Black students. In other words, he made it clear that a tax system more in line with the spirit of the Founding Fathers—and the Bible—could be maintained without neglecting needs such as university education.

Morrill was not alone in his approaches. To tell the truth, in 1895, the Supreme Court handed down a judgment against the 1894 law on the grounds that it would be a step towards "a war of the poor against the rich—a war constantly growing in intensity and bitterness."

However, the so-called progressives decided to continue their plan, and in 1913 they succeeded in having the Sixteenth Amendment replace capitation taxation with progressive taxes. The tax system stopped treating Americans as equal citizens and turned them into groups, an extraordinarily damaging measure for democracy. On the one hand, the very wealthy would increasingly intervene in politics to escape from the increasing fiscal pressure; on the other, entire sectors of the population would be turned into patrons by politicians and, finally, the middle classes would end up paying the bills in terms of employment, economic growth, and prosperity, since the tax increase has the direct consequence of reducing economic and investment growth and increasing unemployment.

As if all this were not enough, the number of politicians determined to conquer and maintain power and to use tax money to create electoral clientele ends up causing a spiral of tax increases that end up destroying democracy. In the end, collecting and collecting more and more becomes one of the first goals of political action. Some true stories will more clearly show what I intend to tell.

Two True Stories That Are Quite Revealing

Let me first tell you a story about an entrepreneur whose initials are M. F. This businessman owned a company, and he was the main distributor of first Airtel and then later of Vodafone in his country. M. F.'s company owned 320 stores in his home country and planned to make a major investment to launch a telephone company through the foreign company. M .F.'s businesses were going so well that he became the owner of the largest private luxury car collection in his country. In 2006, a corrupt tax inspector who extorted taxpayers in collaboration with a law firm opened a tax file on him and seized more than 3 million euros. This action by the corrupt inspector had the direct consequence that, due to the lack of liquidity, M. F. was forced to dismiss three hundred of his employees. As if this were not enough, the Tax Office, the IRS of this country, reported it to the Prosecutor's Office for tax fraud, and the Public Prosecutor's Office agreed with the accusation. As a result of the action of the tax inspector, M. F. was first charged and later tried for this crime. The prosecutor asked for twelve years in prison. None of the tax office's accusations were proven, and almost ten years later, in 2015, the judge acquitted M. F. The acquittal clearly revealed the innocence of M. F., but during the process, the businessman lost a good part of his companies and almost all of his sales.

In fact, the judge also forced the Tax Office to return eight and a half million euros to M. F. that had been deducted from the VAT payment, in addition to a Rolls Royce, an Aston Martin, a BMW, an

Audi, and a Jaguar that had been seized. Then, the Tax Office, in a blatant sample of legal fraud, appealed the ruling to the provincial high court, thereby paralyzing the return. As if that were not enough, between January and September 2016, when the High Court upheld the acquittal, former members of the Province's Customs Service contacted M. F. and guaranteed the immediate return of the eight and a half million if he undertook, in writing, not to take legal action against the city's Tax Office and, in particular, against the corrupt inspector. The businessman M. F. flatly refused to guarantee the impunity of the corrupt inspector. To this day, no justice has been done for M. F., nor has a corrupt inspector who was part of the plot in which members of the Tax Office harassed him has been punished. Lawyers in collusion with corrupt inspectors offered to mediate in exchange for substantial sums of money, and then those sums obtained through extortion were shared between corrupt inspectors and tax lawyers who were even less honest.

In the case of M. F., the first consequence of not accepting the extortion was the seizure of his business accounts and the fact that three hundred people became unemployed. What followed was a judicial ordeal in the course of which the Tax Office seized the property of the businessman and also initiated a court action demanding that he be imprisoned. Ten years later, M. F. was found not guilty, but even at this time he has not been able to avoid the action of officials who have offered to help him recover his assets that had been unjustly seized by the Tax Office in exchange for not taking legal action against the corrupt inspector. M. F., in an exemplary way, refused, but already his life had been ruined by a Tax Office that, in the end, only wanted to collect more to maintain the State apparatus.[1] Certainly, when it is considered lawful to deprive another of his goods for use in a social redistribution, then abuse follows. Is that the exception? No!!! It's the general rule. Let me tell you another of these revealing stories.

1. https://www.farodevigo.es/galicia/2019/01/19/redcom-9-millones-bloqueados-trama/2035491.html; https://www.farodevigo.es/gran-vigo/2019/01/17/caso-redcom-epicentro-investigacion-trama/2034572.html; https://www.elconfidencialdigital.com/articulo/dinero/corrupcion-agencia-tributaria-asi-operaba-trama-inspectores-hacienda-desarticulada-galicia/20190116173527120499.html.

Four officials of the Tax Office—remember that it is the equivalent of the IRS—accompanied by police of the Provincial Brigade of Foreigners and Borders, appeared unexpectedly on March 30, 2017, authorized by an administrative contentious court, in one of the most important brothels in the city. The intention of the Tax Office agents was to extort information from prostitutes that would allow them to collect even more taxes. In order to avoid leaving traces of their actions that could lead to criminal wrongdoing, the Tax Office officials, accompanied by police officers, gave orders to turn off the videos recording what was happening in the brothel. Despite the interest of the members of the Tax Office in erasing the traces of their actions, one of the videos remained on and was able to record what the tax officials did while inside the brothel. This was what one of the officials of the Tax Office told a policeman: "You haven't recorded anything of what we have said to the girls, right? You've just recorded what favors us and nothing else, right?" In other words, the Tax Office official wanted the police to falsify the interrogations. At that point, it was already 12:15 at night, and several officials of the Tax Office had been conducting the tax inspection for seven hours. In his attempt to get the women to confess that they were undercover local workers and not prostitutes who rented the rooms after getting a client, the Tax Office official told one of the women: "This is going to be easy if you collaborate, and if you say what we want to hear, we are going to get through this fast. If you don't tell us, we will take longer, do you understand me?"

In the recording you could see very clearly how prostitutes were pressured, extorted, and threatened by tax officials, who even prevented one of the women from caring for her young son for hours in order to force a confession in the way they wanted. As if this were not enough, two of the members of the Tax Office referred to the bonus they were going to collect while the chief of the operation said that with this inspection "I'll meet the quota for the year."

One of the most serious cases obtained in the recording was that of a young woman named Diandra, to whom National Police officers issued two crime reports and threatened to file them. One of the officials told her as he showed them to her, "That way, next time you'll be quieter." The recordings showed how then a colleague of Diandra separated her from the group and asked her to calm down because "you're going to get hit". "I want to go now, dammit," she replied. The recordings also showed how Diandra grabbed her purse, tried to leave, and then an agent took her back inside the room where she was being held.

At 8 p.m., the National Police officers had concluded that there was no trafficking crime and told the tax officials that it was best to leave. However, the members of the Tax Office decided to continue the extortion they were exerting on the prostitutes. So when the cop said to the head of the Tax Office, "We're going to let the girls go, do you want anything?", the head of the Tax Office replied: "Don't let them go yet."

Since it was impossible to get the women to confess what the tax inspectors wanted, they asked the police to help them in order to cause them greater fear. Thus one of the recordings shows the following dialogue between a policeman and one of the prostitutes:

Police: "They're not the police. They're from the Tax Office. They are going to ask you some questions. I'm just asking you to tell the truth, especially considering your situation."

Girl: "What is my situation? (...) I am totally legal. I am a lawyer in my country. What's illegal about it?"

Police: "I'm just saying that..."

Girl: "Yes, I know what my rights are. I'm a lawyer (...)"

Police: "Your questioning is going to be quick. The way this goes is that we will finish sooner the better you do. The longer you take, the longer we'll take. This is going to be easy if you collaborate and tell us what we want to hear. We're going to go fast. If you don't tell us, we're going to take longer, do you understand me?"

Girl: "Yes."

The recordings also show how the person in charge of the Tax Office operation and a police officer grabbed a girl (Cristina, a Paraguayan national) and took her to a separate room to threaten her that it was best for her to cooperate. The dialogue was as follows:

Police: "Let's see. I'll start from the beginning, or I'll finish, or I'll tell them that you can go, and I'll just catch the foreigners, and you come with me. You're not going to go anywhere nor say anything. Tell it to me and we'll be done in no time. How much do you pay a day to be here?"

Cristina: "The rent of the room."

Police: "Every time you rent, how much do you pay for an hour?"

Cristina: "60."

Police: "And for a half hour?"

Cristina: "30."

Police: "When you enter, how much do you pay with no services?"

Cristina: "We don't pay for the day."

Police: "I don't believe it, and those who live upstairs, don't pay anything?"

Cristina: "Nothing, nothing, I swear. We go in and out, but we don't pay anything if we don't work. It's up to us whether we want to work, but we don't pay for living upstairs."

The recording also showed how the IRS agents were trying to get the girls to tell the version they wanted to hear by threatening economic persecution from the IRS: "What is going to happen to you is that if you say that the money from the clients goes to you (...), in the end, since we know who you are, we will open an inspection on all of you, and we will demand a lot of money (...) and we will start some impressive files on you. That means you can never earn a salary or own property because that debt is going to last a lifetime. And the moment you deposit any money or open an account or try to buy a house, they're going to repossess it. And that's how you're going to end up."

One of the inspectors, in a brutal show of extortion, said to one of the prostitutes, "We're going to start some very important files that are going to cost a lot of money, which is going to generate a debt that you won't be able to pay, and you're going to have that debt forever. You'll never be able to earn a salary because they will seize it. You'll not be able to have anything in your name because they will seize that as well." In another case, the threat from the official from the Tax Office went like this: "In all the State files it's going to show you have a huge debt. What's going to happen to you then, which is what we're talking to you about... if you get what we're saying right now, without writing anything down, just tell us the truth, so we know how much money the company earns, because I'm convinced that all the money is not yours."

According to the recording, one of the policemen said to one of the prostitutes, "What I want to tell you is that we're the police, and we're going after the bad guys, but they'll catch you tomorrow and tell you (...) how can you have an apartment without having declared any earnings, and they will catch you and shoot you and put you in jail."

The recording also includes the following threatening dialogue:

Police: "What nationality are you?"

Girl: "Spanish, from the Canary islands."

Police: "What you're probably going to do is tell me: 'I'm from around here and I'm leaving,' but you're going anywhere or escaping."

Girl: "I don't believe you."

Police: "I mean it."

Girl: "Oh really! Go ahead and do it," she said sarcastically.

Tax official: "No, you're going to have a problem, because the debt will always be there. You'll always have it there...pending."

Police: "I'll come back one day, then you're going to have a hard time, and I'm not going to invite you out for coffee. I'm telling you...we will take you away and we'll find out what this is all about."

Girl: "Oh my goodness!"

Police: "Do you understand what I'm saying?"

The recording also shows how officials even threatened women with falsifying their statements because they did not say what they wanted to hear. Hence, the following dialogue:

Girl: "I'm not going to validate anything you say."

Police: "I'll validate it myself, and if I say that you've told me everything, what then?"

Girl: "Say it, say it, but tell the truth."

Police: "I will say what I want from what you're telling me. You haven't understood anything." (The officials laugh.)

Tax official: "Whatever he wants."

Girl: "Oh, I'm scared!" she said, sarcasm lacing her voice.

Police: "Not wanting to tell me or him anything doesn't seem right to me. I'll come back someday...and have coffee with you."

As if all of the above were a small abuse of power, the tax inspectors went up to the rooms to see them naked. While a tax technician finished making copies of the documentation they took away, one of the recordings shows the following conversation:

Tax official: "Should we go up to the fourth floor now to see if anyone? (...) Because that's where they sleep."

Tax official: "Should we go up to see them? Absolutely, there's nothing else to do here."

A different tax official: "We've already gone up to the fourth floor, and all the beds were unmade."

At the end of the day, the women stuck to their statements, and the Tax Office had to write a report stating that "the answers given coincided in all cases with the explanations given by the company." However, the harassment did not end. In June 2018, the Tax Office notified the owner of the premises of fines of 934,777 euros. In other words, despite the lack of evidence, the tax inspectors decided to seize a million euros from the businessman.[2]

As was to be expected, some of the women reported this illegal intervention to the justice system and filed a complaint for breaking and entering, trespassing, falsification of public documents, coercion, threats, and illegal detention before one of the city's courts. The complaint directed against three national police officers and three tax officials was filed on February 5, 2019 by the court after stating in a writ that "the performance of all the participants in relation to the female 'clients' of the hotel can only be described as totally correct, at no point in the hours recorded in the audio recordings can one discern a bad attitude, arrogance, contempt, pressure, or bad treatment to any of them, and much less a threatening and coercive attitude; on the contrary, the treatment was excellent, proper, and appropriate to the circumstances of entry and search in any police intervention." The story, however, did not end there. The owner of the company noticed, after receiving the document used by the IRS to punish him, that on his computer there were 3,801 files that were not on his computer when the inspectors unexpectedly visited his business. Among these new documents that the IRS placed on his office computer were 185 photographs of naked or semi-naked girls.

The recordings of the actions carried out by the tax officials and the police survived almost miraculously.[3] In fact, the IRS inspector who led the operation wanted to erase all the footage when they realized it had been monitored by the eighteen security cameras on the premises. The Tax Office official himself was aware of the situation and assured one of his colleagues that he had "involved the police." Likewise, he warned the company's lawyer, who appeared in person at the premises, where they tried to take away his cell phone, that if the images were not destroyed, they would have "an incident with the State attorney first thing in the morning." His attitude with the

2. https://www.elconfidencial.com/espana/2019-07-12/inspectores-hacienda-burdel-prostitutas-presiones_2118287/; https://twnews.es/es-news/los-videos-de-un-burdel-que-salpican-a-hacienda-y-policias-te-van-a-fusilar.

3. https://www.youtube.com/watch?v=1hted7P0zZ4.

company's lawyer even led to a writ of protection from the city's own Bar Association.

As if this were not enough, the officials of the Tax Office had to call a colleague, by the name of Álvaro (which does not appear in the inspection report as an official authorized for the operation) and who remained on the premises until three o'clock in the morning trying to destroy the recordings. When they left, they didn't realize there was a double recording system they didn't erase. Thanks to him, we can now know how the Tax Office of that country operates.

The two stories told—and unpunished—form part of a cast that could apply to a multitude of cases. They didn't take place under a communist government, nor in a nation ruled by a dictatorship of any type, let alone in a backward Third World nation. The events took place in one of the first nations of the European Union, and more specifically Spain. The finance minister, Cristóbal Montoro, was a member of a center-right party, but raised taxes beyond the suggestions of the Spanish Communist Party. When he left power, he left behind a terrible wake of professional incompetence and scandalous corruption.[4]

As with all high-tax systems and large political clientele, there comes a time when it is not even legally possible to sustain the gigantic public system and, most especially, its huge clientele, which are indispensable to conquer and maintain political power. Then, in addition to the very high taxes, there is extortion from the tax agencies, an extortion that trickles down particularly to humble social strata, such as prostitutes, and punishes entrepreneurs with frightening consequences. Money must flow into the State apparatus to keep this or that party in power, and it will flow in an increasingly despotic manner. The fact that the stage is a democracy is no guarantee. Moreover, democracy is being destroyed in a way that is hardly reversible thanks to these actions unleashed from power. From the parties, the corruption of the system passes to the State apparatus and permeates the

4. https://www.abc.es/espana/abci-montoro-llevo-equipo-economico-cenas-banqueros-y-empresarios-ibex-organizadas-rato-201706280637_noticia.html; https://www.libremercado.com/2015-04-12/un-doble-informe-destapo-los-favores-de-montoro-a-su-antiguo-despacho-1276543854/; https://www.elespanol.com/economia/empresas/20170430/212478994_0.html.

functioning of the Tax Office, the police, prosecutors, and judges. Perhaps the majority of citizens are unaware of this, but the system in which they live is progressing day by day, perhaps hour by hour, towards a dictatorship that barely retains its earmark as a democracy. However, that economic despotism has not yet reached the bottom. At the same time, there is another major threat to democracy, namely national debt.

CHAPTER VII

THE GROWING STATE INTERVENTION (III): The National Debt

Debt, a Mechanism of Disgrace

Let me begin this chapter with a personal anecdote. Shortly after I was exiled to the United States, I received a call from the bank where I had a checking account. They were asking me to come in for an interview. The person who helped me—a nice, educated middle-aged lady—after offering me coffee, started offering me different banking products. It would be too long to elaborate on her presentation, but I can say that all she presented to me with a smile were ways of getting myself in debt. I had already refused three or four when, finally, I told her that I was not interested in getting into debt, and that when I wanted to buy something, I saved up for it. If I couldn't wait to save up to buy, then it wasn't worth it. The employee continued to insist, and I had to tell her that I was not interested in getting into debt because I was also convinced that going into debt was a disgrace. The woman remained silent for a moment and finally told me, "The truth is that you are right." She paused and added, "You don't know how many people would be spared a lot of suffering if they thought like you." Before I could comment, the employee smiled suddenly and said, "Of course then I wouldn't have a job."

This anecdote, personal and unimportant, says a lot about the world we live in. Indebtedness is not a generous or even balanced response to the needs of individuals or nations. On the contrary, debt is a mechanism of submission to the interests of others that affects individuals as well as nations. It is significant that both the authors of the Bible and the Founding Fathers understood this.

Debt, the Bible, and the Founding Fathers

In Proverbs 22:7 there is a statement that should be written at the entrance of banks and international organizations: "The borrower is servant to the lender." The statement may sound exaggerated and harsh, but it is true. The debtor has given part, at least, of his life to those to whom he owes. Hence the book of Proverbs (17:18; 22:26-27) also points out that adding to one's debt is an act of foolishness that can lead one to lose even the bed in which one sleeps. Only he who refuses to guarantee debts is freed from this situation (Proverbs 11:15). It is not surprising that the Torah taught that a sign of divine blessing is precisely that there is no need to borrow (Deuteronomy 15:6), nor that Jesus taught that incurring expenses that cannot be covered is a sign of foolishness (Luke 14:28). In the end, this horror of debt is the opposite of the wicked who "borrows and does not pay'" (Psalms 37:21).

On that basis, it was not surprising that the Founding Fathers viewed debt as a real disgrace to be avoided. In 1799, Thomas Jefferson wrote to Elbridge Gerry: "I am for a rigorously frugal and simple government, which applies all possible savings from public revenues to be disbursed on ridding itself of national debt." Far from considering debt as normal and even desirable as virtually all current politicians do,

Jefferson was in favor of a government that did not spend and applied any surplus when it had it on totally liquidating debt.

The reason, as Jefferson would explain, in a letter written on July 12, 1816, to Samuel Kercheval, was for the good of the citizens. Indeed, in the text, Jefferson stated: "And to preserve their independence, we must not let our rulers load us with perpetual debt. We must make our election between economy and liberty, or profusion and servitude." Jefferson was more than aware that politicians are inclined to take on national debts. It is never they who pay them, and greater spending can lead to having funds at their disposal to feed political clientele and keep them in power. In the face of this behavior, the author of the Declaration of Independence pointed out something absolutely true, namely that citizens cannot allow politicians to discharge their debt on them. They would have to choose between control of spending and freedom or increased spending and slavery. The text is more than two centuries old and is even truer than when it came out of its author's pen.

Jefferson was also more than aware that this situation did not arise overnight but stemmed from a process in which everything would go from bad to worse. In the same letter, he stressed that "a departure from principle in one instance becomes a precedent for another...till the bulk of society is reduced to mere miserable automatons... And the head horse of this frightful team is public debt. Taxation follows that, and in its train wretchedness and oppression." Jefferson's words could hardly have been clearer. The first thing that comes is a departure from moral principles, and when that happens in one case, soon others follow. The result in the end is that a good part of society is reduced to misery, because like the force of workhouses pulling it along, public debt, taxes, and finally tyranny and poverty appear. Of course, that disturbing reality was never to be denounced by the politicians who benefit from it or by the clientele who take advantage of it, but the reality is that a sequence of absent moral principles, public debt, taxes, poverty, and oppression would become undeniable.

On July 21, 1816, writing to William Plumer, Jefferson restated his theses: "I, however, place economy among the first and most important republican virtues, and public debt as the greatest of the dangers to be feared." Democracy is not characterized, as Piketty would say, by giving whole sectors of society subsidies and grants, raising taxes, and resorting to debt to achieve equality. On the contrary, one of the first and most important of its virtues is to know how to save, and the greatest danger against it is public debt.

Thomas Jefferson's position was not isolated or unique to the Democratic Party he founded. In fact, he was supported by other Founding Fathers. The young republic had to face remarkable challenges, and the economic one was not the least. Alexander Hamilton, the secretary of the treasury, was in charge of this challenge. On January 14, 1790, he submitted a report relating to the public debt. Hamilton's position was blunt. After denying that "public debts are public benefits" because it was "a position inviting to prodigality, and liable to a dangerous abuse," Hamilton made it clear "that he ardently wishes to see it incorporated, as a fundamental maxim in the system of public credit of the United States, that the creation of debt should always be accompanied with the means of extinguishment."

On December 5, 1791, in a report related to manufacturing, Alexander Hamilton repeated his views. Noting that debt accumulation could never be considered "desirable," Hamilton said: "And as the vicissitudes of nations beget a perpetual tendency to the accumulation of debt, there ought to be in every government a perpetual, anxious and unceasing effort to reduce that, which at any time exists, as fast as shall be practicable, consistently with integrity and good faith."

On March 16, 1792, with regard to supplies to be provided for the war against the Indians, Hamilton again stressed the danger of public debt: "Nothing can more interest the national credit and prosperity, than a constant and systematic attention to husband all the means previously possessed for extinguishing the present debt, and to avoid, as much as possible, the incurring of any new debt."

Washington himself, in his farewell address of September 17, 1796, would also address the issue of debt as of national importance. The expected conduct of the rulers would be that of "avoiding likewise the accumulation of debt, not only by shunning occasions of expense, but by vigorous exertions in time of peace to discharge the debts, which unavoidable wars may have occasioned, not ungenerously throwing upon posterity the burthen, which we ourselves ought to bear." Washington's statement is revealing. Generally speaking, there should be no debt that weighs on the nation, but, if that debt were to arise from unexpected wars, strong measures would have to be taken to remove that burden from the shoulders of the citizens.

It must be said in honor of the truth that the struggle against the debt undertaken by the Founding Fathers ended with a triumph, but that did not lead them to lower their guard. On October 11, 1809, Thomas Jefferson wrote from his residence in Monticello to Albert Gallatin: "I consider the fortunes of our republic as depending, in an eminent degree, on the extinguishment of the public debt, before we engage in any war, because, that done, we shall have revenue enough to improve our country in peace, and defend it in war, without recurring either to new taxes or loans, but if the debt shall once more be swelled to a formidable size, its entire discharge will be despaired of, and we shall be committed to the English career of debt, corruption and rottenness, closing with revolution. The discharge of the debt therefore is vital to the destinies of our government."

Thomas Jefferson's statements almost overwhelm one by their enormous lucidity. From his point of view, not ending the national debt could only lead to a chain of misfortunes. It does not only mean losing resources that could be used for the good of the nation without having to resort to new taxes or loans. In fact, the only thing to be expected from the increase in debt was corruption, which would ultimately lead to a revolutionary situation.

The Lesson No One Wants to Learn

Anyone who examines the views on debt held by the Founders of the first democracy of contemporary history can draw very practical lessons. It must be said, however, that the advice that prevents not only the worsening of the national debts, but also the establishment of a corrupt system that will bring democracy to its end, has not been heeded. The desire for State intervention and the benefits that politicians derive from these public funds that they will not have to pay have prevented it.

Today, the nation with the largest public debt on the planet is the United States—a situation that is somewhat less serious because the dollar is the currency of universal exchange and, precisely because of that, a good part of that debt is, in the end, paid for by the rest of the world. The world's second largest public debt nation is Spain. In this particular case, Spain belongs to an economy that is far behind that of nations such as Germany, China, Japan, or the United Kingdom. The outstanding liabilities amount to 1,777 billion euros, which puts the debt at 145% of GDP. According to data published by the Banco de España, public debt increased by 10,470 million in the second quarter of 2019 and set a new record. The debt of the autonomous communities—the inefficient and costly regional governments—increased by 3,706 million, to 300,587 million, 24.6% of the GDP. Of these seventeen autonomous communities, only Cantabria and Madrid reduced their debt in the second quarter compared to the previous one, while the other fifteen increased it. In fact, Catalonia, despite the astronomical amounts of public money from the rest of Spain that have been injected into it, is the most indebted autonomous community. As noted above, these figures make Spain a world runner-up in external debt. In fact, only the United States has more than a trillion dollars of imbalance in the so-called International investment position (IIP) with more foreign liabilities than assets. The IMF document notes that "Spain's extensive external financing needs from both the private and public sectors leave it vulnerable to sudden market changes." In fact, Spain is at the top of the Eurozone's red list, and this summer it has broken a new public debt record. Unfortunately, the very sad case of Spain is no exception.

Debt grips many of the nations of the European Union. The same is true of most of the nations of Africa and Asia and, in a very special way, with those of Latin America. That debt has frightening consequences for national economies, but they go far beyond the economy. An indebted nation is a nation that loses sight of its national sovereignty. An indebted nation is a nation that cannot decide on its present or its future. An indebted nation is a nation that will become easy prey for exploitation. When the payment of the debt becomes difficult or even impossible, the nation ends up in the hands of its creditors and defenselessly assists the process of dismembering its resources for the benefit of obscure interests. In the end, the picture that appears both in the Bible and in the writings of the Founding Fathers is consummated. The corruption of the system has arrived, and with it, bondage and misery. It must be added that this situation has already been experienced by enough nations to make it clear what their most foreseeable future is.

"It Will Never Happen Here..."

The reader may be tempted to think that the picture described in the previous pages will take place south of the Rio Grande or south of the Strait of Gibraltar, but it is impossible for it to be reproduced in his advanced and democratic nation. Yes, this State interventionism can be observed in Somalia and Venezuela, in Vietnam and Cuba, in Chad and Nicaragua, in Angola and Mexico, but it will never, never, never take root in other nations. The author of these lines is not so optimistic. In November 2018, the third annual report on attitudes towards socialism was published in the United States.[1] The information contained in that document was certainly striking. From the

1. https://www.victimsofcommunism.org/2018-annual-report; https://www.victimsofcommunism.org/voc-news/third-annual-report-on-us-attitudes-toward-socialism.

outset, the report concluded that the people of the United States lack a serious understanding of socialism and communism. Three out of four Americans are not able to tell how many people were killed in communist dictatorships. To this was added that 52% of millennials would prefer to live in a socialist (46%) or communist (6%) society, while only 40% would like to live in a capitalist society. Moreover, 26% of Americans have never received any teaching about communism in any educational or professional context. In addition, half of the Americans associate socialism with the welfare states of Western Europe and Scandinavia, but not with the Marxist dictatorships. Such a display of ignorance goes as far as to say that only half of Americans can identify Cuba as a communist country, and 41% do not consider North Korea to be communist. Even more worryingly, one in three Americans associate socialism with health, especially those favorable to the system. Although capitalism is still the favorite system in the United States, half of the Z generation and the Millennials are more favorable to socialism than the Baby Boomers. In regards to the communist danger, 6% consider that it is something of the twentieth century, 43% believe it also affects this century, 33% think it is not a justifiable fear in the twentieth century nor the twenty-first, and 19% believe it was justified in the twentieth century, but not in the twenty-first century. Finally, only one in four Americans associate socialism with "total control," and almost half of the millennials, namely 47%, agree in whole or in part with the restrictions to ensure that what is said in public is not offensive.

In the face of horror, it is a very common reaction to say that "this cannot happen here." On some occasions, that phrase is grounded in reality, especially when the foundations of a nation are solid. The case of the United States is, in this respect, paradigmatic. Based on the spirit of the Reformation with all the biblical values it recovered, the American system has functioned far better than that of the nations south of the Rio Grande, who owe their current situations to the Roman Catholic Counter-Reformation, and also better than that of most European nations. However, that system was faced with a number of circumstances that seriously endangered it. First of all, the youth, the famous millennials, not only suffer from an overwhelming ignorance of what communism is, they have come to identify socialism with the achievements of northern European societies and the remedy for the problems facing society. Secondly, progress in this direction is facilitated by massive immigration from Latin America, an immigration that comes from a Hispanic culture in which clerical assistance adds to the faith in the socialism of Cuba and Venezuela and often to a deep resentment against the United States. It is still a bloody paradox that people who have fled north to rid themselves of the pernicious effects of interventionist political systems are now seeking to implant similar systems of public spending, corruption, and patronage on the soil of the United States. Finally, that change can be facilitated by the growing conviction that those who are not willing to agree with the theories of what is politically correct must be silenced, a thesis that is enthusiastically embraced by many millennials. However, State interventionism is not the only danger that threatens democracies. Undoubtedly, a State that spends, recruits, maintains clientele, and gets into debt is a State that will annihilate democracy and will NOT bring justice. That national agenda represents the great internal danger, without a doubt, but the external one, which counts on it as an ally, is even more formidable and has no intention of giving up on annihilating democratic systems and nations. It is an agenda that goes much further in its fight against freedom and that is taken up not only by the Left but also by the Right. We will dedicate the next part of the book to it.

PARTE III

THE GLOBALIST AGENDA

CHAPTER VIII

THE GLOBALIST AGENDA (I):
What It Is and How It Is Imposed

What Is the Globalist Agenda?

On October 23, 1995, an event took place that was ignored in all its significance by the vast majority of the media and political circles. Marking the fiftieth anniversary of the United Nations and the Council of Foreign Relations, a number of political leaders of international significance came together with the intention of being able to deliver their respective speeches. The occasion was striking because, with a few exceptions such as Vaclav Havel, a former Czech dissident, the rest were people who had repeatedly spoken out against the United States. Now, with the end of the Cold War, everyone was flocking to New York City, the world capital of capitalism, to meet with American financiers. At that meeting, Fidel Castro, the Cuban dictator, would take an historic photo with David Rockefeller, one of the symbols of multinational capitalism. The image would travel the planet, but it was much less known that Peggy, David's daughter, had frequently visited Cuba since 1985 or that David Rockefeller would meet Castro the next day at the Foreign Relations Council building on Park Avenue.[1] For many it might seem a simple gesture of social courtesy or an incomprehensible act, but it would be David Rockefeller himself who would perfectly explain his conduct in 2002 in his *Memoirs*.

Millionaire, philanthropist, habitual participant in the highest circles of power, David Rockefeller would make the following confession: "Some even believe we—the Rockefellers—are part of a secret cabal working against the best interests of the United States, characterizing my family and me as 'internationalists' and of conspiring with others around the world to build a more integrated global political and economic structure—one world, if you will. If that's the charge, I stand guilty, and I am proud of it."

Rockefeller's statement was highly relevant not only for its sincerity but for its forcefulness. Faced with the accusation that he was developing an agenda that was not that of the United States and that was even against the interests of this nation, an agenda that he expressed in his cordiality to the Cuban dictator Fidel Castro, David Rockefeller declared himself guilty and also proud to be so. Faced with the accusation of being an internationalist who conspired with others around the world, he pleaded guilty and proud to be one. Faced with the accusation of building a global political and economic structure that was advancing towards a single world, he pleaded guilty and proud to be so. At the beginning of this century, as soon as the 9/11 attacks had been carried out, Rockefeller had no qualms about publicly acknowledging that he supported a globalist agenda whose purpose was to subject the world to a new order that even conflicted with the interests of nations such as the United States.

David Rockefeller was not exaggerating. His family, his foundation, and he himself were a key part of a globalist agenda that had begun decades earlier, but one that at the beginning of this century was already beginning to present itself in a somewhat more open way.

1. David Rockefeller, *Memoirs* (New York, 2002), p. 405.

The purpose of that agenda is clearly stated in his *Memoirs* as to its ultimate objective. That goal implies, first and foremost, the elimination of nations as independent and sovereign entities and of the cultures on which they are based. Secondly, it seeks to seize its easily plundered wealth to the extent that nations will have become mere protectorates. Thirdly, this control over politics and the economy will also lead to the imposition of an antifamily policy that will make it possible to drastically reduce the population and leave individuals defenseless. Finally, all of the above will be combined with a major offensive against Christianity in order to subdue or crush it, because as it represents a scale of values contrary to this universal despotism. The development of these goals will be seen in more detail in the next pages.

How Is the Globalist Agenda Imposed?

The plan of the globalist agenda is certainly very ambitious and, apparently, it is inevitable that it was going meet with enormous resistance insofar as it clashes with national interests and seeks to shape global reality. The truth, however, is that it has made inexorable progress, and it has done so thanks to the concentration of resources and the provisions emanating from international entities. By 2020, large conglomerates such as Comcast, The Walt Disney Company, AT&T, and Viacomcbs exert extraordinary control over much of what the world's populations consume in information and entertainment. In addition, there are other smaller but gigantic groups such as Bertelsmann, Sony Corporation, News Corp, Fox Corporation, Hearst Communications, MGM Holdings Inc., the Globo Group, and Lagardère Group. Altogether, a dozen companies account for 80% of global media production, and their influence can be considered greater when we consider that in other nations such as China, Russia, or India they do not have anywhere near absolute control. In practice, the mergers, alliances, and participation of the media have turned the information market into a set of oligopolies that make up a growing risk to the accuracy and neutrality of information in the written, broadcast, and televised press, as well as the entertainment industry.

It was Thomas Jefferson[2] who once claimed that "the only security of all is in a free press. The force of public opinion cannot be resisted when permitted freely to be expressed. The agitation it produces must be submitted to. It is necessary, to keep the waters pure." That reality has never been as distressing as it is today.

Jefferson was quite right, but the truth is that from television programs to cartoon films, from press agencies to the written press, from radio to documentaries and films, everything is concentrated in the hands of a few people. Not surprisingly, even in the absence of such data, a Gallup poll conducted in 2019[3] shows that, in the United States, only 41% of the population believe that the media—written press, radio, and television—report "fully, accurately, and fairly." The figure is four points lower than 2018. Quite significantly, the figure is 69% among Democrats—a party that enthusiastically supports aspects of the globalist agenda—while in the case of Republicans it stands at just 15%. However, it is not just a question of the party. Truth be told, only 36% of independents trust the media. If this happens in a nation based on freedom of the press from birth and with considerably open legislation regarding freedom of expression that is determined to resist monopolies, it is easy to draw conclusions about what happens in the rest of the world where political groups or family members control the media in regimes that can be either democracies as well as dictatorships. In fact, in Europe, with the nuances desired for each nation, communication is controlled in a huge way by four media groups—RTL Group, CEME, Modern Times Group, and Sanoma. In nineteen of the European nations, the four mentioned multinationals are the first four reference groups, and in another seventeen, they are

2. Thomas Jefferson to Lafayette, November 4, 1823.

3. https://news.gallup.com/poll/267047/americans-trust-mass-media-edges-down.aspx.

among the main ones. Significantly, Pan European Boradcasting operates as a brand, and its components are based in the United States. These pan-European groups include Discovery, Viacom, Warnermedia, and The Walt Disney Company.

There can be little doubt that this overwhelming media hegemony can change the public opinion of entire nations in areas that have never been prone to them. Thus, for example, a pro-family public opinion can be shaped in favor of gender ideology, a positive view of homosexuality, or support for transgender people. Nothing difficult considering how easy it has been historically to use the media to start a war or the way they are used by intelligence services.[4]

Secondly, the action of international organizations that are not derived from democratic mechanisms or originate from popular will is essential for the advancement of the globalist agenda. David Rockefeller himself mentions several in his *Memoirs*, and it is only fair that he do so. Among them, the Council on Foreign Relations occupies a prominent place. Founded in 1921, with the intention of supporting the League of Nations, a direct antecedent to the UN, it theoretically sought to inform American citizens about the world reality. The reality is that it set out very clear political guidelines. Among them, Winthrop Aldrich, uncle of David Rockefeller, supported the intervention of the United States in the Second World War. Similarly, it was essential in shaping the doctrine of containment and was already defending population control in the 1950s. As expected in a globalist institution, the debates have been dominated by bankers—David Rockefeller has been on the board of directors since 1949—financiers, and lawyers joined by representatives of the media, academia, and NGOs. In the 1980s, it had added human rights, environmental degradation, and economic development to its causes. In other words, virtually none of the areas from which the globalist agenda is driven were left out. Since 2001, he maintained close relations with the Cuban dictatorship....[5]

4. Udo Ulfkotte, *Presstitutes* (Middletwon, 2019).
5. D. Rockefeller, *Memoirs*, p. 410.

Another global forum is the Bilderberg Club.[6] Its first meeting was held in May 1954 at the invitation of Prince Bernard of the Netherlands, under the guidance of Joseph Retinger.[7] The name of the hotel where the event took place would give the name of the group. At that first event, there were fifty—eleven Americans among whom was David Rockefeller—from eleven Western nations. In this case, professional origins included people from the world of economics and the media, but there were also politicians and trade unionists. The Bilderberg Club was on the verge of disappearing due to a corruption scandal that took place in 1976. Prince Bernardo was accused of offering Lockheed contracts with the Dutch defense ministry in exchange for a reward. That year, the Bilderberg Club did not hold any meetings, and it was thought that its story was over. That was not the case. In 1977, it resumed its meetings, which have been attended by a larger number of people—several aspiring to power in their own country—who will not reveal what happened at the meetings.

No less important than these two entities is the Trilateral Commission. Founded in the early 1970s, it was intended to extend global dominance beyond what the United States could undertake. It was the product of David Rockefeller and Zbigniew Brzezinski from Poland—who would serve as director—to which Western Europe and Japan were added (the first meeting was held in Tokyo in October 1973). Significantly, an obscure Georgia governor named James Earl Carter was present at the first meeting. In December 1975, Carter announced that he would run for the United States presidential election. When he arrived at the White House—with a campaign set against Washington and against the establishment—he appointed fifteen members of the Trilateral to work in his administration. Brzezinski, in fact, became the national security adviser. The fact that the United States financed the Taliban and Osama bin Laden is due to his closeness to the presidency. Although Brzezinski could not be

6. The reference book on this entity continues to be the work of Daniel Estulin, *The True Story of the Bilderberg Group* (Walterville, 2009). Though unrecognized, much of what has been written on the subject later is taken from Estulin.

7. On Retinger, see: *Joseph Retinger, Memoirs o fan Eminence Grise* (Toronto, 1972).

said to have defended the interests of the United States more than his historical resentments as a Pole allowed, the influence of the Trilateral did not decrease. In April 1984, all its members were received by President Ronald Reagan at the White House. Contrary to what ordinary citizens may think, the foreign policy of recent decades has owed much more to the work of people like Brzezinski than to the action of the Congress or the Senate. When the results of the work of these entities are contemplated, in whose formation there is not the slightest trace of democracy, the progress of the globalist agenda can be understood.

CHAPTER IX

THE GLOBALIST AGENDA (II):

Its Icons (I): George Soros

The Omnipresent George Soros

The globalist agenda has been largely secret for decades. Indeed, much of its success rests on the fact that its leaders are not recognized. Despite this, however, the reality is that Györgi Schwartz, better known as George Soros, has been one of the visible faces of the globalist agenda for a few years. Born on August 12, 1930, in Hungary, into a Jewish family, the young Györgi had no problem collaborating with the Nazi occupiers just as they were carrying out the deportations of Jews to Auchswitz. That fact—certainly scandalous—has been acknowledged by Soros himself, claiming that he never felt guilty.[1] After World War II, Soros went to England, where he studied at the London School of Economics, graduating with a bachelor's degree, and then he obtained a master's degree in Philosophy. It has been discussed whether Soros received support from the Rothschilds and, quite possibly, that aspect will never be

1. https://www.youtube.com/watch?v=X9tKvasRO54.

clarified. It is true that in 1969 he founded his first hedge fund known as Double Eagle. From this company would emerge its second hedge fund in 1970, the Soros Fund Management. Before the end of the decade, Soros had managed to bring the sterling pound to its knees, earning the nickname of "The Man Who Broke the Bank of England," and making a billion-dollar profit in that incident. It was a speculative operation that would later be repeated successfully against various Asian currencies of which only the Chinese, which had come out in defense of the Hong Kong currency, managed to resist the attack. As he would come to recognize later, he did not stop to think about the effects that these operations could have on people.[2] By then Soros had already become an outspoken financier of political causes. According to some estimates, by 2017 Soros had spent no less than $12 billion on those endeavors. Soros' power, however, has extended beyond simply financing the globalist agenda on an international scale. It implies promoting political programs in presidents of governments, launching legislative changes in different nations, and having an extraordinary influence in international organizations that go beyond philanthropy and are always channeled towards the imposition of the globalist agenda. Thanks to the billions of dollars spent by Soros, massive and illegal immigration, gender ideology, drug legalization, global warming theses, and merciless speculation have been fueled in all parts of the world except those where there has been a clear resistance to their agenda, such as Orbán's Hungary, Putin's Russia, or Xi's China. Listing all these episodes far exceeds the purpose of this book, but it is essential to give some examples in order to capture, even roughly, the role of George Soros in the globalist agenda.

Soros, Advisor to Governments

On May 31, 2018, a motion of censure began in the Spanish Parliament that ended on June 1 with the resignation from the government of

2. https://www.youtube.com/watch?v=Alyi7PjZljI.

president Mariano Rajoy for corruption. Whether Rajoy should have been prosecuted later on several criminal charges is currently under discussion, but the truth is that his downfall resulted in Pedro Sánchez, general secretary of the Spanish Socialist Workers Party (PSOE), becoming president of the government. That same month, Pedro Sánchez met with George Soros in Moncloa, the seat of the Spanish government's president. The meeting was not on the president's public agenda, lasted about an hour and a half, and two other unidentified people were present. In addition, when it took place there was more than sufficient evidence that Soros was collaborating and financing the Catalan nationalists who had staged a *coup d'état* in Catalonia and that even one of their organizations received 1.6 million euros over the course of two years from the Catalan nationalist government.[3] In other words, the newly appointed president was meeting in a special way with someone who had helped forces seeking to dismember the nation.

What could justify that meeting with someone who had maintained relationships with some coup leaders against the Constitution and the territorial integrity of Spain is something that has not become known to date. However, three months after that meeting with Soros, in September 2018, Sánchez was promoted in New York by a group of entrepreneurs at the Soros Fund Management, which included Soros' chief investment officer, Dawn Fitzpatrick. At that time, Dawn Fitzpatrick managed $25 billion, being responsible for the funds of the Open Society Foundation, to which Soros has allocated $18 billion in recent years.

Soros' meeting with Sánchez had taken place a month after Soros warned that another major financial crisis was brewing in Europe. On that occasion, Soros had attacked the member states of the European Union and stated that the European Union should give the go-ahead to Spain's and Italy's budgets to deal with their deficit and debt goals.

3. https://www.elmundo.es/comunidad-valenciana/2018/05/15/5af9b016268e3e71298b45f7.html; https://cronicaglobal.elespanol.com/politica/george-soros-financio-impulso-proces_137477_102.html; https://okdiario.com/investigacion/especulador-soros-dio-solo-ano-300-000-grupos-mas-radicales-del-separatismo-catalan-3092935.

Pedro Sánchez was, of course, sensitive to Soros' agenda. On his trip to New York to attend the Climate Summit, he pledged to spend a large sum on the fight against global warming.[4] It was only the first step, because Pedro Sánchez has since developed, step by step, all the content of the globalist agenda.

On other occasions, Soros has not privately issued guidelines to politicians but has published in different media what national governments are supposed to do. So in June 2018, *El Confidencial* published an article by George Soros advising what Italy and the European Union should do.[5] In the aforementioned article, Soros pointed out that "after a crisis that has lasted three months, Italy already has a government based" on what he calls "a disturbing coalition between the Five Star Movement and the League." According to Soros, "it is possible that the government will collapse and that elections will be held this year or, more likely, at the beginning of next year." The Hungarian-born philanthropist added that the EU could not try to "teach Italy a lesson," because, in this case, the "Italian electorate that, consequently, will re-elect the Five Star Movement and the League, thus reinforcing its majority." Undestandably, Soros attacked the immigration policy carried out by the Italian government, which is firmly opposed to the uncontrolled entry of immigrants and a supporter of border control. Thus, Soros stated quite controversially in the article that the Italians regretted the existing immigration policy in Italy and referred to the Dublin III Regulation, claiming that it applies to all member States and that it maintains that refugees are the responsibility of the country in which they land first. According to Soros, this situation caused "a disproportionate impact for Italy, due to the international norm that requires vessels that rescue refugees on the high seas to land them in the nearest safe harbor, which in practice means Italy." In the magnate's view, the EU "should alter the Dublin III rules and agree to pay the bulk

4. https://elpais.com/sociedad/2019/09/23/actualidad/1569239746_777826.html.

5. https://blogs.elconfidencial.com/mundo/tribuna-internacional/2018-06-13/union-europea-ayuda-italia-inmigracion-desintegracion_1578320/.

of integration and support for migrants who are disproportionately trapped in Italy."

As expected, the article took the opportunity to accuse the Hungarian Prime Minister, Viktor Orbán, of having won the last elections, basing his campaign on the claim—according to Soros, false and ridiculous—that he wanted to flood Hungary with immigrants. According to Soros, part of the solution would be for the EU to finance a Marshall Plan for Africa, which would sink it even further into debt, and stressed that it was necessary to "constructively influence the next Italian elections," and for this, Emmanuel Macron and Angela Merkel should "assume leadership and persuade dissident forces in the EU to follow them." After attacking Poland and Hungary—two nations especially opposed to the globalist agenda—Soros insisted that "the EU has little chance of avoiding disintegration, unless the Franco-German alliance is maintained" and the 2019 European Parliament elections and the selection of the next president of the European Commission are controlled. Can anyone consider it normal—and appropriate—for a millionaire to tell the nations of the European Union what they have to do to the point of setting forth the course of actions that would determine the outcome of the national elections of some of its members? It is doubtful, but, in any case, it is very difficult not to see a totally unacceptable interference in a democracy. All in all, Soros's actions go even much further.

Soros, Promoter of Campaigns

The influence of George Soros in other cases goes beyond that of government and extends to other levels of society. This is the case, for example, of Argentina and its campaign to legalize the drug trade. In 2009, a group of eighty Argentine magistrates informed that the supply and demand of drugs "shows unprecedented levels" in the Spanish-American country, also pointing out that drug rings "in many cases received political, administrative, and judicial protection."[6] This judicial protest was happening at the same time that both the government and forces linked to Kirchnerism were promoting the decriminalization of drugs. This drive towards the decriminalization took place simultaneously when there was a dramatic growth in drug use and the arrival of drug dealers in Argentina. In addition, drug use has been decriminalized in Argentina for twenty years, so the entire current campaign only made sense as a way to spread the marketing of drugs. The truth is that, despite the propaganda of some politicians and the media about the so-called "harm reduction" that would imply the legalization of drug possession, the data from different nations where this measure has been applied indicate exactly the opposite.

It is significant the manner in which George Soros'[7] shadow has loomed in the background behind the debate over drug decriminalization. Since 1992 George Soros has pursued a policy of liberalizing the drug consumption and drug trade in Europe and America. The way to promote this measure has been, as in the cases of abortion, gay marriage, or uncontrolled immigration, the insistence that drug use is one more human right that must be recognized in national legislation. In this way, Soros played a role in the legalization of marijuana in Uruguay.[8] Likewise, Colombia, Jamaica, and Paraguay have appeared as other Soros target nations to legalize the growing of marijuana for commercial purposes. The same is happening in Argentina where the Cannabis Avatora Sociedad del Estado company intends to commercialize the cultivation of marijuana and has even already requested financial aid from the United States.

Drug use is one of the worst scourges afflicting our society today. It is certainly one of the most lucrative forms of trafficking, and it is no less true that it has involved the submission of institutions and

6. https://www.ultimahora.com/jueces-argentinos-denuncian-la-proteccion-los-narcos-y-el-aumento-la-venta-drogas-n200652.html.

7. https://www.taringa.net/+tsindrogas/george-soros-y-su-lobby-para-despenalizar-las-drogas_16m5g9.

8. https://www.bbc.com/mundo/noticias/2013/12/131216_george_soros_marihuana_jgc.

governments that carry it out. It is precisely these two circumstances that make it even more dangerous, because they can end up causing the annihilation of a society and the loss of sovereignty of a nation.

In order to deal with the terrible consequences of drugs, it is not possible to argue, as if it were a human right, for their legalization. If we really want to put an end to drug trafficking and its tragic effects, the measure is not to legalize them even partially, in the same way that it would not reduce the number of violations to consider their use legal from midnight to two in the morning, nor would it put an end to theft by making it legal only on Saturday afternoons. To end drug trafficking, the way is through greater border control, better coordination among police forces, greater international collaboration, and isolation from those governments and institutions that profit from drug trafficking.

Far from being a human right, as Soros claims, drug use is a true plague, and the way to eradicate it is not to tolerate and encourage it, but to go after it forcefully to stop it. It is precisely for this reason that it is not surprising that among the objectives of the globalist agenda, of which George Soros is one of the protagonists, is not only gender ideology, the expansion of abortion, or massive and uncontrolled immigration, but also the expansion of drug use supposedly as a human right.

Soros and His Influence in International Organizations

Soros' real influence, surely, cannot be calibrated down to the last detail, but it is unquestionably extraordinary for a person who has not been elected to any office, who has no popular support, and who seeks to impose himself on the institutions in a more than dubiously democratic manner. The extent to which that influence is real can be inferred from the fact that the Soros entities themselves boast about it. For example, in 2017, the Open Society European Policy Institute and the Open Society network, both entities reporting to George Soros, published a list with European Parliament MPs likely to support the values of the Open Society by billionaire George Soros.[9] The list that goes by the name of "Reliable Allies in the European Parliament" included the names of 226 members (of a total of 751) who potentially supported Soros and his campaigns to promote ideology gender, abortion, open door immigration, and the erosion of national sovereignty.

Contrary to what might have been expected, Soros' trustworthy Members of the European Parliament (MEPs) were not only located on the Left, but went from the Right to the extreme Left, including members of pro-independence forces. An example of what Soros' influence means in the European Parliament can be seen when examining the different nations that are represented. For example, in the case of Spain, no less than 24 MEPs appeared on the list. Among those MEPs is first and foremost Marina Albiol of the Izquierda Plural Left (Plural Left), who is included for her support of gender ideology, abortion, immigration, and minorities. Her colleague from the Catalan sector was Ernest Urtasunal, who is also presented as a supporter of gender ideology and abortion. In the same political line were also Javier Couso of La Izquierda Unida (United Left) for his support of abortion, minority rights, and gender ideology; as well as Paloma López Bermejo, who was described as a supporter of gender ideology and abortion. This was also the case of Mayor Ángela Vallina, who was presented as an advocate of gender ideology and abortion.

For the PP (Partido Popular, "The People's Party"), a center-right party in office in Spain at the time, were included in the list Agustín Díaz de Mera for his role in immigration policy; Rosa Estaràs for her support of gender ideology, who was applauded not only for being progressive, but she was willing to oppose the theoretical guidelines of the PP; and Santiago Fisas, who presented himself as a supporter of the gay agenda, calling himself a "progressive" with a heart willing to oppose his party line.

9. file:///C:/Users/Cesar/Desktop/USA/Radio3/-Europe-OSI%20Brussel%20EU%20Advocacy%20calendar-European%20Elections-reliable%20allies%20in%20the%20european%20parliament%202014%202019%20(1).pdf.

Among the PSOE politicians (Partido Socialista Obrero Español: "The Spanish Socialist Workers' Party"), the first opposition party, appeared, first of all, Irache García Pérez, who presented herself as a defender of gender ideology—who was already known for that position—and abortion. A relevant place was also occupied by Enrique Guerrero Salom, who held important positions during the government of socialist José Luis Rodríguez Zapatero and was considered of interest in areas such as the post-crisis economy. Also from the PSOE and then Secretary General of the Socialist Youth (JJSS) appeared Sergio Gutiérrez, who was recommended for supporting gender ideology, immigration, minorities, and, significantly, taxes. No less important within the PSOE were Juan Fernando López Aguilar, former secretary of Rodríguez Zapatero, who was considered important in matters related to immigration; and Elena Valenciano, also considered a supporter of abortion and gender ideology.

Belonging to the progressive alliance of socialists and democrats was Eider Gardiazábal, who was seen as a possible ally on regional matters.

Podemos ("We Can"), a communist party with close ties to dictatorships in Iran and Venezuela, also had several MEPs whom Soros considered allies. The most prominent was obviously Pablo Iglesias, number one in the party, but he was joined by Teresa Rodríguez, who was seen as a supporter of gender ideology and abortion, or Lola Sánchez, also described as an advocate of gender ideology.

Ciudadanos ("Citizens"), a center-left party, also had its quota of MEPs potentially allied with Soros, represented by Fernando Maura and Javier Nart. There even appeared on Soros' list the UPyD (Unión, Progreso y Democacia: "Union, Progress, and Democracy"), a party practically extinct in Spain, but which contributed to Maite Pagazaurtundua.

Unsurprisingly, nationalists also appeared in Soros' list. That was the case of Jordi Sebastiá de Compromís, who was presented as a defender of gender ideology; a member of the Catalan nationalists—who have been financed on different occasions by Soros—and who were represented by Josep-Maria Terricabras of Esquerra Republicana de Catalunya (ERC: "The Republican Left of Catalonia"); Ramón Tremosa i Balcells of Convergència (Convergècia Democràtica de Catalunya: "The Democratic Convergence of Catalonia"); and Izaskun Bilbao of the Basque Nationalist Party (PNV: "Partido Nacionalista Vasco") who was mentioned for her support for nationalism, gender ideology, and minority rights.

It is, of course, difficult to know to what extent politicians on the list are fully, partially, or minimally open to George Soros' suggestions, actions, campaigns, and objectives. But the fact that agencies dependent on the magnate were allowed to publish the list of MEPs whom they considered open is very revealing. That Soros can confidently believe that more than a third of the European Parliament will fulfill his objectives leads one, of course, to entertain serious doubts as to the representativeness of that Parliament and the reasons for which the candidates were elected to it.

No less disturbing is the fact that they are politicians of all kinds, ranging from the extreme Left to the Right, and even secessionists. Given such facts, it can only be deduced that few parties are solid guarantees to defend the interests of the citizens, because even the extreme Left would gladly collaborate with a millionaire like George Soros, and the right would turn its back on the interests of its nation in favor of the globalist agenda.

Even more revealing and disturbing are the reasons why Soros believes he will win the support of these politicians. The fundamental cause is that they coincide with his globalist agenda in areas such as the implantation of gender ideology, the massive spread of abortion, and a lax immigration policy. All these aspects, which are a direct threat to Western culture, will presumably be supported by a sizeable sector of the European Parliament, whatever the color of its members. Undoubtedly, it is a more than serious subject to reflect on the real representativeness of our politicians, the real agendas that govern nations, and those who really direct international politics.

Soros and the Internal Politics of the United States

In the previous pages, we have seen how Soros's influence in favor of the globalist agenda has spread over supranational organizations, American societies, and European nations. Not even the United States is protected from his actions and, to a large extent, that makes sense. Naturally, there is no lack of analysts who consider that Soros is, substantially, an agent of American foreign policy, a policy that they view as characterized by intolerable interventionism. Such an analysis does not correspond to reality. To tell the truth, Soros has taken many steps to also control the policy of the United States by aligning it with the globalist agenda. David Horowitz and Richard Poe have amply documented how Soros has taken over Democratic Party politics and influenced its development.[10] Indeed, he even used the attacks of 9/11 to advance his ideas in his 2002 book *George Soros on Globalization*. For example, he took up again his idea of a bank that would control world credit, as he had already pointed out in 1998.[11]

Be that as it may, there can be little doubt that Soros has identified President Trump as one of the enemies of his globalist agenda. This was clearly seen from the very inauguration. Just when the inauguration took place, there was a women's march on Washington. In a revealing way, *The Guardian* defined the march as a "spontaneous" action in favor of women's rights. Similarly, VOX, another left-wing medium, defined it as a "huge, spontaneous groundswell." In clear parallel to these statements, the manifesto of the march affirmed that The Uprising of Women = The Uprising of the Nation.

Despite the claims, the march was not a women's march, nor was it at all spontaneous. On the contrary, it was the march of the women opposed to Trump and was paid for by important anti-Trump organizations. In fact, George Soros was subsidizing or maintaining

10. D. Horowitz y R. Poe, *The Shadow Party. How George Soros, Hillary Clinton and Sixties Radicals seized Control of the Democratic Party* (Nashville, 2006).
11. George Soros, *The Crisis of Global Capitalism* (1998), pp. 28, 155.

relationships with at least fifty-six organizations that sponsored the march. Among the organizations receiving money from Soros that were involved in the Women's March was Planned Parenthood, which was directly responsible for millions of abortions. Likewise, among the supposedly nonpartisan organizations that received money from Soros and supported the March was National Resource Defense, which takes advantage of the global warming position. It was also the case of the MoveOn.org movement, which fiercely supported Hillary Clinton in the last election, and the National Action Network. This group of entities that supported the March was also supported by the Council on American-Islamic Relations, which is strongly opposed to reforms such as women not being forced to wear veils, and the Arab-American Association of New York, whose executive director Linda Sarsour is also opposed to a reform that would allow Muslim women not to wear headscarves.

Soros and the Pope

To conclude, without being exhaustive, this brief list of Soros' areas of influence, another of the visible faces of globalization must be identified. We are referring to Pope Francis. According to data published by Wikileaks, George Soros has been counting for years on "*engaging the Pope on issues of economic and racial justice*" by adding the Vatican to his globalist agenda.[12]

The aforementioned alliance was brought to light, for example, on page 16 of the leaked book of the May 2015 meeting of the OSF's North American board of directors, where it pointed out that $650,000 had been given to finance the pope's visit to the United States. The text further noted that "Pope Francis' first visit to the United States in September will include a historic speech in Congress, a speech at the United Nations, and a visit to Philadelphia for the

12. https://gaceta.es/noticias/soros-soborno-los-obispos-durante-visita-papa-eeuu-24082016-1725/; https://www.religionenlibertad.com/opinion/51575/iglesia-cae-manos-soros.html.

'World Meeting of Families.' To take advantage of this event, we will support activities organized by PICO to engage the pope on issues of economic and racial justice..."[13] The text went on to say that such a goal will have "the influence of Cardinal Rodriguez, the pope's chief adviser" and that "a delegation will be sent to visit the Vatican in the spring or summer to enable it to listen live to the poor Catholics of America."

The goal of Soros' collaboration with the Vatican also included influencing the 2016 U.S. elections to ensure the presidency of Soros' chosen candidate, who was none other than Hillary Clinton. Thus, the document also stated that Soros' money "will support FPL's media, strategies, and public opinion actions, including developing a survey that shows that Catholic voters are receptive to the pope's message about economic inequality, and getting media coverage to convey the message that being "profamily" requires addressing growing inequality.

By using the papal visit to reinforce Pope Francis' strong criticism of what he calls "*an economy of exclusion and inequality*," Soros' organizations should shift national paradigms and priorities in the 2016 presidential campaign race. In helping to achieve Soros's goals, apart from Cardinal Rodriguez Madariaga, a personal friend of Pope Francis, there was mention of an entity called PICO, which is a network of left-wing religious organizations founded in 1972 by John Baumann, a Jesuit. In fact, one of PICO's initiatives aims to redistribute income by demanding that "*leaders in the faith take up positions on the boards of large banks.*"

The Soros-based *Open Society Institute*, in fact, describes PICO as "*a network of congregational-based community organizations that elevates the voices of people of faith and faith leaders to the public debate about national priorities*," and cites other Soros funding besides the core collaboration. In addition, Soros also funds FPL, *Faith in Public Life*, another organization of Left-leaning clergy, which warmly supported Pope Francis' visit to the United States, defends

13. https://adelantelafe.com/jefe-del-papa-wikileaks-papa-soros-una-alianza-profana/.

gender ideology, and, according to one Soros entity, provides survey results as requested in advance by Soros. Among those polls is one that allegedly shows that Catholic voters are receptive to Pope Francis' message about economic inequality.

The data presented in this chapter is not intended to be an exhaustive description of George Soros' activities. It does show, at least, part of his agenda and also how he manages to move it forward through various avenues. However, as we will see in the next chapter, Soros is not the only icon of the globalist plan.

CHAPTER X

THE GLOBALIST AGENDA (III): Its Icons (II): Pope Francis

Before Pope Francis

Pope Francis is one of the great icons of the globalist agenda today. For some, this is an aberrant phenomenon that would indicate a confrontation within the Roman Catholic Church. Such reasoning may ease the consciences of some restless Roman Catholics, but the reality is that the support that the current pontiff provides to the globalist agenda and to a world government is not something new, but has clear and unquestionable antecedents in the popes that preceded him.

Thus, on January 1, 2004, one of the most relevant diplomatic initiatives of John Paul II's pontificate took place when he launched the idea of a new world order.[1] Accompanied by the Secretary of State, Cardinal Angelo Sodano, and by the president of the Pontifical Council for Justice and Peace—both of whom had expressed their "pity" for Saddam Hussein, who had been captured the previous month—the

1. https://www.theguardian.com/world/2004/jan/02/catholicism.religion.

pope stated emphatically that "more than ever, we need a new international order that draws on the experience and results achieved in these years by the United Nations." The statement was of enormous relevance, first, because it was delivered before the representatives of the diplomatic missions accredited to the Holy See; second, because it clearly referred to a new world order that would go beyond what the United Nations had portrayed up until then; and finally, because, supposedly, "it would be able to provide solutions to the problems of today." In other words, this new world order would go far beyond the system of existing international organizations and, of course, nations.

Such an affirmation carried an enormous weight of importance not because of the number of Roman Catholics on the planet or because of the pontiff's moral authority that does not extend beyond his church, who even within his church is openly challenged by millions of Catholics in specific respects. The importance derives from the fact that the Holy See is a State with observer status at the UN and diplomatic representation in more than one hundred and seventy countries. In other words, its capacity to act as a lobby for certain interests is not insignificant.

The line of support for a new world order expressed by John Paul II continued in a more accentuated way with his successor Benedict XVI. In 2009, his encyclical *Caritas in Veritate* (Love in Truth) referred expressly and imperatively to the need for a government that is able "to manage the global economy, to revive the economy hit by the crisis; to avoid any deterioration in the present crisis and the greater imbalances that would result from it; to provide timely and comprehensive food security and peace; to ensure the protection of the environment and to regulate immigration: for all this, there is an urgent need for a true global political authority."

The passage could hardly have been clearer and more revealing. Faced with the problems that countries might be up against, the solution advocated by the pope was not adequate action by their respective governments or international cooperation in individual cases. On the contrary, the goal should be the establishment of a world government that would deal, for example, with some of the inalienable powers of the nation, such as the regulation of immigration. To tell the truth, a good part of the globalist agenda was outlined in these phrases from Benedict XVI.

In October 2011, the Vatican took a further step towards the globalist agenda.[2] Thus, the Pontifical Council for Justice and Peace published a document entitled "Towards Reforming the International Financial and Monetary Systems in the Context of Global Public Authority." The document attacked the free market economy. It was not difficult, because the Holy See had always spoken out against the free market system—to the chagrin of not a few Catholics—and it was easy to quote Paul VI or John Paul II along with popes from the last four centuries. In fact, the Holy See was consistent with its record of opposition to freedom. Precisely for this reason, the text spoke of the need to establish a "world political authority" with broad powers to regulate the financial markets and to put an end to the "inequalities and distortions of capitalist development." Of course, one could ask what would be left of capitalist development if it were controlled by a world political authority.

As for the creation of the new world government, it was obvious from the above-mentioned document that it would be built on the basis of emptying national governments of their powers. As the document noted, "this transformation will be made at the cost of a gradual, balanced transfer of a part of each nation's powers to a world authority and to regional authorities."

In case anyone was left in doubt about the meaning of the document, at the press conference where it was presented, Cardinal Peter Turkson, president of the Pontifical Council for Justice and Peace, stated that "the basic sentiment" behind the protests of the Occupy Wall Street movement was in harmony with the social teaching of the Catholic Church or "the basic inspirations can be the same." Of course, one must ask what remnants of democracy can remain in any

2. https://catholicherald.co.uk/news/2011/10/28/vatican-calls-for-global-government-to-oversee-markets/.

nation that surrenders its economic sovereignty to a world government, that condemns the free market, and that believes that the world should be governed by the principles of the Occupy Wall Street movement. In either case, all this was a reality before the arrival of Pope Francis to the papal throne.

Furthermore, it should be noted that it cannot be said that John Paul II or Benedict XVI started from scratch. In 1963, in his encyclical *Pacem in Terris*, Pope John XXIII advanced similar concepts. Thus, for example, he wrote: "Today the universal common good presents us with problems which are global in their dimensions; problems, therefore, which cannot be solved except by a public authority with power, organization, and means that are coextensive with these problems, and with a global sphere of activity. Consequently, the moral order itself demands the establishment of some similar form of public authority." It is possible that the death, very close in time, of John XXIII and the conclusion of Vatican II by his successor overshadowed these claims, but in the second half of the twentieth century, the Holy See had decided to embrace the idea of a world political authority charged with solving, supposedly, problems that remain in the sphere of nations. John Paul II and Benedict XVI went further in that direction by taking advantage of such situations as the war in Iraq or the world economic crisis. Pope Francis would elaborate on it precisely at the height of his insistence for the globalist agenda, but for anyone who knew the background of the previous popes or of Francis himself, it should not have come as a surprise.

The Ideological Background of Pope Francis: Praise for the Castro Dictatorship

In 1998, a book entitled *Dialogues between John Paul II and Fidel Castro* was published in Buenos Aires.[3] The text had no major rele-

3. *Diálogos entre Juan Pablo II y Fidel Castro*, Buenos Aires, 1998.

vance and was limited to the homilies of John Paul II and the speeches of Fidel Castro, all of them delivered during the pontiff's visit to Cuba. However, the book had a prologue by Jorge Maria Bergoglio, Archbishop of Buenos Aires, which was extraordinarily revealing. In the following pages, we will see how more than twenty years ago, the ideological position of the future Pope Francisco was more than defined. Thus, he points out that "since the Encyclical *Laborem Exercens*, John Paul II has made a notable contribution to opening up the dialogue between Christianity and Marxism. He considers that the Marxist system is the starting point to be able to reveal and visualize the limits and the obstacles erected against the realization of a humanistic project."[4] Bergoglio maintained that John Paul II "is willing to listen, but specifically needs and wants to listen to the truth of the Cuban people, of its government, of the revolution, of religion, and of the relationship between Church and State."[5] From that dialogue between John Paul II and Fidel Castro, the existence of "basic convergences" between the positions of the two had emerged.[6] Not surprisingly, Bergoglio stated that the two "through their speeches were able to dialogue, confront each other, agree, and ultimately leave a wide margin of tolerance open."[7] On this basis, it could be said that "not everything will be the same after his (the pope's) departure, but the dialogue will have been established between the Church and Cuban institutions."[8]

This positive view of the relations between the pope and the Cuban dictator gave way to an analysis of the economic reality in which Bergoglio accepted the theses put forward by the Castro dictatorship. Thus, he stated that "Cuba has, for example, finances that have been battered by the impossibilities and atrophies of the economic model, foreign debt, the commercial obstacles of the US embargo, and credit difficulties."[9] The supposed fault of the United States in the disastrous

4. *Diálogos...*, p. 13.
5. *Diálogos...*, p. 14.
6. *Diálogos...*, p. 14.
7. *Diálogos...*, p. 15.
8. *Diálogos...*, p. 16.
9. *Diálogos...*, p. 20.

state of the Cuban economy was underlined when Bergoglio maintained that "another source of economic distress is the so-called *brain drain*, mainly to the United States."[10] In the end, Bergoglio quoted almost literally John Paul II, who had blamed the economic situation suffered by Cuba on "the unjust and ethically unacceptable restrictive economic measures imposed from outside the country."[11]

Given this background, it is not surprising that Bergoglio stated without blushing that "since 1990, when Fidel Castro proposed *a strategic alliance between Christians and Marxists*, he has not ceased in his intentions to find and demonstrate convergences, or points of connection, between Catholicism and the postulates of the revolution."[12] In case there is any doubt about what this means, Bergolio pointed out that "his two thoughts converge in addressing the *important questions of today's world, and this gives us great satisfaction*."[13]

In a further gesture of flattery towards the Cuban dictator, Bergoglio added, "Fidel Castro went beyond the mere search for convergences by making an explicit recognition of the pope's work in that comparison and highlighting the importance of achieving peaceful coexistence and tolerance."[14] But as if that were not enough, Bergoglio maintained that "there is no other country in a better position to understand the mission of the pope, since the work carried out by the pontiff coincides with that preached by the Cuban government, especially with regard to the equitable distribution of wealth and the aspirations of globalization of human solidarity.",[15] It is truly disturbing to think that the Vatican and the Cuban dictatorship, as Bergoglio stated, coincide in the distribution of wealth and in the globalization of solidarity.

There can be no doubt that Bergoglio felt very close to the Cuban dictatorship, since in the following pages he stated, among other

10. *Diálogos...*, p. 21.
11. *Diálogos...*, p. 22.
12. *Diálogos...*, p. 23.
13. *Diálogos...*, p. 23.
14. *Diálogos...*, p. 24.
15. *Diálogos...*, p. 24.

things, that "the doctrine of Karl Marx is very close to the Sermon on the Mount."[16] In his speech, he described as "genocide" and "economic asphyxiation" the embargo imposed by the United States since 1962,[17] pointing out that the pope had condemned "blockades or embargoes,"[18] and, above all, he maintained that "the vindication of the rights of man that the Church constantly demands—food, health, education, among others—are within the scope of the concept of human rights to which Fidel Castro adheres and is proud to defend in Cuba."[19]

On this basis, it is not surprising that Bergoglio argued that "there are many hypotheses of Fidel Castro's willingness to obtain a transition agreed upon on the basis of papal mediation. It is logical that he sees the Church as an ally to proceed with the change in a gradual and nontraumatic way. An agreed transition, with the pope himself as its supervisor, would be a dignified, successful, and acceptable solution."[20]

This closeness of the Holy See to the Castro dictatorship, with which it wishes to collaborate, even assuming the Cuban propaganda regarding the embargo and pointing out the enormous similarities between both world views, appeared in the Bergoglio text together with some fierce attacks against the free market system. The future Pope Francisco stressed that the "doctrine (of the Catholic Church) has repeatedly condemned liberal capitalism."[21] As reasons for this condemnation, Bergoglio stated that "the fundamental principles of the capitalist system are based on free competition and free markets. Undoubtedly, these principles dwell in the emancipated man, in the utilitarian individual, making possible for the economy to act in a way that does not recognize society as a whole."[22] It is certainly revealing that the same person who praises Fidel Castro condemns

16. *Diálogos...*, p. 25.
17. *Diálogos...*, p. 25.
18. *Diálogos...*, p. 26.
19. *Diálogos...*, p. 26.
20. *Diálogos...*, p. 31.
21. *Diálogos...*, p. 46.
22. *Diálogos...*, p. 47.

the free market system at the same time. The condemnation, however, did not seem disinterested, because it went on to point out that "it is imperative that the economy be subordinated to other aspects of human life, which are dikelogically higher, such as culture, morals and religion."[23] The panorama that Bergoglio presented as desirable is, in the end, coherent with the historical trajectory of the Roman Catholic Church. Once again, freedom is viewed with distrust, if not open aversion, while the alliance with an absolute power that totally controls the life of its subjects and subordinates it to conditions that are not even remotely those of freedom is viewed with pleasure.

Within this left-wing orthodoxy, Bergoglio categorically stated that "the postulates of neoliberalism cannot be admitted and considered Christian."[24] In fact, for Bergoglio, neoliberalism is "precisely at the antipodes of the Gospel."[25] In the end, "John Paul II...has sent a message to those *superpowers* that pressure, exclude, and isolate the Cuban people in the context of the world economy."[26] It was certainly revealing that Bergoglio could openly declare himself to be an enemy of the free market economy and, at the same time, lavish praise on the Cuban dictatorship by assuming its propaganda and condemning not the excesses of Castro's tyranny, but the embargo decreed by the United States. That archbishop was made a cardinal in 2001 and elected pope in 2013.

Bergoglio as Pope

In 1452, Pope Nicholas V, wishing to strengthen relations with the kingdom of Portugal, which was the major power in the world, issued a bull of certainly striking content. In it, the King of Portugal was literally authorized to "invade, search, capture, defeat, and subdue all

23. *Diálogos...*, p. 47.
24. *Diálogos...*, p. 48.
25. *Diálogos...*, p. 49.
26. *Diálogos...*, p. 49.

Saracens and pagans of any kind...and condemn them to perpetual slavery and to appropriate for himself and his successors the kingdoms, duchies, counties, principalities, dominions, possessions, and goods and use them for his use and benefit." The papal bull, which would be followed by another similar one three years later, was of enormous significance because it provided legitimacy for the beginning of one of the blackest pages in the history of humanity: the slave trade from the African continent. That the fact of capturing, enslaving, and exploiting millions of human beings, whose only crime was to be non-Catholic Africans clashed head-on with Jesus' teaching, is more than obvious, but Pope Nicholas V was merely acting in accordance with the centuries-old behavior of the institution he governed. On the one hand, he could refer to charity and, on the other hand, he had political interests that placed good relations with Portugal in first place to the point of justifying the massive commission of crimes against humanity. Such a fact, which can cause understandable unease in many Roman Catholics, was, however, due to a centuries-old consistent practice , since the Vatican is its own State—as recognized by international law—that puts its interests in power before the moral principles it claims to defend and that, on many occasions, even adapts its principles to its interests. The very election of the popes has been historically determined by power relations between the aspirants[27] and by the desire to give the Holy See a situation of greater influence even if this meant legitimizing the capture of Africans to make them slaves or signing a concordat with Hitler.

Bergoglio was elected pope for several reasons. The first was that he came from the only part of the world where the Roman Catholic Church not only has economic, political, and social influence, but where the majority of the population holds to this position. In Africa and Asia, the Roman Catholic Church has a witnessing presence, and in Europe, it has regressed dramatically in recent decades. Secondly, Bergoglio was Latin American, but a nonethnic Latin American.

27. Examples of these power struggles between the tenth and fifteenth centuries can be found in E. R. Chamberlin, *Los malos papas* (Barcelona, 1970).

Neither mestizo nor mulatto, any European or American could identify with him racially, which is logical, because, in the end, he was the son of Italian immigrants to Argentina. Thirdly, Bergoglio was the ideal person to maintain ideal relations with the dictators of so-called twenty-first century socialism. Not only Fidel Castro, but also Evo Morales, Hugo Chávez, Daniel Ortega, and Rafael Correa could feel more than comfortable with a pope who condemned the free market, who attacked the United States, and who considered that there were enormous similarities between Catholic social doctrine and Castro's communism. Moreover, at the time of his election, it seemed that such regimes would continue over time and even spread to other nations. In fourth place, Bergoglio was an apparently ideal character to try to neutralize the advance of the evangelical churches in Latin America, churches that have displaced the Roman Catholic Church in entire areas of the subcontinent, as is the case of the Amazon. Finally, Bergoglio could perfectly embody the support for the globalist agenda that had already been advanced by pontiffs such as John XXIII, John Paul II, or Benedict XVI. It must be acknowledged that Bergoglio, who became Pope Francis, has been fully suited to that mission.

On May 24, 2015, the encyclical letter *Laudato si* was published, which totally fit within the globalist view. That same year, in case there might be any doubt, Pope Francis, in a letter to the Catholic bishops, stated: "Climate change is real and dangerous. A new system of global governance is needed to address this unprecedented threat. This new political authority would be in charge of reducing pollution and developing poor countries and regions."[28] In a very revealing way, the pontiff linked the desire for a world government with the affirmation of climate change and the desire for control of the global economy.

In 2017, Pope Francis repeated his support for a world government and in statements to the Italian newspaper *La Repubblica*, he stated

28. https://verdadyvida.org/francisco-pide-un-nuevo-gobierno-mundial/.

that the United States of America has "a distorted view of the world" and that Americans must be governed by a world government, as soon as possible, "for their own good."[29] This was a statement that could only be considered a real threat to American democracy. Certainly, Pope Francis' sympathies lay elsewhere. So it is not surprising that that same year, on June 14, he appeared with Ayatollah Al-Milani, the Dalai Lama, and Rabbi Abraham Skorka in a video supporting the same globalist position.[30]

In May 2019, at a meeting with the Pontifical Academy of Social Sciences, Pope Francis again signaled his support for the idea of a supranational government.[31] The pope's statement attacked what he called the "excessive claim to sovereignty by nations" by insisting that "often precisely in areas where they are no longer able to act effectively to protect the common good." Pope Francis also insisted that "both in the encyclical *Laudato si* and in the Address to the Members of the Diplomatic Corps this year, I drew attention to the global challenges facing humanity." Then, in full harmony with the globalist agenda, Pope Francis pointed out that these global challenges are "comprehensive development, peace, care for the common home, climate change, poverty, wars, immigration, trafficking in persons, organ trafficking, protection of the common good, and new forms of slavery." In case there might be any doubt about what this meant, Pope Francis expressed the concern of the Roman Catholic Church about the attitude of anti-immigration currents and regretted that this "hinders the achievement of the Sustainable Development Goals approved unanimously at the United Nations General Assembly on September 25, 2015." The pope then spoke out against the assimilation of immigrants, considering that this is not true integration. The pope also stressed in

29. https://www.thetrumpet.com/12819-pope-calls-for-new-world-government.

30. https://apnews.com/f79dd15461f24e6297f439d254be8a26/Global-religious-leaders-join-for-online-friendship-appeal; https://articles.aplus.com/a/pope-francis-dalai-lama-elijah-interfaith-institute-make-friends?no_monetization=true.

31. http://www.vatican.va/content/francesco/es/speeches/2019/may/documents/papa-francesco_20190502_plenaria-scienze-sociali.html.

the above-mentioned communication that "the national State is no longer capable of providing for the common good of its people on its own," and that a supranational authority is therefore needed to address this issue. Consistent with this globalist vision, he added that "when a supranational common good is clearly identified, it is necessary to have the appropriate authority, legally and consistently, that is capable of facilitating its implementation." The justification for such a supranational entity would be, according to Pope Francis, "the great contemporary challenges of climate change, new forms of slavery, and peace." According to the pope, "This universal common good, in turn, must acquire a more pronounced legal validity at the international level."

At this point, one could either be for or against Pope Francis, but one cannot accuse him of not speaking clearly on certain issues. Of course, it was already more than revealing that he had clamorously kept quiet in the face of the ferocious advance of gender ideology or very serious moral problems, while at the same time defending the fight against climate change as a major objective.

Pope Francis clearly manifested himself as a fierce and persistent defender of the globalist agenda that seeks to impose a supranational government that aspires to deprive nations of their powers until they are practically empty of content, trying to justify these steps by appealing to more than debatable issues such as global warming, which has as one of its roadmaps the Sustainable Development Goals approved by the United Nations General Assembly in 2015.

The undivided and express support of Pope Francis to this United Nations document can be clearly understood by where it is found, because among its goals is the implementation of gender ideology throughout the planet, and it does so, expressly, by pointing out that the fifth objective, after quality education and before clean water and sanitation, is gender equality.

On this basis, it comes as no surprise that on November 11, 2019, the Holy See initiated a two-day seminar in which, in collaboration with the Rockefeller Foundation, it presented the stated purpose of fighting against the loss and waste of food.[32] The seminar was organized by the Vatican's Academy of Sciences, attended by more than forty experts and religious leaders, and was intended to conclude with a declaration outlining the guidelines to be followed by public authorities and the private sectors of society. Pope Francis himself supported the initiative from his Twitter account, stating that "we must put an end to the culture of waste, we who ask the Lord to give us our daily bread. The waste of food contributes to hunger and climate change."

It is a real mystery to know the relationship between food waste and climate change, but it's no secret that behind the Vatican and Rockefeller Foundation conference was also the UN and, more specifically, the new head of the UN's food and agriculture agency, Dongyu Qu. As the Chancellor of the Pontifical Academy, the Argentine Marcelo Sánchez Sorondo, would point out during the opening statements that the seminar was intended to establish priorities included in "the Sustainable Development Goals (SDG) of the United Nations." Not surprisingly, on that basis, the head of the FAO (Food and Agriculture Organization of the United Nations) announced that one of the goals of the seminar was the reduction of carbon dioxide emissions. Participants at the seminar said that food waste "is harmful to the planet because of greenhouse gas emissions." According to the organizers, the conference wanted to come up with "a declaration calling for a joint public and private policy for action; a coordinated communication effort to mobilize civil society and religious communities." Similarly, the conference sought to set "a path towards a plan of action and global commitments."

The Rockefeller Foundation now supports in a significant way a global plan that would potentially change the world by 2030. Among its seventeen global goals are spreading gender ideology as the fifth, supporting the theses of the climate warming advocates as the thirteenth, and globalizing energy control as the seventh, tenth, and

32. https://www.youtube.com/watch?v=oeMwp23GKr8; https://www.sol915.com.ar/vaticano-la-fundacion-rockefeller-se-unen-desperdicio-alimentos/; https://infovaticana.com/2019/11/12/el-vaticano-y-la-fundacion-rockefeller-juntos-contra-el-desperdicio-de-alimentos/.

twelfth. The same seventeenth goal is to establish alliances to advance these goals, a task that the Vatican has joined with undeniable enthusiasm. However, this is by no means the only initiative of the Holy See to implement the globalist agenda.

The Pact of the Catacombs for the Common House

In 1965, some forty Latin-American bishops, who were participating in the Second Vatican Council, took advantage of the occasion to reach a unique pact. After celebrating Mass in the catacomb of Domitila, they signed a pact—to which more bishops later adhered—in which they committed to dedicate themselves in a special way to the poor and to "hard-working and economically weak and underdeveloped persons and groups," to promote the "advent of another new social order, one worthy of the children of man and the children of God." The text was signed by the so-called "red bishop" Hélder Câmara as well as by bishops such as Antônio Fragoso, Luigi Betazzi, Manuel Larraín, Leonidas Proaño, Vicente Faustino Zazpe, and Sergio Méndez Arceo. It is not surprising, therefore, that it became the basis of the movement of collaboration with the left-wing and communist parties that, four years later, was presented as liberation theology. Conceived as a fusion of Roman Catholicism and Marxism,[33] liberation theology would have an extraordinary relevance during the following years. This liberation theology defended the revolution in Latin America and played a relevant role in the implementation of the Sandinista regime in Nicaragua and in the actions of the communist guerrillas in El Salvador and Guatemala, even including pockets farther south in the continent that always maintained a positive view of Fidel Castro's dictatorship in Cuba.

Liberation theology was losing its influence as a result of the failure of the communist parties in America, although the Sao Paulo

33. Leonardo Boff and Clodovis Boff, *Cómo hacer Teología de la liberación* (Madrid, 1985), p. 40ff.

Forum included among its goals to resurrect it. Thus, on March 21, 2013, barely a week after being elected pope, Francisco received the Argentinian Nobel Peace Prize Adolfo Pérez Esquivel, who gave him a copy of the Pact of the Catacombs at the request of the Spanish bishop and liberation theologian Pedro Casaldáliga. The request was that he "try to listen, reflect, and reach an agreement, a reconciliation with the Latin American theologians."[34] In July 2014, Leonardo Boff, a liberation theologian who clearly expressed that his view was a fusion of Marxism and Catholicism, stated in an article entitled "The Pact of the Catacombs as lived by Pope Francis" that the Pact of the Catacombs contained the ideals presented by Pope Francis.[35] Not long after, taking advantage of the Amazon Synod, a group of bishops signed the so-called "Pact of the Catacombs for the Common House."[36]

During a Mass celebrated by Cardinal Claudio Hummes and also attended by Cardinal Pedro Barreto, about forty bishops, accompanied by other synod priests, advisers and experts of both sexes, as well as some of the participants in the Amazon Common House signed a new Pact of the Catacombs for the Common House. The Pact of the Catacombs for the Common House was literally signed "for a Church with an Amazonian face, poor and servant, prophetic and Samaritan." The text stated that "we, the participants of the Pan-Amazonian Synod, share the joy of living among numerous native peoples, quilombos and river dwellers, migrants, communities on the periphery of the cities of this immense territory of the planet."

The text then paid homage to liberation theology by stating that "we recall with gratitude the bishops who, in the Catacombs of Santa Domitila, at the end of the Second Vatican Council, signed *the Pact for a Servant and Poor Church*. We remember with reverence all the

34. https://www.lavoz.com.ar/noticias/mundo/perez-esquivel-papa-pacto-catacumbas.

35. http://www.servicioskoinonia.org/boff/articulo.php?num=651.

36. https://www.vidanuevadigital.com/documento/pacto-de-las-catacumbas-por-la-casa-comun/; https://www.vaticannews.va/es/vaticano/news/2019-10/casa-comun-en-centro-nuevo-pacto-catacumbas.html; https://jesuitas.lat/es/noticias/1653-padres-sinodales-firman-historico-pacto-de-las-catacumbas-por-la-casa-comun; https://www.youtube.com/watch?v=t_12SxMZSjI.

martyrs who are members of the base ecclesial communities, of the pastoral and popular movements; the native leaders, the female and male missionaries, the laity, priests and bishops, who shed their blood for this option for the poor, to defend life and to fight for the safeguarding of our Common House." He went on to point out his decision "to continue their fight with tenacity and courage. It is a feeling of urgency that imposes itself in the face of the aggressions that today devastate the Amazon territory, threatened by the violence of a predatory and consumerist economic system."

The goal of the pact was "to assume, in the face of extreme threat of global warming and the depletion of natural resources, the commitment to defend the standing Amazon jungle in our territories and with our attitudes. From it come the gifts of water for a large part of South American territory, the contribution to the carbon cycle and the regulation of the global climate, an incalculable biodiversity and a rich socio-diversity for humanity and the entire Earth." In addition to this goal, they determined to "recognize that we are not owners of Mother Earth, but rather her sons and daughters... Therefore, we commit ourselves to an integral ecology, in which everything is interconnected, the human race and all creation because all beings are daughters and sons of the Earth."

Likewise, the new Pact of the Catacombs had as its goal "to renew in our churches the preferential option for the poor, especially for the native peoples, and, together with them, to guarantee the right to be protagonists in society and in the Church. To help them to preserve their lands, cultures, languages, histories, identities, and spiritualities." Similarly, the new Pact of the Catacombs indicated as its goal "to walk ecumenically with other Christian communities in the inculturation and in the liberating announcement of the Gospel, and with other religions and people of good will, in solidarity with native peoples, with the poor and the small, in defense of their rights and in the preservation of the Common House."

Another goal indicated by the new Pact of the Catacombs was to "recognize the services and real Diakonia of the large number of women who direct communities in Amazonia today and to seek to reinforce them with an adequate ministry of women leaders of the community." Likewise, the new Pact of the Catacombs affirmed as its mission that of capturing "peripheries and migrants, workers and the unemployed, students, educators, researchers, and the world of culture and communication."

After affirming its desire to "reduce the production of waste and the use of plastics, to favor the production and commercialization of agro-ecological products," the new Pact of the Catacombs affirmed that the bishops placed themselves "alongside those who are persecuted for the prophetic service of denouncing and repairing injustices, of defending the land and the rights of the little ones, of welcoming and supporting migrants and refugees." Finally, the text concluded by stating that in the Eucharistic Bread "creation tends towards divinization, towards the holy wedding feast, towards unification with the Creator himself," with the text concluding with the date in the Catacombs of Domitila, Rome, October 20, 2019.

Liberation theology was, without any doubt, theology, but it was a theology aimed at establishing communist dictatorships in Latin America, totally intertwined with the action of subversive and guerrilla groups and blatantly sympathetic to the theses of the Cuban dictatorship through works such as *In Cuba* by the Nicaraguan priest Ernesto Cardenal or *Fidel and the religion* by the Brazilian priest Frei Beto. That same line was expressed, as we have already seen, by a person known then as Bergoglio and now as Pope Francis in the prologue of the book *Dialogues between John Paul II and Fidel Castro*, where he assumed all the communist propaganda on the Cuban tragedy and even went so far as to affirm that, except for atheism, the Castro dictatorship was similar to the Catholic social doctrine.

Liberation theology was defeated at every turn on the battlefield and, when the revolutionary experiments failed, it was gradually extinguished in a way that was not infrequently painful and even ridiculous. It is now returning to the globalist agenda as a new force that can unleash misery, pain, and death on hundreds of millions of Latin

Americans. With clear references to Pope Francis and to what was referred to in the Amazon Synod, the new Pact of the Catacombs defends four very clear pillars of the globalist agenda. The first one is climate warming, assuming the thesis of global warming and going to ridiculous extremes such as qualifying human beings as children of Mother Earth the same way it happened in pre-Christian religions or trying to reduce the use of plastics or increase the production of agro-ecological products. The second is uncontrolled immigration. Again, these immigrants—referred to by the politically correct term of migrants—become a target and an ally for schemes of social disruption. They are expected, as are the indigenous people whose spiritual worldview is honored, to become instruments of a concrete policy. The third is gender ideology to which tribute is paid here in a more limited way and through a specific section devoted to women who are promised to become community leaders. The fourth, finally, is to deprive national sovereignty of its content, which is achieved by bringing together elements that can be clearly used against it, such as illegal immigrants and indigenous communities, and also as expressly stated, by seeking to remove the management of areas of their territory from State powers, as is the case with the Amazon.

These four pillars of the globalist agenda will be advanced, according to the new Pact of the Catacombs, through the recruitment of young people or the use of the media as well as through the defense of subversive elements, as was done in the past by the supportive hierarchy of liberation theology with the guerrillas and the condemnation of capitalist development. In fact, it makes sense because the slowing down of economic growth would mean the end of enormous masses who, by becoming middle classes, would not be able to increase the ranks of totalitarianism.

The document was signed, moreover, when, among other circumstances, the indigenous people were bringing the government of Ecuador to its knees; young people were subverting the situation in Chile in a prodigiously frightening way; a president who was in favor of gender ideology was staging a coup d'état in Peru; George Soros was impatient because the globalist agenda was not moving fast enough; and Pope Francis had no problem with the Amazon Synod being inaugurated with pagan ceremonies performed by a shaman,[37] although some Catholic faithful would later throw some of the indigenous images into the river.[38]

The new Pact of the Catacombs for the Common House is not a mere theological document. On the contrary, it is a program of political action with religious legitimacy similar to the liberation theology that shed so much blood in Latin America over decades. The threat now is not less, and it could even be said that the danger to the freedom and prosperity of the people is much greater. However, more serious than the new Pact of the Catacombs was to be revealed by the recent Amazon Synod.

The Amazon Synod

In 1890, John Henry Newman published a book in which he sought to justify the changes that the Roman Catholic Church had experienced in its beliefs and practices over the centuries. He wrote: "In the course of the fourth century two movements or developments spread over the face of Christendom, with a rapidity characteristic of the Church: one ascetic, the other ritual or ceremonial. We are told in various ways by Eusebius, that Constantine, in order to recommend the new religion to the heathen, transferred into it the outward ornaments to which they had been accustomed in their own. It is not necessary to elaborate on a subject which the diligence of Protestant writers has made familiar to most of us. The use of temples, and these dedicated to particular saints, and ornamented on occasions with branches of trees; incense, lamps, and candles; votive offerings to heal from illness; holy water; asylums; holydays and seasons, use of calendars,

37. https://infovaticana.com/2019/08/20/el-sinodo-cuenta-ya-con-las-bendiciones-del-chaman-amazonico/.
38. https://www.aciprensa.com/noticias/roban-polemicas-imagenes-del-sinodo-amazonico-y-las-arrojan-al-rio-tiber-video-61653.

processions, blessings on the fields; sacerdotal vestments, the tonsure, the ring in marriage, turning to the East, icons that came later, perhaps the ecclesiastical chant, and the Kyrie Eleison, are all of pagan origin, and sanctified by their adoption into the Church.[39] Newman's text was particularly interesting because it contained three relevant statements. The first was that in the fourth century, the Roman Catholic Church had allowed in its practice a true transfusion of paganism that persisted until the very nineteenth century in which Newman wrote; the second was that such permissiveness was due, fundamentally, to the desire to increase its power, something that would derive from the fact that the pagan population would feel comfortable with that paganization of Christianity; and the third was that such immense absorption of pagan elements was unimportant, since they were sanctified for adoption by the Church. This last point can be discussed in the same way that one can question whether a poison ceases to be a poison simply because it is poured into a glass of water, but what cannot be denied is that the Roman Catholic Church absorbed en masse a considerable set of pagan practices, and it did so to increase its social and political influence in a largely pagan world. These are undoubtedly facts that need to be reflected upon. By the way, the author of these lines wrote them when he had already converted to Catholicism. Later, he was made a cardinal by Pope Leo XIII, and in October 2019, he was officially canonized. It is difficult not to find parallels in that conduct with what happened at the so-called Amazon Synod, one of the central events in the development of the globalist agenda.

On January 19, 2018, Pope Francis visited the Amazon and began a journey that resulted in the celebration of the Amazon Synod during the month of October 2019, which lasted for twenty-one days. The final document of the synod is comprised of a whole program of political action with supposed spiritual legitimacy. At the outset, it makes reference to the fact that "the atmosphere was one of open, free, and respectful exchange of ideas between the bishops who are pastors

39. J. H. Newman, *An Essay on the Development of Christian Doctrine* (London, 1893), p. 373.

in the Amazon, missionaries, laymen and women, and representatives of the indigenous peoples of the Amazon." The document also praises the fact that "there was a notable presence of people from the Amazonian world who organized acts of support in different activities, processions, such as the opening with songs and dances accompanying the Holy Father, from Peter's tomb to the synodal hall."

The document adds that "the territory and its inhabitants are disappearing, especially the indigenous peoples. The Amazon rainforest is a 'biological heart' for the increasingly threatened earth. It is a frenzied race to the death. Radical changes are urgently needed as well as a new direction in order to save the forest. It is scientifically proven that the disappearance of the Amazon biome will have a catastrophic impact on the planet as a whole!" Likewise, the document points out, in a programmatic way, that "the celebration ends with great joy and the hope of embracing and practicing the new paradigm of integral ecology, the care of the 'common house and the defense of the Amazon."

The document goes on to qualify those "attacks against nature" and "threats against life: appropriation and privatization of natural assets, such as water itself; legal logging licenses and the entry of illegal loggers; predatory hunting and fishing; unsustainable mega-projects (hydroelectric plants, forest licenses, massive logging, single-crop farming, highways, waterways, railways, and mining and oil projects); pollution caused by the extractive industry and city dumps; and, above all, climate change."

After endorsing the theses of the climate change advocates, the document focuses on the so-called "migrations," which allegedly demand "cross-border pastoral care...capable of understanding the right to free movement of these peoples." Having affirmed a more than debatable right to free movement without borders, the document points out that "the life of the Amazonian communities not yet affected by the influence of western civilization is reflected in the belief and rites regarding the action of the divine spirits, which are summoned in innumerable ways, with and in the territory, with and in relation to nature (LS 16, 91,

117, 138, 240). Let us recognize that for thousands of years they have cared for their land, their waters, and their forests, and have managed to preserve them until today so that humanity may benefit from the enjoyment of the free gifts of God's creation."

It is significant that, after affirming that the spirits have cared for the Amazon for thousands of years, the document states that in the Amazon, "relationships between Catholics and Pentecostals, charismatics and evangelicals is not easy. The sudden appearance of new communities, linked to the personality of some preachers, contrasts strongly with the principles and the ecclesiological principles and experience of the historical churches and can conceal the danger of being swept away by the emotional waves of the moment or of confining the experience of faith in protected and reassuring environments."

Even more revealing is the fact that, after praising the action of the spirits and criticizing the action of the evangelicals because they create "protected and reassuring environments"—how can this reality be considered as something negative?—the document states that "in the Amazon, inter-religious dialogue takes place especially with indigenous religions and Afro-descendant cults. These traditions deserve to be known, understood in their own expressions and in their relationship with the forest and Mother Earth."

At this point, the document once again focuses on the "phenomenon of migration" and then turns to the young people whom it defines "with indigenous faces and identities, Afro-descendants, river dwellers, gatherers and cultivators, migrants, refugees, and others." To these young people, the Roman Catholic Church intends to give "adequate accompaniment and appropriate education." Precisely then, the document recognizes what it calls "new family formats: single-parent households headed by women, an increase in separated families, civil unions and reunited families, a decrease in institutional marriages," an affirmation that is, to say the least, striking from a Roman Catholic perspective.

The document then focuses on the situation of indigenous people. Thus, it affirms that "it is necessary to defend the right to the city of all people," insisting that "special attention should be given to the reality of the indigenous people in urban centers, as they are the most exposed to the enormous problems of juvenile delinquency, lack of work, ethnic struggles and social injustices." In that same vein, the document states that "it is necessary to defend the rights to self-determination, demarcation of territories, and free and informed prior consultation," adding that "at all times respect for their self-determination and their free choice about the type of relationships they want to establish with other groups must be guaranteed at all times."

In the same indigenous line of thought, the document states that "motivated by integral ecology, we wish to strengthen the already existing sources of communication in the region with a view to encouraging and promoting integral ecological conversion. To this end, we must collaborate in the training of local communicators, especially indigenous ones" with the purpose of creating "an All-Amazon Church communication network."

The document goes on to add to the environmentalist theses by affirming that "integral ecology is not one path among many that the Church can choose for the future in this territory, it is the only possible path, because there is no other viable route for saving the region." After this affirmation, the document states: "We embrace and support campaigns of divestment from extractive companies responsible for the socio-ecological damage of the Amazon, starting with our own Church institutions and also in alliance with other churches; c) we call for a radical energy transition and the search for alternatives."

Then right after, ignoring the sovereignty of the different nations over their territory, the document affirms that "the protagonists of the care, protection and defense of the rights of peoples and the rights of nature in this region are the Amazon communities themselves. They are the agents of their own destiny, of their own mission. In this scenario, the role of the Church is to be an ally. They have clearly stated that they want the Church to accompany them, to walk with them, and not to impose on them a particular way of being, a specific form of development that has little to do with their cultures, traditions and spiritualities. They know how to take care of the Amazon, how to love and protect it; what they need is for the Church to support them."

After affirming that "the Church recognizes the wisdom of the Amazon peoples about biodiversity, a traditional wisdom that is a living and ever-present process," the synodal document points out that "there is an urgent need to develop energy policies that drastically reduce the emission of carbon dioxide (CO2) and other gases related to climate change. New clean energies will help to promote health. All companies should establish ways of monitoring their supply chains to ensure that the products they buy, create or sell are produced in a socially and environmentally sustainable manner."

As if these statements aimed at intervening in national economies were not enough, the document goes on to say that "we propose to define ecological sin as an action or omission against God, against one's neighbor, the community and the environment... We also propose to create special ministries for the care of the 'common house' and the promotion of integral ecology."

This desire to establish specific political structures is even more evident when the document goes on to state that "as a way of repaying the ecological debt that countries owe to the Amazon, we propose the creation of a world fund to cover part of the budgets of the communities present in the Amazon to promote their integral and self-sustaining development and so also to protect them from the predatory compulsion to extract their natural resources at the behest of national and multinational companies."

In the same line of interventionism in the economic life of the peoples, the synodal document states that "we should reduce our dependence on fossil fuels and the use of plastics, changing our eating habits (excess consumption of meat and fish/seafood) and adopting a more modest lifestyle...promote education in integral ecology at all levels, promote new economic models and initiatives towards a sustainable quality of life..." and "create a pastoral socio-environmental office."

After enthusiastically subscribing to the theses of the global warming advocates, the document goes on to make several concessions to gender ideology. Thus, it affirms that we should "value 'the role of women, recognizing their fundamental role in the formation and continuity of cultures, in spirituality, in communities and families. Their leadership must be more fully assumed in the heart of the Church, recognized and promoted by strengthening their participation in the pastoral councils of parishes and dioceses, and also in positions of governance."

After assuming the debatable term "femicide," the text affirms about women that "the Church commits to defend their rights and recognizes them as protagonists and guardians of creation and of our 'common house,' pointing out that "we want to strengthen family ties, especially for migrant women." Likewise, she points out that "we ask that an instituted ministry of 'women community leadership' be created."

In an understandable continuation of those interventionist theses that would control the economy, development, and borders, and that would use State structures in addition to students, migrants, and women, the document also refers to education, affirming that "it should include disciplines such as integral ecology, ecotheology, theology of creation, Indian theologies, ecological spirituality, the history of the Church in the Amazon, Amazonian cultural anthropology, and so on." Finally, the document, after defending the creation of a specifically Amazonian rite, concludes by considering itself "under the protection of Mary, Mother of the Amazon, venerated with various titles throughout the region."

The final document of the Amazon Synod is hardly a religious text; on the contrary, it is an emphatic plea in favor of globalist goals. It is significant that it contains hardly any references to papal documents, Roman Catholic theologians, or texts from the Bible, but, on the contrary, it reproduces, defends, and promotes the globalist agenda.

The synodal document thus begins with inclusive language that is grammatically unacceptable but is an inescapable feature of that globalist agenda. It then reproduces the position of the global warming advocates in a totally uncritical, sectarian, and dogmatic manner. The document even sets forth specific guidelines on economic and energy policy and educational indoctrination in that regard.

No less significant than the enthusiastic support for the global warming advocates' theses is the way in which the synodal document refers to the so-called migrations. The text not only denies governments the right to establish borders, but also insists that migrations cannot be contained by borders and that those who instigate those migrations should be supported. The consequences of such a view, which was totally contrary to the law, could be truly frightening.

No less significant is the set of concessions to feminism adopting inclusive language, referring to the empowerment of women, and even pointing out that their leadership position must be enhanced even in the ecclesial sphere, something truly remarkable within the Roman Catholic Church. It is also revealing that, while national governments are being robbed of their governing rights, the document affirms indigenous peoples' right to self-determination by sowing the seeds for countless future political conflicts.

All of this goes hand in hand with a direct attack on the evangelicals, who, by the way, make up 80% of the inhabitants of the Amazon, and a series of concessions to the paganism of the indigenous people, such as recognizing that the spirits they worship have cared for the Amazon for centuries, such as insisting that inter-religious dialogue must be linked above all to indigenous paganism, or creating a special Amazonian rite. In a barely concealed way, the document makes clear which spiritual views can be integrated into the globalist agenda and which are clearly incompatible.

The Amazon Synod has been a true milestone for the massive extension of the globalist agenda in Latin America, and it is significant that it has taken place at the same time as an outbreak of social conflicts in the area and the advance of the Left in some relevant nations.

Far from being a religious text, the document of the Amazon Synod advocates an easily recognizable globalist agenda.

It adopts the view of gender ideology to ridiculous extremes, such as considering that indigenous women are especially worthy of interest, who are alone and have migrated to the city.

It adopts the idea of global warming to the point of pretending that policies will be set in place that will have dire consequences for the well-being of the region.

It adopts the globalist view of migration by denying the legitimacy of borders.

It adopts a globalist view regarding the use of minorities—in this case, indigenous and young people—that can be used to weaken national governments. Thus, it looks at young people, but especially at those belonging to certain sectors who can be instrumentalized, and at indigenous people in order to emphasize a principle of self-determination that would make the political structures of the nations of Latin America even more fragile.

It adopts the globalist view of economy by calling for measures that would bring economic growth to a halt in Latin American nations and bring about their subsequent poverty.

It adopts a policy of stripping nations of their sovereignty so that the Amazon, in which the Roman Catholic Church has a minority representation, is governed internationally and without borders.

It adopts the globalist view in a strategic zone whereby outside nations would decide on the region's development and where the majority of the population has already stopped being Roman Catholic to become evangelical. In fact, José Luis Azcona, bishop emeritus of Marajó, in the Amazon delta, pointed this out.[40] Certainly, the bishops debated the reasons for the growth of evangelicals and the decline of Roman Catholics.[41]

In other words, the document adopts a complete globalist agenda, an agenda that can only have dire consequences not only for Latin America, but for the planet as a whole. This enthusiastic support

40. https://infovaticana.com/2019/08/25/la-amazonia-ya-no-es-catolica/.

41. https://www.aciprensa.com/noticias/obispos-debaten-por-que-los-protestantes-crecen-en-la-amazonia-y-los-catolicos-no-25972.

for the globalist agenda pursued by the Roman Catholic Church is strongly reminiscent of the way it supported Constantinianism in the fourth century. In fact, just as in the fourth century it accepted in its midst an infinite number of pagan practices because that allowed it to expand its power, it has now not only absorbed the globalist agenda, but has also paid tribute to the spirits worshipped by the indigenous people, and has demonstrated its willingness to engage in spiritual dialogue, especially with those same shamans who performed their religious ceremonies before Pope Francis and who placed images of Pachamama, Mother Earth, in Roman Catholic churches.

Above and beyond what millions of decent Roman Catholics may think and feel, the reality is that by making a choice between good and evil, the Holy See has officially placed itself on the side of the most sinister, most terrifying and most totalitarian evil.

Pope Francis: a Gay-friendly Pope?

All the aspects described in the previous pages clearly show that Pope Francis, following a line already present in previous pontiffs, is an active protagonist and defender of the globalist agenda. These aspects, however, escape many of the Roman Catholics who cling to the idea that the pope cannot change aspects of morality. This illusion does not correspond to reality, since the Holy See has indicated that it supports the millennium goals. In fact, there are sufficient indications to ask whether the pope has not taken considerable steps to, for example, embrace the ideology of gender even in aspects such as the acceptance of homosexual relationships.

Thus, in 2018,[42] the American Jesuit James Martin declared at a meeting of his order that Pope Francis has deliberately chosen bishops in favor of homosexuality to change the attitude of the Roman Catholic Church towards homosexuality. Far from being just another

42. https://infovaticana.com/2018/11/09/james-martin-el-papa-nombra-obispos-gay-friendly-para-cambiar-la-iglesia-sobre-los-lgbti/.

Jesuit, Father Martin is a consultant for Vatican communications and, above all, is a cleric esteemed enough by Rome to have been the most relevant speaker at the recent World Meeting of Families in Dublin, invited by Bishop Kevin Farrell. In fact, Bishop Farrell is responsible for the Dicastery for the Laity, Family and Life, and he wrote the prologue to the Jesuit's most famous book entitled *Building a Bridge*.

During the Ignatian Family Teach-in for Justice 2018, Father James Martin stated that, in order to understand the change towards homosexuality experienced by the Catholic Church, "just look at what has happened in the last five years, since Francis was appointed as pope." To show the reasons for his claim, Jesuit James Martin pointed out the following: "To begin with, notice Pope Francis' comments about LGBT people such as 'Who am I to judge?'" His five most famous words were in response to questions about gay people, weren't they? He's the first pope, as you know, to pronounce the word 'gay' in a sentence." Jesuit Martin also stated that Pope Francis "has gay friends, and he has spoken about how he wants gays to feel welcome in the Church. That's a lot to take in."

In case there might be any doubt about what he was saying, Jesuit Martin added, "He has also appointed pro-LGBT bishops and archbishops and cardinals, such as Cardinal Tobin, the archbishop of Newark, who, for example, celebrated a 'Welcoming Mass' for LGBT Catholics in his cathedral. That's a trend." According to Martin, the trend was "unstoppable," and he encouraged his listeners to identify themselves as "LGBT Catholics" to help bring about change.

The Jesuit also cited as evidence of Pope Francis' pro-gay agenda his behavior during the recent synod, supposedly focused on youth, which he considers "a great step forward." According to Jesuit Martin, "Last week, for example, at the Youth Synod in the Vatican, bishops and experts from around the world were gathered...to talk about young people. And LGBT issues were discussed more openly than at any previous synod." Jesuit Martin pointed out that "in its final document, the synod delegates spoke about coming alongside LGBT people, about listening to them and recognizing the work of many people in the Church who serve this community." Martin regretted that at the synod, where Pope Francis waved a cross with the rainbow flag, the acronym LGTBI was avoided in the text because of, he said, opposition from some American dioceses and especially those from sub-Saharan Africa and India. However, according to Jesuit Martin, "In general, the Church has made progress on these issues. The Church is learning." In a very revealing way, Martin's words coincided with Archbishop Carlo Maria Viganò's[43] denunciations; although, far from considering the facts as something negative, he presented them as a positive move forward. Viganó had gone even further by revealing that Pope Francis had lied about sexual abuse by the clergy.[44]

The Jesuit case was far from an exception. Cardinal Reinhard Marx, President of the German Bishops' Conference, claimed on February 3, 2018, that, for him, Catholic priests could perform "blessing" ceremonies for homosexual couples.[45] In statements to the German radio station Bavarian State Broadcasting, Cardinal Marx said that "there can be no rules" on this issue, and that the decision as to whether a homosexual union should receive the blessing of the Roman Catholic Church should lie in the hands of "a priest or a pastoral minister." In the interview, conducted in the context of Cardinal Marx's tenth anniversary as Archbishop of Munich and Freising in Germany, the prelate also pointed out that the specific liturgical form of that blessing, or other form of "encouragement," was quite a different matter. Asked if he was really saying that he "could imagine a way to bless homosexual couples in the Catholic Church," the cardinal replied "yes," adding that, however, these could not be "general solutions." Cardinal Marx was not reprimanded, and, in fact, in December 2019, he again reiterated that the Roman Catholic Church could bless homosexual unions.[46]

43. https://infovaticana.com/2019/09/11/vigano-denuncia-que-se-esta-construyendo-una-nueva-iglesia/.

44. https://www.dw.com/es/exembajador-del-vaticano-acusa-al-papa-de-mentir-sobre-abusos-sexuales/a-49132792.

45. https://www.aciprensa.com/noticias/cardenal-marx-en-algunas-regiones-se-podria-permitir-sacerdotes-casados-97798.

46. https://www.aciprensa.com/noticias/cardenal-aprueba-ceremonias-de-bendicion-de-parejas-homosexuales-37536 and https://infovaticana.com/2019/12/24/cardenal-marx-bendecir-las-uniones-homosexuales-es-licito/.

It is not surprising that the news sparked the enthusiasm of entities such as gay Christians.[47]

It's not just about priests and bishops. There are powerful indications that it is Pope Francis himself who is supporting the acceptance of homosexual behavior within the Catholic Church. This has recently come to light thanks to the testimony of a homosexual priest who claims to have received a call from Pope Francis, in which he told the priest he wanted him to walk with deep interior freedom and gave him the "power of the keys."[48] The pope thus granted the priest freedom to practice homosexuality. It is not surprising that the priest says he is not sorry for having committed homosexual acts, but rather for having followed the teaching of the Roman Catholic Church on homosexuality. So far, the Holy See has not denied the statements of the homosexual priest.

The facts may be disturbing to millions of bona fide Roman Catholics, but the reality cannot be denied. If there is one undisputed icon of the globalist agenda besides the tycoon George Soros, it is Pope Francis and with him the Holy See. The next chapters will be dedicated to the specific dogmas of this globalist agenda.

47. https://www.cristianosgays.com/?s=Reinhard+Marx.

48. https://www.lifesitenews.com/news/openly-gay-priest-claims-pope-francis-affirmed-his-homosexuality-in-private-phone-call.

CHAPTER XI

THE DOGMAS OF THE GLOBALIST AGENDA (I): Global Warming

What Is Global Warming (or Climate Change)?

Global warming is a theory. Although its supporters—whom we call in this book "global warming advocates"—insist that it is an indisputable truth, and although unscientific bodies, such as the Vatican, claim that it cannot be denied, the reality is that the theses of global warming are debatable and, indeed, are discussed,[1] moreover, by leading scientists.[2] What do global warming advocates maintain? First, we are experiencing a process of global warming—or climate change—that is perceived on the planet. Second, this warming has never existed before. Third, this warming is a direct consequence of human action. Fourth, it must be controlled because, otherwise, the catastrophic consequences of this warming will affect the planet and human and

1. Of interest are the works of the climatologist Tim Ball, *Human Caused Global Warming. The Biggest Deception in History. The Why, What, Where, When and How it Was Achieved* (2016) and *The Deliberate Corruption of Climante Science* (Mount Vernon, 2014).

2. Of special interest in this regard is the documentary *La gran estafa del calentamiento global*, https://www.youtube.com/watch?v=NWmMOoyCNYs.

animal life.[3] The Intergovernmental Panel on Climate Change (IPCC) has disseminated this view in a special, if not unique, way. In its Fifth Assessment Report, the IPCC concluded that "it is *extremely likely* that human influence has been the dominant cause of the observed warming since the mid-twentieth century." The greatest human influence would be the emission of greenhouse gases such as carbon dioxide, methane, and nitrous oxide. This circumstance would force us to set up supranational authorities that, over and above the sovereignty of individual governments and nations, would establish the guidelines for a world economy and for each particular country. In the case of the United States, this view of State control has crystallized in the so-called Green New Deal through two resolutions—resolution 109 of the chamber promoted by Alexandria Ocasio-Cortez—and resolution 59 of the Senate promoted by Ed Markey. Markey's resolution failed miserably in the Senate. Among the people of the United States, climate change is a thesis believed with true enthusiasm by Democratic supporters, but is being viewed with skepticism by the Republicans. In fact, the belief in global warming has become for many a true religion to the point of declaring even the end of the world, as if it were a millennial cult. For example, at the beginning of 2019, Representative Alexandria Ocasio-Cortez pointed out that global warming is "our World War II" and stated emphatically that the world will end in twelve years if we do not correct global warming.[4]

The reality, however, is that the claims of the advocates for global warming lack a solid foundation. First, if we really are experiencing global warming; in any case, it is not something exceptional in the history of this planet and of human beings. In the past, both have gone through major warming periods.[5] One of these periods coincided

3. IPCC AR5 WG1 Summary for Policymakers 2013, p. 17.

4. https://www.newsweek.com/alexandria-ocasio-cortez-climate-change-world-will-end-12-years-un-report-1300873.

5. Of special interest, regarding the history of periods of global warming and cooling, are the works of archaeologist Brian Fagan, *The Great Warming. Climate Change and the Rise and Fall of Civilizations* (New York, 2008) (on global warming during the Middle Ages) and *Idem*, Brian Fagan, *The Little Ice Age. How Climate made History, 1300-1850* (New York, 2000) [over centuries of cooling between warm periods].

with the end of the ice ages, another with the Mycenaean period—for the reader to understand, that was during the Trojan War—another with the first-century BC during the time of Julius Caesar and the Wars of Gaul, and another with the Middle Ages. On all these occasions, the human race survived the warming and certainly did not cause it, because cars, factories, or industries did not exist in any of these three historical periods. Second, it is obvious that these cyclical periods of warming had nothing to do with human activity and that the reason was natural and related to the sun. The reason for this being so logical is because life would be extinguished on Earth if the light of the sun disappeared, and also because this star is the greatest source of heat. Third—and this is a sadly neglected aspect—the forecasts on global warming climate change, as is often the case in millenarian sects, have not come to pass by a long shot in the last two decades as we shall see below.

Unfulfilled Prophecies

On February 25, 2001, the supplement *Crónica* of the Spanish newspaper *El Mundo* published in its Issue #280 a report entitled PREDICTIONS | BETTER NOT FULFILLED. In the mentioned text it indicated what would happen in 2020 according to what the scientists had claimed at that time. The text, signed by Paco Rego, contained the following statements in its headlines: "2020: The Mediterranean without beaches AND THE NORTH of Spain is dotted with palm trees; people do not wear coats in winter due to the rise in temperatures.... This will be life as we know it if the UN report comes to pass." The report went on to describe what the situation of the planet would be in the year 2020 according to the theses of the defenders of global warming. It stated: "In one of the geographical charts, updated to mid-2020, there is no longer any trace of many of the beaches lapped by the waters of the Mediterranean and the Atlantic. The level of their waters, as predicted by the

Intergovernmental Panel on Climate Change (IPCC), has risen to cover a large part of European coasts."

The text also explained that in 2020 "heat waves will raise thermometers above 40 degrees. Due to the increase in temperatures (between 1.4 and 5.8 degrees Celsius), cold areas have become hot and vice versa. In the north of Spain, the landscape is dotted with palm trees, and people go without their coats in the winter. The alpine glaciers have disappeared. The few that remain are still retreating, which will add more water to the oceans."

In the same vein as claimed by the IPCC, the report stated that in 2020, "The rising of the seas is not the only deadly gift that the twentieth-century's greenhouse effect has left us. Global warming has also triggered the rate of marine evaporation, contributing to an increase in the number and violence of storms and hurricanes, as well as causing other weather imbalances." The report also pointed out that in 2020 "all this has had an impact on food, especially agriculture, as well as on the way we dress and plan our holidays."

In case there was any doubt that these conditions would be those experienced in 2020, the text stressed: "The predictions made by the 3,000 scientists of the IPCC have stood the test of time well." One of them warned: "The consequences of this warming will be paid by all of humanity." This is what is happening twenty years after that global alarm that many preferred to ignore."

Along those same lines, the report stated that in 2020 "more and more water is being seen on the maps of the planet. Nearly 300 islands have sunk to the bottom of the Pacific, swallowed up by rising ocean levels. In Europe, the deltas of the Rhine, the Ebro, and the Guadalquivir have already disappeared, drowned by the unstoppable rise of the seas. Amsterdam looks like Venice. The effects of global warming have completely disfigured the physiognomy of the coasts." The text also stated that "on the other side of the Iberian Peninsula, the Mediterranean threatens the survival of some of its islands, such as Sicily or Corsica, where thousands of people are facing rising waters that have seriously endangered their fishing and agricultural resources."

Among the forecasts, the report also pointed out that in 2020, "Inland, the toxic mist, which like a shroud covers large cities and suffocates the lungs of their people, continues, twenty years later, to spray the Old Continent with its poisons. There were those who doubted that this acid rain would last for so long. But, unfortunately, most of the forecasts from the US National Center for Atmospheric Research did not fail, nor did those that spoke of longer and extremely torrid summers."

Similarly, the report also noted that in 2020, "This has led some tropical diseases, such as malaria and cholera, to find new victims among us. It was written, as Felix Hernandez, one of the greatest experts on climate change at the Spanish National Research Council, had said. More and more cases of skin cancer, cataracts, and tuberculosis are appearing in hospitals, as well as more people with heat stress, which has caused the death lists among the population to increase."

Furthermore, in 2020, "The string of floods and droughts have also caused the contamination of drinking water with fertilizers and sludge, contributing to the spread of infections. Most of the cases result in vomiting and severe diarrhea, which sometimes kill people, especially the elderly and children." And, of course, the impact on the economy was devastating, because, in 2020, "global warming has greatly dampened the spirits of tourists. The Mediterranean and Atlantic beaches, where just over two decades ago most Europeans and Spaniards went to, today are one of the places now infested by insects from Africa. There's not much sand left. The sea has swallowed it up. In Torremolinos, in Huelva, in Benidorm... A copy of the prediction was made back in 1999 in a report for the World Wildlife Fund by British climatologist David Viner from the University of East Anglia in the United Kingdom. Snow tourism, once one of the major winter attractions in Europe, is scarce today because of the increased thawing."

The impact on rivers and seas by 2020 was, according to the report, truly devastating: "With the heat rising, the sea is also rising at a rate of between 4 and 10 centimeters per decade. And although it may seem little, it is more than enough to affect a large part of the rivers. Ours don't even look like the ones you see in books anymore. Evaporation, caused by the high temperatures, pollution, and the overexploitation of the rivers' waters for irrigation, has reduced the courses of the Ebro, Duero, and Tajo until they are practically dead rivers."

And to all these disasters was added the immense scourge of hunger. Thus, in 2020, "At midday, all the television stations begin their news programs with the shocking information: 1,600 million people around the world are suffering from hunger. Exactly twice as many as those who suffered the same conditions at the end of the twentieth century." Not surprisingly, "At that time, acid rain had already washed away 50% of the trees in large regions of Europe, the air in major cities was reaching intolerable levels of pollution, and Spain was losing, through erosion, 1,000 million tons of land per year."

Possibly, where the report reached a peak was when it mentioned a number of people who, in a supposedly scientific way, had predicted all those disasters that were supposed to happen in 2020. Thus, the text pointed out that "today, as we enter 2020, almost half of the fertile soil that still remains in our country is about to be depleted. This is in line with the fears of the United Nations advisor, Teresa Mendizábal, who two decades ago claimed that 40% of the territory was suffering from land leprosy or desertification." This was a statement made before announcing that in 2020 "grains, corn, and pastures, as some studies already predicted in those years, will take the brunt of it. Especially in the Mediterranean countries, where large areas of crops have been invaded by mega-cities. These settlements, responsible for more than 80% of the reduction in plant cover, have compelled us to make use of genetic engineering, which has made it possible to multiply harvests and thus compensate for the lack of fertile land. This is the ultimate triumph of transgenic fields."

It is almost touching to contemplate the predictions made by global warming advocates almost two decades ago. It is touching because not a single one of them has been fulfilled, not even remotely. Certainly, those truly spectacular errors do not seem to have had any impact on the professional development of those who proclaimed them. Teresa Mendizábal, Director of the Environment of CIEMAT (Spanish National Research Council), Management Advisor of the Center for Energy and Environmental Research; Director of the Department of the Environment of the Center for Energy, Environmental and Technological Research (CIEMAT) and advisor to the United Nations Convention to Combat Desertification, does not seem to have suffered any repercussions for painting a future that has nothing to do with reality. The same can be said of the Spanish global warming advocate Félix Hernández.

As for David Viner, he has managed to move on from teaching in the university to different positions in different British government agencies such as Natural England or the British Council—where he earned a higher salary—and in 2012 he became Senior Climate Change Advisor to Mott MacDonald, a company with interests in over 140 countries.

In none of the three cases did the failure to make a single correct prognosis hurt them. On the contrary, it even seems to have served for their promotion, advancement, and higher salaries. Their case has certainly not been exceptional. Nor is there any news of anyone in the Intergovernmental Panel on Climate Change or the United States National Center for Atmospheric Research being held accountable for such gross errors. Rather, the sentiment is that all those who failed so badly in their predictions have been rewarded.

After more than two decades, it is more than obvious that the forecasts of the global warming advocates have failed miserably, but it is also more than undeniable that they are more popular than ever thanks to politicians, financiers, journalists, and academics who have found a way of life in global warming.

The truth is that this should come as no surprise, because the most popular global warming advocate of all time, former US Vice-President Al Gore, said as early as January 26, 2006, that we had ten years left to take drastic action on our carbon dioxide emissions, or the world would reach a point of no return. He made those predictions during the Sundance Film Festival, where he presented his documentary *An*

Inconvenient Truth. Gore's documentary earned him an Oscar and the Nobel Peace Prize. However, the truth is that almost a decade and a half after its premiere, his prophecies have not been fulfilled. In fact, temperatures have not varied much and, to top it off, they have remained below the lowest predictions of climatic models. However, as in the millenarian sects, the faithful of global warming have kept predicting that the end of the world is near. Even twelve years away. Despite all this, there is reason to believe that the very defenders of the global warming theses *may not* believe in them.

From Greenpeace to Obama

It was 1971 when in the city of Vancouver, Canada, a group of young people decided to change the world and save it from the threats to the environment. That's how they founded an organization called Greenpeace. Among the initial group of scientists, activists, and journalists was Robert "Bob" Hunter, a very active journalist who became its visible face, its president, and one of the most powerful voices in the history of environmentalism; Paul Watson, a twenty-year-old sailor turned defender of aquatic fauna; and Patrick Moore, the only one who, because of his academic background, was an ecologist. After beginning its campaigns against whalers, especially the Soviets, Greenpeace's public impact continued to grow. At one point, in the 1980s, Greenpeace even broadcast a documentary entitled *The Apocalypse According to Greenpeace*, which laid out the catastrophic future that awaited the planet at the end of the twentieth century, and defended the actions of politicians such as the American Al Gore. The documentary was broadcast on television stations around the world, but, significantly, not a single one of the predictions came true. Meanwhile, the organization was undergoing remarkable changes.

In 1977, in an action promoted by Patrick Moore, and supported, although not without complaints, by Hunter, Greenpeace ended up expelling Watson from its midst. A few months later, Hunter, overwhelmed by what was happening, chose to hand over the presidency of Greenpeace to Patrick Moore. In 1985, Hunter and other members decided it was time to stop Moore, with whom they did not share the view of the organization that gave the impression of being suspiciously utilitarian. The mechanism for doing so was to create Greenpeace International, forming separate chapters and granting Moore the leadership in Canada. After a few years, and with Hunter's return to activism, Moore decided to leave the organization. He didn't believe in the climate change thesis at all and was convinced that Greenpeace had become an organization fundamentally guided by a profitable political agenda. By this time, Watson had created his own organization dedicated only to protecting marine species, the Sea Shepherd Conservation Society, an NGO whose logo bears a pirate skull, that fights against the capture of marine animals, which resorts to violence at times.

In 2005, Bob Hunter died after having returned to journalism and environmental reporting he had pursued in his earlier days. Thus, Greenpeace looked little or nothing like it had been in the beginning, although, despite not being right in its forecasts, it had managed to reach the category of a more than lucrative business and had become one of the icons of climate change. It was a lesson that few people grasp and one that has, least of all, been assimilated. It was not something exceptional. Let's look at a very significant example.

In 2015, the President of the United States, Barack Obama, announced to the UN that the greatest threat to the human species was climate change.[6] In doing so, he provided extraordinary support for the global warming advocates' theses. Four years later, Obama announced the purchase of a home in Martha's Vineyard.[7] It was a property owned by Wyc Grousbeck, the owner of the Boston Celtics. During the summer of 2019, Obama rented the house and was so

6. https://obamawhitehouse.archives.gov/president-obama-climate-action-plan; https://obamawhitehouse.archives.gov/the-record/climate.

7. https://www.forbes.com/sites/kathleenhowley/2019/12/08/barack-and-michelle-obama-buy-marthas-vineyard-estate/#3909ecda3167; https://www.townandcountrymag.com/leisure/real-estate/a30169311/barack-michelle-obama-buy-marthas-vineyard-house/.

pleased with it that he decided to buy it. The property is valued at $ 14,850,000[8] and has twenty-nine waterfront acres. It also has seven bedrooms, a swimming pool, a place to cook outside, a kitchen for a chef, vaulted ceilings, and two wings of the building for guests. The views are impressive, especially from the Jacuzzi located on the second floor.

However, what is relevant is not the character of the house but the fact that, in a very significant way, Climate Central, a subsidized entity during the Obama presidential period, includes that property among those that will end up underwater in this century as a result of climate change. In other words, if the claims from climate change believers are true, former President Obama is not only going to lose $15 million, but he is also risking his life and that of his family by acquiring this property.

So far, regardless of what you think of President Obama, there is no reason to think that he suffers from some type of mental disorder that would lead him to endanger his own life and that of his family. There is, of course, the possibility that former President Obama knows that the predictions of the global warming advocates will not come to pass; that is, nothing, in fact, has happened yet.

One of the great advantages of history is that it allows us to understand to what extent many of the theses defended today have already been refuted in the past and, therefore, there is no point in raising them today. The ones wielded by the global warming advocates can be grouped undoubtedly into that sad and pitiful group. It is not just the fact that those of us who are a little older can remember how countless forecasts have not even come close to being fulfilled. It is also about seeing how those who defend these theses behave. The fact that all of the three original founders of Greenpeace ended up outside the organization, and one even continues to express his opposing views to the theses of the global warming advocates is quite significant. But the fact that Al Gore wastes an enormous amount of energy

8. https://nypost.com/2019/08/22/barack-and-michelle-obama-are-buying-15m-estate-in-marthas-vineyard/.

in his mansion in a truly colossal way[9] or that Obama decides to spend almost fifteen million dollars on a mansion that, supposedly, will be flooded by the rising waters due to the effect of climate change is even more revealing. It is particularly serious that among the objectives of the global warming advocates' sect, the recruitment of children and young people holds a special place.

Greta Thunberg and the Greenpeacers

The year was 1384, when the chronicles of the city of Hamelin in Germany recorded this sentence: "It is now one hundred years since our children left." The reference, although a century old, is the oldest one related to the disappearance of the children of the town of Hamelin. The legend—which already existed at that time—stated that a flutist had rid the city of rats by luring the pesky rodents with the sound of his flute until they sank into a river and drowned. Not being paid for his work, the pied piper decided to take advantage of a party where all the inhabitants of Hamelin had gathered, in order to make an appearance again. However, this time, the piper did not take the rats with him but rather the children. This fact, of a certain historical nature, has been the subject of various interpretations. The most plausible is that, after the collapse of Danish power in Pomerania, someone managed to take the children of Hamelin to the area to repopulate it. To this day, for example, there are still traces of the migration carried out so massively by mere children. We do not know if the person who dragged all the children of Hamelin behind him used a flute to take them away, but what seems undeniable is that he managed to drag them behind him, causing a trauma in Hamelin, a trauma that was remembered a century later in all its vividness, a trauma that came from parents who had been unable to protect their

9. https://nationalcenter.org/ncppr/2017/08/01/al-gores-inconvenient-reality-the-former-vice-presidents-home-energy-use-surges-up-to-34-times-the-national-average-despite-costly-green-renovations-by-drew-johnso/; https://www.washingtonexaminer.com/al-gore-used-over-20-times-more-energy-to-power-his-home-for-a-year-than-the-average-american-report.

children from manipulation. Today, the globalist agenda has among its main objectives the recruitment of children and adolescents. Greta Thunberg is proof of the veracity of this thesis.

Greta Thunberg, a young Swedish woman who is only sixteen years old, has become one of the best-known faces of global warming advocates. In a recent speech to the UN, she accused world leaders of stealing her "dreams" and her "childhood" with empty words.[10] Greta said, on that occasion, that "we are at the beginning of mass extinction, and all they talk about is money and fairy tales of never-ending economic growth. Along with fifteen other children, Greta Thunberg filed a formal complaint with the UN Committee on the Rights of the Child, accusing Argentina, Germany, France, Brazil, and Turkey of violating children's rights by not taking sufficient action to address global warming. Significantly, the children's complaint did not include nations such as China and India, which are among the biggest polluters.

Greta has become a true icon of global warming, but her complaint and those of other children soon provoked negative reactions from various world leaders. For example, Australian Prime Minister Scott Morrison[11] accused Greta Thunberg of subjecting Australian children to "unnecessary anxiety." In Morrison's words, "We have to let children be children...we have to put some context into this. French President Macron, who initially supported Greta Thunberg, has also distanced himself from her, noting that "these radical positions will eventually create antagonisms in our societies.[12] Similarly, Brune Poirson, France's minister of ecology, also criticized Greta Thunberg, saying, "I don't think we can mobilize the population with despair, almost with hate, creating divisions that may be irreparable." Poirson also pointed out that "it is important that you mobilize, but what are the solutions you're putting on the table? I don't know."

10. You can see the recording at https://twitter.com/reuters/status/1176170629588029441; https://www.gq.com/story/greta-thunberg-un-how-dare-you.

11. https://www.newsweek.com/australian-prime-minister-scott-morrison-greta-thunberg-impress-people-overseas-1478772.

12. http://www.rfi.fr/en/france/20190924-macron-hits-back-greta-thunberg-antagonistic-activism-despair-un-climate-conference.

Even Angela Merkel, who had formally praised Greta Thunberg, said, "I would like to take the opportunity to strongly contradict her on one issue. She did not correctly address the fact that technology and innovation, especially in the energy conservation sector, increase the chances of achieving our goals."

Similarly, Vladimir Putin said he welcomed the concern of the younger generation about current problems, including ecological ones, but condemned their use "in someone's personal interest."[13] According to Putin, "No one has explained to Greta that today's world is complex, very diverse, developing rapidly, and people in Africa and many Asian countries want to have the same level of well-being as in Sweden. But how do you do that? By forcing them to use the solar energy that is available in Africa? Has anyone explained how much that is going to cost?" According to Putin, adults should try harder not to "expose teenagers to extreme situations and protect them from unnecessary emotions."

The criticisms expressed by politicians had already been preceded by those made by scientists. The director of the World Meteorological Organization, Petteri Taalas,[14] denounced that climate extremists and "catastrophists" were attacking scientists in order to drag them towards an extremist point of view. According to Taalas, to achieve this, "they resort to threats." Similarly, Taalas accused the global warming advocates of selectively choosing the reports of the UN Intergovernmental Panel on Climate Change that resemble "religious extremism."

Similarly, Benny Peiser,[15] director of the Global Warming Policy Foundation in London, said that "Europe's political leaders are increasingly concerned about losing their climate agenda to eco-fanatics and extremists." Peiser also said that "Greta's apocalyptic mass movement

13. https://www.youtube.com/watch?v=i2U4e9Yjgbo; https://www.youtube.com/watch?v=1CnyqLogH0Y/

14. https://www.climatedepot.com/2019/09/11/shock-head-of-world-meteorological-organization-slams-climate-doomsday-claims-it-is-not-going-to-be-the-end-of-the-world/.

15. https://www.theepochtimes.com/leaders-of-france-germany-and-australia-rebuke-greta-thunberg_3097308.html;https://www.thegwpf.com/political-leaders-turn-on-greta-thunberg-as-she-sues-france-germany/.

is turning millions of French, German, and European children and adolescents against their own governments, institutions, and countries, transforming them into a resentful and angry mob." According to Peiser, "Officials and politicians are beginning to raise their voices because they fear they may lose control over this increasingly dangerous tiger they thought they could ride forever."

It is striking that today children and young people, who are, time after time, undisciplined and unable to tidy up their rooms, organize their school activities, or even their leisure time, are trying to put the world in order. One could think that they are a kind of super-generation that has emerged with more intelligence than those of their elders, with more social commitment, with more nobility. One might think so, but the reality is that mere observation makes it clear that this is not the case.

On the contrary, when we consider Greta and the Greenpeacers, we only see children who lack nothing materially, who live considerably better than the immense majority of children on the planet, and who demonstrate a truly rampant ignorance of what they are pontificating about. This scandalous ignorance allows them, for example, to attack nations such as Turkey or Argentina and to remain totally silent about China or India despite the immense polluting capacity of these two economic giants.

Furthermore, their message does not contain a single rational or practical element but is limited to voicing immense resentment against the elderly, against governments, and against institutions. Millions of children are thus subjected to the new and totalitarian globalist religion and, more specifically, to its global-warming sector.

No one who retains a modicum of common sense can escape the fact that this gigantic manipulation is accomplished by a pied piper, as already happened with the medieval village of Hamelin. That flute player dragged the children along in favor of his own interests, but the responsibility of the parents in the misfortune of their children is not small. For decades, those parents have not known how to deal with a piper they even called for at the time.

They have not educated their children in solid moral principles but have allowed the piper to do it through various means and an education system that is increasingly degenerate. They have not spent time with their children but have let that time be filled by the piper with his tunes. They have not taught discipline and industriousness to their children but have spoiled them in many cases because the mothers felt guilty for not being by their side as in the past. They have not taught them about God and their responsibility to Him because they themselves, though being religious, have not had a personal encounter with the Almighty but, at most, have limited themselves to the practice of rites and ceremonies. In the end, what we have after decades of misconduct and bad education are generations of spoiled children who accuse those who spoiled them of having destroyed their childhood and who sow resentment with extreme bitterness. They are Greta and the Greenpeacers, poor unhappy souls who dance to the sound of the pied piper and succumb to their own annihilation.

The reality is that the global warming advocates' theses aim to achieve two fundamental objectives. The first is to get as much public and private money as possible through economic funding to NGOs, universities, academic bodies, political parties, and the media. The second is to control the economy from above in order to make it subservient to a small elite group that will end up governing the very miserable destinies of the human race. In both cases, the threat to freedom is truly colossal. The theses of the global warming advocates—enthusiastically embraced by Pedro Sánchez, Pope Francisco, Al Gore, and Barack Obama, the Left, and the radical sector of the Democratic Party in the United States—are not true, but neither are they innocent, and they all form an essential part of a sinister and totalitarian globalist agenda.

CHAPTER XII

THE DOGMAS OF THE GLOBALIST AGENDA (II): Gender Ideology

What Is Gender Ideology?

The dogmas of the globalist agenda are intertwined with each other as in any religion. In fact, it should not be surprising that the global warming theses are joined, although it seems irrational, by gender ideology.[1] In fact, they are all influenced by a more aggressive propaganda to which hardly anyone dares to offer the slightest resistance. It is interesting, of course, to compare this phenomenon with what happens with other ideologies. Of course, there are still people who defend the socialist economic model, but after the fall of the Berlin Wall and the disappearance of the Soviet Union at the end of the last century, it is obvious that it is very difficult to defend, and, of course, you will always find discordant voices that deny the wisdom of continuing to maintain that position. "Gender ideology" seems, however, to have succeeded in silencing virtually everyone, even those who hold

1. https://www.lavanguardia.com/vida/20191211/472180062442/ribera-cop25-cumbre-clima-negociaciones-genero.html.

a Christian worldview. In fact, it has been filtering through even into church bodies with disturbing success.

"Gender ideology" claims that the "biological fact" (a somewhat ridiculous way of pointing out that someone is male or female) is not decisive, is reversible, and should even be viewed as another episode of the class struggle, if you prefer, of the oppressed against the oppressors. Only in this case, the oppressed class is supposedly made up of women or of homosexuals as opposed to heterosexual men.

From this point of view, any vindication of feminists or homosexuals would be totally legitimized, since they are historically oppressed groups, and the concept of the family would be blurred to the point of having hardly any recognizable traits in common with what we find in the behavior of Humanity since it took its first steps on earth. However, the gender ideology goes even further. Surpassing the ambition of communism or Nazism, it aims to change human nature, whose origin it attributes not to a natural origin, but rather a political one. In other words, what any midwife has known as soon as she sees the child whose delivery she helped—be it male or female—is totally denied by gender ideology and attributed to social context. Possibly, there are few texts where this view has been made clearer than in Beatriz Preciado's *Counter-sexual Manifesto.*[2] In the face of natural sexuality, Preciado proposes what she calls "countersexuality." Her definition is truly revealing:

> "Countersexuality is not the creation of a new nature, but rather the end of Nature as an order that legitimizes the subjection of some bodies to others. Countersexuality is, first of all, a critical analysis of gender and sex differences, a product of the heterocentric social contract, whose normative performatives

2. The different editions of the text can be found on the Internet. You can see in the references that I include that her Manifesto is supported by the media and also by organizations such as the Henry Dunant Foundation: www.sertao.ufg.br/up/16/o/Beatriz_Preciado_-_Manifiesto_contra-sexual_(2002).pdf?1373809656; https://periodicoelamanecer.files.wordpress.com/2013/08/beatriz-preciado-manifiesto-contra-sexual-periodicoelamanecer-wordpress-com.pdf; www.fundacionhenrydunant.org/images/stories/biblioteca/Derechos%20Sexuales%20y%20Reproductivos/Beatriz%20Preciado-%20Manifiesto%20contrasexual.pdf.

have been inscribed in bodies as biological truths. Secondly, countersexuality aims to replace this social construct that we call Nature with a countersexual construct. In the framework of the countersexual contract, bodies recognize themselves not as men or women, but as speaking bodies, and they recognize others as speaking bodies."

In other words, gender ideology will mean the end of Nature and with it the end of the sexes as we know them. Instead of men and women, we will arrive at an ideal society in which there will be "speaking bodies. The "systematic deconstruction of the naturalization of sexual practices and the gender system" will be carried out in this countersexual society. The reason for this is that "sex, as an organ and practice, is neither a precise biological place nor a natural drive. Sex is a technology of heterosocial domination that reduces the body to erogenous zones according to an asymmetric distribution of power between the genders (female/male), making certain affections coincide with certain organs, certain sensations with certain anatomical reactions. Human nature is an effect of social technology that reproduces in bodies, spaces, and discourses the equation: nature = heterosexuality."

It is hard to believe that such an affirmation can be made, but the truth is that, according to the text, sex is neither something natural nor an impulse of Nature. On the contrary, it is a technology of heterosocial domination. Thus, according to the cited work, "men and women are metonymic constructions of the heterosexual system of production and reproduction that authorizes the subjugation of women as a sexual labor force and as a means of reproduction. This exploitation is structural, and the sexual benefits that heterosexual men and women extract from it force them to reduce the erotic surface area to the sexual reproductive organs and to privilege the penis as the only mechanical center of production of the sexual impulse." In other words, since their appearance, the sexual organs that have been linked to the human race are nothing more than a system of subjugation of women.

Along the same lines, the manifesto adds: "Because heterosexuality is a social technology and not a natural founding origin, it is possible to reverse and divert (modify the course, mutate, cause to shift) its practices in the creation of sexual identity."

Naturally, such reasoning clashes with something as obvious as the existence of clearly differentiated sexual organs that indicate who is male and who is female. Precisely because of this, this reality must be denied outright and so it is stated: "Sexual organs as such do not exist. The organs that we recognize as naturally sexual are already the product of a sophisticated technology that prescribes the context in which the organs acquire their significance (sexual relations) and are used properly, in accordance with their 'nature' (heterosexual relations)."

It is understandable that if the function of the sexual organs is denied because they reveal that there are two natural sexes, then a substitute for that natural reality must be sought. And this is precisely what has happened, and it is found precisely in an organ that, without a doubt, is common to both men and women: "The anus is the erogenous space to be enhanced. It is the neutral space for all "speaking bodies" and it has three characteristics: 1) The anus is the universal erogenous center located beyond the anatomical limits imposed by sexual differentiation where roles are reversible; 2) it is a zone of privileged passivity, a center of excitement and pleasure that did not figure into the pleasurable anatomical points, 3) the anus constitutes a technological working space; it is a factory for the reworking of the countersexual body."

From this view—which is certainly striking, but not without clarity—the so-called *Principles of the Countersexual Society* are derived. These principles are as follows:

1. The countersexual society demands that the masculine and feminine names corresponding to the biological categories on ID cards be erased, as well as all administrative and legal forms of a legal nature. They would be open registrations for free exchange of speaking bodies.

2. To avoid the reappropriation of bodies as male and female in the social system, each body would bear a new name that escapes gender nomenclature, whatever the language...
3. Following the abolition of the heterocentric reproduction system, the countersexual society imposes:
   - The abolishing of the marriage contract...
4. Universalization of practices stigmatized as abject...
   - Resexualizing the anus as a universal countersexual center
   - Disseminate, distribute, and put into circulation the new codes for stimulation. The first period is the massive establishment of other prostheses for pleasure: fingers, vibrators, cucumbers, carrots, arms, legs, etc.
   - Parodying and simulating new orgasmic forms, not related to romanticism, can reveal the benefits of violence and pain within the speaking bodies.
5. The countersexual relationship will be valid and effective for a limited period of time. It should never involve the whole life of the speaking body...
6. The countersexual society will never lead to the act of reproduction... Methods of contraception and termination of pregnancy will be distributed everywhere and will be compulsory for every speaking body.
7. Countersexuality denounces, pursues, and punishes psychiatric, medical, and legal policies that prevent sex changes. It will facilitate sex changes for transvestites...
8. The constrasexual society decrees that constrasexual activities shall be considered as social work, which shall be a right and an obligation for any speaking body and that these practices shall be practiced regularly a number of hours per day.
9. The countersexual society demands the abolition of the nuclear family... Individual bodily relationships and group practices will be established and implemented and taught through countersexual images and texts.

10. The countersexual society promotes the modification of traditional educational institutions and the development and implementation of a countersexual pedagogy...
11. The countersexual society demands that every sexual act be potentially viewed as work. Therefore, any practice of constrasexuality should be elevated to art and discipline. This would entail the formation of new university centers committed to the learning of different countersexual and post-body disciplines.

Beyond its claim to make the anus the center of the sexual experience of both sexes or its call for a sexuality based on objects rather than natural organs, the manifesto of countersexuality sets forth an extraordinarily clear ideological vision. It is not—as many would expect—a text in favor of supposed women's or homosexual rights. On the contrary, it is much more ambitious in its aims. After manifesting a deep hatred for natural sexuality and the natural division into sexes, it announces a program to end the very sexual nature of the human race. First of all, such a reality must be denied by insisting that the different sexes are due to a decision of power whose purpose is to exploit women. Second, such a denial of sexual difference must include political measures, such as name changes, assistance for sex changes, the prohibition of any assistance to people with sexual identity problems, the abolition of marriage, the suppression of the family, indoctrination in schools and universities, and even the pursuit of imposed sexual practices that displace natural ones.

After an examination of this paradigmatic text one might think that it is no more than the work of a deranged mind or the pages of a dystopia like Aldous Huxley's *A Brave New World, 1984* by George Orwell, or Yevgueñi Zamiatin's *We*. Reality, however, is not in the future but in the present. At the beginning of 2020, a new government was formed in Spain by socialists and communists. This new government defined itself from the outset as an instrument of the globalist agenda and showed its close ties to George Soros.[3] The Ministry of Equality, created to be headed up by Irene Montero, the partner of the communist Pablo Iglesias, was from the first moment a faithful reflection of what gender ideology would mean. Thus, all the senior positions were occupied solely and exclusively by women. It would appear that equality means that all senior positions belong to the same sex and that this is the female sex.[4] The new Minister of Equality, Irene Montero, appointed as the regional deputy of Podemos ("We Can") Beatriz Gimeno to head the Women's Institute, and the former president of the LGTBI Federation Boti Garcia for the General Directorate of Sexual Diversity. The two were married in 2005 at the Madrid City Hall in one of the first gay marriages in the capital. Both have been living gender ideology for decades. Gimeno was president of the FELGTB (Spanish Federation of Lesbians, Gays, Transsexuals, and Bisexuals) between 2003 and 2007 and responsible for the area of Equality of Opportunity for Podemos in the community of Madrid. She has also served two terms as a member of the Assembly of Madrid for Podemos. Boti Garcia, who will now serve as the newly created director general of Sexual Diversity and LGBTQ, was previously the director general for Equal Treatment and Diversity. Beatriz Gimeno's political positions are clearly revealing. In 2013 she wrote an article stating that heterosexuality is not natural. In it she pointed out[5]: "It is essential to assume that homosexuality and heterosexuality are not equivalent, nor are they different ways of living out sexuality, but rather they are systems that fulfil different social functions. Heterosexuality, the regulatory system par excellence, is not the natural way of living out sexuality, but is a political and social tool with a very specific function that feminists denounced decades ago: to subordinate women to men." Gimeno added that heterosexuality "aims

3. https://okdiario.com/espana/sanchez-reune-secreto-moncloa-mayor-especulador-del-mundo-george-soros-2484178; https://casoaislado.com/pedro-sanchez-se-hace-un-selfie-con-el-hijo-de-george-soros-defensor-de-la-inmigracion-ilegal-masiva/.

4. https://www.larazon.es/espana/20200114/m6owbviphjct5l5bisrwu7h5zy.html.

5. https://www.actuall.com/familia/podemos-asigna-el-instituto-de-la-mujer-a-una-extremista-que-justifico-la-quema-de-iglesias/.

to contribute to the unequal distribution of power between women and men, thus constructing a category of oppressors, men, and one of the oppressed, women." Gimeno also pointed out that "male power has been exercised over women, over all women, through the institution of heterosexuality," concluding that "heterosexuality is the main tool of patriarchy." Gimeno's lesbian position is so extreme that in the same article she also attacked men, even homosexuals, saying that "while lesbianism can be lived as a liberating condition, this is impossible for men." She also pointed out that "the male condition means belonging to the gender that holds all the power. Being gay means giving up, or being deprived of, some of the male privileges, though never all or none in the event that the homosexuality does not become visible." In her attack on male homosexuals, Gimeno went on to say that "the interest of male homosexuals is to depathologize male homosexuality, but to depoliticize it as well, since they, as men, have nothing to gain from the disappearance of patriarchy." Gimeno also pointed out that "it is true that heterosexuality also oppresses gays, but that is precisely the goal of the homosexual liberation movement: to stop oppressing them as gays, but to leave untouched the benefits they receive as men."

In 2011, Gimeno also wrote that "human rights and capitalism are incompatible." In December 2017, Gimeno, in another article published in another ultra-left digital magazine, CTXT, stated that "we need a new pact that breaks with this social, economic, and political model but also with this patriarchal model that is constitutive of democracies, and liberal entities." It is obvious that if a high-ranking official of any government in the West demanded that all members of that government be white and could not include blacks, we would experience a scandal. If a high-ranking member of any government in the West demanded that all members of that government be men and they could not include women, we would experience a scandal. If a high-ranking official in any government in the West demanded that all members of that government be heterosexual and could not include homosexuals, we would experience a scandal. If a high-ranking official in any government in the West demanded that all members of that government were of one religion and could not include those of others or non-believers, we would experience a scandal. In each and every case, it would be shouted that such a person could not hold public office because he or she discriminated against different people and denied diversity. It is also very likely that they would be prosecuted for a hate crime. However, if a female minister appoints only women to senior positions, not a word is said, and it is even considered a sign of progress. If a female director of a major state institution claims that heterosexuality is unnatural, not a word is said, and it is even considered a sign of progress. If that same person claims that even homosexual men are unacceptable because they are male, not a word is said, and it is even considered a sign of progress. Such circumstances are a glimpse of what the gender ideology in power means and show that the manifesto we have been discussing for a few pages can inspire concrete policies from within that power.

Unfortunately, what is set out in the manifesto is much more. It is, in fact, the record of an agenda that has been developing for decades. The first step, possibly, was to destroy the separation between the natural and the unnatural, the healthy from the sick. This step was taken in the United States at the beginning of the 1970s and also took place within the scientific community. Quite significantly, the action owed more to Saul Alinsky's[6] subversive tactics than to scientific analysis.

When Homosexuality Stopped Being Contrary to Nature

The term *homosexuality* is recent in historical terms. In fact, it was coined in 1869 by the Hungarian psychologist Karoly Maria Kertbeny (or Benkert), himself a pioneer of the homosexual movement.

6. S. Alinsky, *Rules for Radicals: A Pragmatic Primer for Realistic Radicals* (New York, 1971).

Throughout history, judgment on homosexuality has undergone several variations, but always on the basis of a moral consideration of what was considered natural or unnatural. In general, ancient cultures judged it to be morally reprehensible. Egyptians, Mesopotamians, and Aryans looked upon it with disdain if not open contempt, while for the people of Israel it was included in the list of a series of behaviors unworthy of the people of God that extended from adultery to bestiality to theft or idolatry (Leviticus 18:22). The classical cultures of China and India also viewed homosexual behavior in a very negative light.

In classical antiquity, in Greece, some form of homosexual behavior—male and non-penetrative—was tolerable, but not, of course, all homosexual practices. In fact, negative references are not uncommon in Hellenic sources, and there were even laws, for example, in Athens that explicitly condemned it.[7] The Greek physicians, in turn, considered it a mental illness.[8] In Rome, it was harshly criticized by authors such as Tacitus[9] or Suetonius as a sign of moral degeneration and even civic decadence.[10] Christianity maintained the same line against homosexual practices found in the Old Testament. It is not surprising that the condemnation of homosexual practices[11] was common among the Fathers of the Church, and that in the oldest documents of ecclesiastical discipline, it appears as one of the sins punishable by excommunication. On this basis it is not surprising that the medieval world—both Jewish, Christian, and Muslim—condemned homosexual practices and even legally punished them, even though later in daily life it was as tolerant—or as intolerant—of this behavior as of others also considered a sin. This attitude was overwhelmingly prevalent in the East and West for centuries to come. Essentially, the negative view of homosexuality was related to natural, religious, and moral mores—if

7. http://local.droit.ulg.ac.be/sa/rida/file/2000/macdowell.pdf.

8. https://www.ncbi.nlm.nih.gov/pubmed/28541240.

9. *Anales* 14; 15.37.

10. *Julio* 2, 45, 49; *Nerón* 28-29; *Galba* 22.

11. *Didajé* 2-3, written at the end of the first century, is possibly the first Christian condemnation of homosexuality contained outside the New Testament.

homosexuality were general it would end the species—and not to a medical or psychiatric qualification. A homosexual could commit reprehensible acts that were even described as contrary to nature and perverse. However, his behavior was not identified with a mental disorder or a physical disorder. In fact, such a judgment would have to await the consolidation of psychiatry as a science.

Starting from a view that considered heterosexual behavior as natural, which if we merely look at statistical criteria, there is nothing that disputes that. Psychiatry included from the beginning the homosexual inclination—and not only the acts as was the case with theological judgments—among the illnesses that could and should be treated. Richard von Kraft-Ebing, one of the fathers of modern psychiatry of whom Freud recognized himself as an offshoot, even considered it a degenerative disease in his *Psychopathy Sexualis*. In a way not so difficult to understand, not even the arrival of psychoanalysis would change that judgment.

It is true that in 1935 Freud wrote a compassionate letter to the American mother of a homosexual in which he assured her that "homosexuality is certainly not an advantage, but neither is it something to be ashamed of, nor is it a vice, nor is it a degradation, nor can it be classified as an illness."[12] However, his scientific works are less flattering not only for the practices, but even for the mere condition of being a homosexual. For example, in his *Three Essays on the Theory of Sexuality* (1905), Freud included homosexuality among the "perversions" or "sexual aberrations," to use his terms, in the same way as hair and foot fetishism or sadistic or masochistic practices. In Freud's view, homosexuality was a manifestation of a lack of sexual and psychological development that resulted in a person becoming stagnated in a behavior prior to heterosexual maturity. Among the causes of what he called "inversion" could be a discouraging experience with a "normal" sex object, i.e., heterosexual. In a similar sense, and even with harsher nuances, the other great figures of psychoanalysis, Adler

12. The English translation of the letter can be found at https://en.wikisource.org/wiki/A_Letter_from_Freud_(to_a_mother_of_a_homosexual).

and Jung, also spoke out. Adler considered homosexuality to be a failure like prostitution and criminality and placed its origin in a feeling of inferiority related to one's sex. Jung, convinced that the goal of human beings was heterosexual marriage, saw homosexuality as the consequence of a process of psychic maladjustment and development. Later, psychoanalysts not only did not modify these assessments but even accentuated them while applying treatments considered curative against the homosexual inclination.

In the 1940s, for example, Sandor Rado maintained that homosexuality was a phobic disorder towards people of the opposite sex, which made it susceptible to being treated like other phobias. Starting from their analysis derived from working with a considerable number of homosexual patients, Bieber and other psychiatrists, as early as the 1960s, claimed that homosexuality was a psychological disorder derived from family relationships during the Oedipal period. Charles Socarides, during that same decade and in the following one—in fact until his death—would defend, on the contrary, the thesis that homosexuality originated in a pre-oedipal period and was therefore much more pathological than had been thought up until then. Socarides is a kind of black beast of the gay movement to this day, but it is difficult to think of anyone in the field of psychiatry who has studied the homosexual question more thoroughly and exhaustively. For Socarides, homosexuality is "a neurotic adaptation to unconscious fears." The homosexual is not born that way. According to Socarides, such a statement would only be a rationalization of his fears.[13]

Interestingly, the relativization of these medical judgments came not from the field of psychiatry but from figures from sciences such as zoology (Alfred C. Kinsey), whose theses were totally denied by psychiatric science and from whose methodology many disturbing elements have been discovered. Understandably, and based on this history, the DSM (Diagnostic and Statistical Manual of Mental Disorders) included homosexuality in the list of mental disorders.

13. Charles W. Socarides, *Homosexuality. A Freedom to Far* (Phoenix, 1995), pp. 16ff.

However, in 1973 homosexuality was removed from the DSM in the midst of what U.S. Congressman W. Dannemeyer would call "one of the most depressing stories in the annals of modern medicine."[14]

The episode has been widely reported by one of its protagonists, Ronald Bayer, a well-known sympathizer of the gay cause, and certainly constitutes a remarkable example of how political militancy can interfere with scientific discourse by shaping and altering it.[15]

According to Bayer's testimony, since the 1970 convention of the American Psychiatric Association (APA) was to be held in San Francisco, several homosexual leaders agreed to carry out a concerted attack on the organization. This was to be an undeniable effort to sabotage the annual meetings of the APA. When Irving Bieber, a noted authority on transsexualism and homosexuality, was conducting a seminar on the subject, a group of gay activists stormed the campus to oppose his presentation. As they laughed at his words and mocked his presentation, one of the gay activists shouted at him: "I've read your book, Dr. Bieber, and if that book talked about black people the way it talks about homosexuals, you'd be drawn and quartered and you'd deserve it."[16]

To equate racist prejudice with a medical diagnosis was the worst kind of demagogy, and it is not surprising that those present expressed their displeasure at this demonstration of force. It was only the beginning. When the Australian psychiatrist Nathaniel McConaghy referred to the use of "aversive conditioning techniques" to treat homosexuality, gay activists began shouting at him calling him "vicious" and labeling such action "torture." One even stood up and said, "Where did you do your residency, Auschwitz?"[17] The protesters then indicated their desire to intervene by saying that they had waited five thousand years while one of them began to read a list of "gay demands." While the activists accused psychiatrists of using their profession as

14. http://www.city-data.com/forum/psychology/1768160-if-youre-self-described-gay-man-10.html.
15. Ronald Bayer, *Homosexuality and American Psychiatry. The Politics of Diagnosis* (New York), 1981.
16. *Idem, Ibidem*, p. 102.
17. *Idem, Ibidem*, pp. 102-3.

an instrument of oppression and torture, most of the doctors left the room in outrage. However, not everyone thought so. In fact, some psychiatrists found unexpected incentives by the gay pressures. Dr. Kent Robinson, for example, met with Larry Littlejohn, one of the gay leaders, and told him that he believed such tactics were necessary because the APA systematically refused to let gay activists appear on the official program.[18] He then turned to John Ewing, chairman of the programming committee, and told him that it would be wise to give in to the claims of the gays because otherwise they would "not just end up taking over a portion" of the APA's annual meeting. According to Bayer's testimony, "Noting the coercive terms of the petition, Ewing quickly agreed, stipulating only that, in accordance with APA convention regulations, a psychiatrist chair the proposed session."[19]

That the APA was suspicious of who it was dealing with is clear from the fact that it hired security experts to prevent further demonstrations of gay violence. It didn't help. On May 3, 1971, a group of gay activists broke into the psychiatrists' annual meeting, and its leader, after taking over the microphone, told them that they had no right to discuss the issue of homosexuality and added: "You may take this as a declaration of war against you.[20] According to Bayer, the gays then used false credentials to flood the hall and threatened those in charge of the presentation on treatments for homosexuality to destroy all their material if they did not proceed to remove it immediately. This was followed by a panel developed by five gay activists in which they defended homosexuality as a lifestyle and attacked psychiatry as the most dangerous enemy of homosexuals in contemporary society.[21] Since the vast majority of psychiatrists were more or less competent, but certainly not used to being told what to do by their patients or characterized by the dominating violent pressure tactics of organized groups, the victory of the gay lobby was resounding.

18. *Idem, Ibidem*, p. 104.
19. *Idem, Ibidem*, p. 104.
20. *Idem, Ibidem*, pp. 105-6.
21. *Idem, Ibidem*, pp. 108-9.

In fact, by 1972, it had managed to assert itself as a forced presence at the annual meeting of the APA. The following year was the year of the great offensive to have the APA remove the mention of homosexuality from the DSM. Presentations by psychiatrists specializing in the subject such as Spitzer, Socarides, Bieber, or McDevitt[22] were drowned out by reducing their speaking time to a ridiculous quarter of an hour while gay leaders and some politically correct psychiatrists made statements to the press announcing that the doctors had decided that homosexuals were not abnormal. Finally, Kent Robinson's alliance, the gay lobby, and Judd Marmor, who had ambitions to be elected president of the APA, submitted for discussion a document aimed at removing the mention of homosexuality from the DSM.[23] Its approval, despite the propaganda and pressure, got no more than 58% of the vote. This was certainly a qualified majority for a political decision, but a bit overwhelming for a scientific analysis of a medical problem. Nevertheless, a large number of APA members were not prepared to give in to what they considered an intolerable and violent intrusion by gay militancy.

In 1980, the DSM included among the mental disorders a new homosexual affliction known as ego-dystonic disorder. The term referred to that homosexuality that caused persistent grief to its sufferer. In reality, it was a compromise solution to appease psychiatrists—mostly psychoanalysts—who still considered homosexuality a psychic illness and who thought it a medical and moral obligation to offer adequate treatment to those who suffered from it. This was a merely temporary triumph over gay pressure.

In 1986, gay activists succeeded in expelling that ailment from the new DSM and even obtained a new triumph by having pedophilia—sex with children—excluded from the list of psychological disorders. In the United States, at least statutorily, homosexuality—and pedophilia—had ceased to be an ailment that could be treated psychiatrically. It is a separate issue that thousands of psychiatrists accepted

22. *Idem, Ibidem*, pp. 114.
23. *Idem, Ibidem*, pp. 132-37.

that step, because the reality is that so far they have continued to insist that political ideology—in this case that of the gay movement—cannot dictate their decisions to science and that, because the APA has consented to it, such behavior has only served to deprive the sick of the treatment they needed.

No matter what you think about it—and the lack of medical unanimity should be a good reason to opt for prudence in terms of conclusive opinions—the truth was that the final decision affirming that homosexuality was not a psychological disorder had been based more on political action—and not on the best kind—than on a scientific consideration of the evidence. Ethically and scientifically, therefore, it was not very different from historical aberrations such as the condemnation of Galileo or the purges carried out by Lysenko in Stalin's Soviet Union.

The most important thing, however, was not the final result, even though it was significant, but the fact that it had become clear that political pressure from the gay lobby, using Alinsky's tactics, could twist the arm of any segment of society including the scientific one.

Marriage Is No Longer What It Used to Be

The next assault on the shaping of society came with the push to legalize same-sex marriage and the adoption of children by gay couples. Historically, homosexual relationships have generally been short on duration, welcomed open unions, and held little or no interest in legal formalization. Not only that. It was even common for homosexual couples to boast about the freedom of their unions compared to marriages. The change in approach is striking and is related not to the conquest of a "right to marry," but rather to the desire to undermine the natural family as an institution that must be annihilated. In fact, the battle for gay marriage had its first success in the Netherlands in 2000 and in Roman Catholic Belgium in 2003. However, it came to a standstill there without giving the impression that its example would be followed.

In 2005, the legalization of homosexual marriage in Spain, promoted by the government of the socialist José Luis Rodríguez Zapatero, a well-known defender of socialist dictatorships and narco-dictatorships, in whose ranks were notorious homosexuals, implied a leap forward insofar as its influence could be extended over Latin America and also the rest of the European Union. On the other hand, the step taken by Spain held a special relevance, first, because, being mainly a Roman Catholic nation, it seemed to demolish any objection of this type in other countries of similar sociology such as the Latin American republics and, second, because the step was already linked to educational indoctrination through the subject of Education for Citizenship. Not only was homosexual marriage imposed legislatively in spite of heated popular protests, but it also opened the way for the brainwashing of society from kindergarten onwards.

In the same year as in Spain, Canada legalized marriage between same-sex couples, but it was not until the end of the decade—Sweden (2009), Norway (2009), Portugal (2010)—that more cases occurred within the European Union. Over the next decade, nations were added on both sides of the Atlantic with methods not infrequently of dubious legality, but of undeniable effectiveness: Argentina (2010), Iceland (2010), Denmark (2012), France (2013), Brazil (2013), England and Wales (2013), New Zealand (2013), Uruguay (2013), Scotland (2014), Luxembourg (2014), Ireland (2015), Finland (2015), Greenland (2015), Colombia (2016), Germany (2017).

A particular case within this legal evolution was the United States. Eleven years after the legalization of homosexual marriage in Massachusetts, and after it had been rejected by referendum and unanimously in different states, the Supreme Court issued a debatable decision that opened the door to it throughout the nation. Significantly, the deciding vote—5 to 4—came from a conservative justice. The basis for the decision was a more than dubious interpretation of the Fourteenth Amendment. Thus it was argued that limiting marriage to heterosexual couples violated the guarantee of equal protection under the law. The argument was very weak and, in fact, could serve in the future to legalize polygamy as well—why restrict marriage to monogamous people?—or unions with minors or close relatives. The approval of homosexual marriage—with all that it implies of the erosion of the natural family—has not been the conclusion of the process but just another milestone in the advancement of gender ideology.

Gender Ideology Comes to Education

After achieving supposed scientific support for homosexual practices, after legally establishing that same-sex marriage is the same as natural marriage, a period has begun in which social indoctrination, first, and the persecution of dissidents, later, have become widespread. Along with educational programs aimed at indoctrinating children, adolescents, and university students in gender ideology; along with the propaganda poured out in that regard by the media in which refusal to accept the new dogma is unthinkable without serious consequences, rules have been adopted that prevent the existence of dissidents.

As happened in the time of the socialist Rodríguez Zapatero, Spain has once again placed itself at the forefront of advances in gender ideology, and this time it has done so even with governments belonging to right-wing forces. These circumstances show that, contrary to what many believe, the Right no longer provides a guarantee of defense of moral principles. Simply put, gender ideology has been embraced by the entire political arena. Thus, various norms approved by their autonomous communities governed by the Left and the Right, under the excuse of avoiding discrimination, have not only imposed educational programs on gender ideology and prohibited psychological treatments to get out of homosexuality, but also include penalties—including loss of employment and prison—for those who do not submit. The simple refusal to teach gender ideology in an educational institution or the formulation of criticism can have terrible consequences. When we see all of this, one understands that what has been pointed out in the text so far is not at all a delusion but a concrete program of action.

Gender Ideology Reaches the Churches

The last step in this social imposition of gender ideology concerns the churches. That they should be the most solid bastion against gender ideology is obvious, but the fact that this is not always the case is undeniable. It is not just that some renowned theologians have been writing books to defend their hypotheses and, of course, the legality of homosexual relations or the agenda of current feminism. To that sad chapter we must add the so-called inclusive editions of the Bible where any reference to the teaching of the Word of God on homosexuality has been erased or the translation has been molded to gender ideology. This is the case of the Queen James Bible or the Inclusive Bible. Also the books of the so-called queer theology that maintains, in many cases, that God himself or, at least, Jesus is homosexual. One of the most disturbing cases of this type of literature is *The Subversive Gospel* by Thomas D. Hanks, published in Spanish by a publishing house that for years was conservative.[24] Hanks was a missionary until, at one point, he decided to "come out of the closet," break up his marriage, and start living an open life as a homosexual. *The Subversive Gospel* is a commentary on the New Testament, but with a LGTBI tone to the point that it goes so far as to affirm that John was the homosexual lover of Jesus or that Jesus blessed homosexual relations when he cured the centurion's servant, since both were lovers. Certainly, the book is a blasphemous and repugnant read, but the worst thing is not only the author's evil perversion of the Bible, but the fact that the book, along with others of a markedly liberal theological nature, has been published by a publisher that once could be trusted, but has now lost the slightest trace of spiritual integrity. It is

24. https://www.amazon.com/-/es/gp/product/8482676644/ref=ppx_yo_dt_b_asin_title_o00_s00?ie=UTF8&psc=1; https://www.youtube.com/watch?v=rhUI6YHxnsc.

obvious that the past is no guarantee against apostasy in favor of gender ideology.

This deplorable infiltration of gender ideology and its defenders into publishing houses, such as the one mentioned above, and in educational institutions, such as the SEUT in Spain, has been accompanied by the infiltration of supraecclesiastical entities. In this regard, I must discreetly point out a particularly serious case that has occurred in a nation located in southern Europe. The leadership of the federation, which includes a considerable number of evangelical religious entities in Spain (FEREDE), decided to keep within its ranks a denomination that marries couples of the same sex and even defends homosexual relations and gender ideology as part of its program of social activity.[25] In the face of protests from some of the federation's members who considered such behavior unacceptable because it made a mockery of Bible teaching and was a clear apostasy, the leaders not only backed down but also condemned what it called inflexibility and intolerance among those who wanted to be faithful to biblical principles. It was not an exceptional action, but the continuation of a regrettable path begun long ago. A few years earlier, the same federation had decided to withdraw a book from circulation that made a negative reference to gender ideology, and had done so because, otherwise, it would not have been able to collect a number of grants promised to it by the government, a government fiercely committed to advancing the agenda of the gay lobby.[26] It is hard to think of cases of apostasy so scandalous. This is undoubtedly an example of the abandonment of biblical principles that we will most likely have to contend with more and more. In the end, it is the action of ecclesiastical institutions willing to accept conduct that clashes head-on with what is taught in God's Word just to keep the applause—and the money—coming from the world. It is true that, in these cases, the rate charged, as a rule, is much higher than thirty pieces of silver. The great advantage of Protestantism over Roman Catholicism in

25. https://www.youtube.com/watch?v=rhUI6YHxnsc.

26. Information provided by the author of the removed work to the author of this book.

this type of situation is that the final decision of each faithful believer is made on the basis of the Bible and not on the basis of the decisions of a hierarchy. Ordinary believers can regretfully, but with a clear conscience, stop buying books from the fore-mentioned publisher, or stop belonging to FEREDE, or being a member of a church that has decided to marry homosexual couples. That kind of a break is much more difficult for the common Catholic, who ends up, many times, deceiving himself to continue under the wing of his confession of faith despite the actions of the Holy See.

Of course, this imposition of gender ideology is already having terrible consequences on democratic freedoms, and everything points to the establishment of an ideological dictatorship that will be very costly to resist. It has also begun to eat away at the foundations of many ecclesiastical institutions in a way that is extremely harmful. However, it is not just a question of first eroding and then destroying our freedoms or certain religious bodies. Since society is based on countless basic groups made up of different families, the fact that the family is being replaced by the practice of what the Bible calls "abomination" logically has terrible consequences.

Gender ideology fulfills various functions of enormous relevance for the globalist agenda. First, it erodes the natural family, precisely the last bastion that human beings have to defend themselves in the most difficult situations of life. Revolution, war, economic crisis, and social disorder can be more easily confronted when the protection provided by the family is in place. Without it, the individual is an unconnected atom at the mercy of the social current. Nothing can satisfy a totalitarian project more than to be free from the danger of any kind of resistance, because it only has to dominate an unconnected herd. Secondly, gender ideology is a powerful instrument for terminating legal gains that are indispensable for the survival of the democratic system or even any political system. The division of society into sexes—instead of equality of the sexes before the law—and the establishment of laws that punish adolescents more than men—annihilating the equality of all citizens before the law—splits the nation by preventing all citizens from considering themselves members of the nation, because solidarity with any of the followers of the rainbow flag is greater than with those who rally under the national flag. In the end, the lesbian from Washington considers herself to be closer to the lesbian from the Ukraine than to the heterosexual woman from her own nationality and city. The phenomenon is not by chance, but sought after, and involves creating supranational ties that are no longer protected under the red flag but under the rainbow flag. Thirdly, the imposition of gender ideology allows the masses to be educated in the acceptance of the absurd by depriving them of a rational criterion. Let me give an example of this. If an extremely thin daughter of one of the readers went to her father and told him that she looked like a hippopotamus and did not intend to eat, any responsible parent would take her to a specialist for treatment. It wouldn't matter what the daughter looked like because the objective reality is that she was thin, and she had to accept that reality for her own sake and not engage in behaviors that would harm her. Her anorexia had to be treated, not accepted. Let us consider, however, that the daughter appeared before her father and told him that she is no longer Charlotte, but Charles, because she feels like a man. In that case, the propaganda of gender ideology does not allow the concerned parent to take her to a doctor to treat gender dysphoria, but forces them to accept what is clearly false, under pain of being branded as fanatical and cruel. Today, many parents accept that their children will start hormone treatment at an early age, which will cause irreversible damage to themselves, and expose themselves to a much higher suicide rate than children who do not have gender dysphoria[27] just because they do not confront gender ideology. Politicians even willingly accept such irrational behavior by condoning the statements of an eight-year-old transgendered woman.[28] It is hard to think of a greater example of collective brainwashing. Whichever way you

27. https://cnnespanol.cnn.com/2018/09/13/suicidio-adolescentes-hombres-transgeneropropensos-estudio/; https://www.telemundo62.com/noticias/local/suicidio-en-la-comunidad-transgenero-filadelfia-pensilvania/79510/.

28. https://www.lavanguardia.com/vida/20191203/472043167659/nina-transexual-conquista-asamblea-extremadura-nadie-arrebate-felicidad.html.

look at it, the continuation of freedom and democracy is more than compromised by gender ideology. Finally, gender ideology pursues another goal born of the spread of homosexuality—sterile by definition—and the hatred sown in women against men. This is one of the most ambitious goals of the globalist agenda, that of reducing the world's population. We will devote the next chapter to this topic.

CHAPTER XIII

THE DOGMAS OF THE GLOBALIST AGENDA (III): Population Reduction

The Goal of Population Reduction

In 1972, the book *The Limits to Growth* was published. It was a report commissioned to MIT by the Club of Rome. The main author of the text was Donella Meadows, a biophysicist and environmental scientist, specializing in systems dynamics. The work would have an extraordinary impact to the point of selling more than thirty million copies in thirty languages. In fact, the success would last for decades and lead to sequels such as *The Limits to Growth: The 30-Year Update* in 2004 and *2052: A Global Forecast for the Next Forty Years* in 2012. The text came to a very significant conclusion: «*If the current increase in world population, industrialization, pollution, food production, and natural resource exploitation remains unchanged, it will reach the absolute limits of growth on Earth over the next hundred years.*" The solution to that challenge was "zero growth" in both the economy and population.

The Club of Rome lacked any democratic legitimacy. No one had elected them. No one had entrusted it with this task according to a democratic procedure. Nor did anyone guarantee its scientific trustworthiness. However, the text would become a clear model by the end of the year of its publication thanks to the *Stockholm Declaration*, an agreement created after the United Nations Conference on the Human Environment, held in Stockholm in June 1972. Twenty years later, *Beyond the Limits of Growth* was published, which stated that humanity had already exceeded the carrying capacity of the planet to sustain its population. Updates to the report would abound with the same theses. In particular, the 2012 text would assume the thesis that the situation is desperate and that the only way to deal with global warming and an alleged shortage of resources would be an internationally planned economy and a drastic reduction in population.

In its most extreme form, this desire to reduce the world's population—one of the essential dogmas of the globalist agenda—finds its manifestation in the so-called Movement for Voluntary Human Extinction. Founded in 1991 by Les U. Knight and based in the United States, this group calls on the human race to refrain from reproduction in order to reach the gradual extinction of the human species. Les U. Knight had concluded that most of the misfortunes suffered by the planet were due to human beings, which led him to join the Zero Population Growth organization, now known as *Population Connection*. At the age of twenty-five, Knight underwent a vasectomy because he was convinced that the extinction of the human race was the best solution to the Earth's environmental problems. In 1991, Knight also began publishing the VHEMT newsletter, known as *These Exit Times*. In its pages, it urges against reproduction. The position is certainly extreme, but, interestingly, no more dramatic than that set by the globalist agenda. In fact, this agenda has been promoting other mechanisms of population reduction for decades that, as is the case with gender ideology, are masked as rights that must be incorporated into the internal laws of nations.

The Advance of Abortion

In the course of classical antiquity, in a very significant way, the Hippocratic oath, taken by medical doctors, obliged them by Apollo, Asclepius, Higueia, and Panacea not to cause abortions. Of course, there were abortions, and, on top of that, the abandonment of children already born—children who often were taken by traffickers and turned into slaves—was considered as something normal. The birth rate policies of some Roman emperors tried to counteract, even in part, this perception. However, it was precisely Christianity that would radically change that behavior. By defending life as a gift from God and offering a compassionate embrace to the weakest, Christianity excluded abortion from socially acceptable behavior and even punished it.

The repudiation of abortion was, for centuries, undeniable even though not all legislation was equally as rigorous. For example, Lord Ellenborough's Act of 1803 made abortion after childbirth a capital offense, while it punished pre-birth abortion with various penalties. In 1861, the English Parliament ratified the outlawing of abortion, but by this time, in the United States, the efforts of various physicians belonging to the American Medical Association had imposed a battery of legislation that placed most abortions outside the law. This view had parallels in other nations.

Significantly, among the most vocal opponents of abortion were some of the suffragettes and feminists of the late nineteenth and early twentieth centuries. This was the case with Elizabeth Cady Stanton, Mary Wollstonecraft, and Margaret Sanger. The latter case is especially notable because Margaret Sanger is cited today—by Hillary Clinton, for example—as a justification for gender ideology. Fewer things are further from the truth. Sanger wanted the circulation of contraceptive methods—something that was not considered very acceptable at the time—and suffered from seeing many women's situation, but, like other proto-feminists, she abhorred abortion. All of them easily understood that abortion was not and could not be a kind of feminine right, but only a male imposition intended to free future male parents from all responsibility for their actions.

Such a view changed radically with the establishment of the first totalitarian dictatorship in history—that of the Soviet Union. In 1920, Lenin proceeded to legalize abortion, and his initiative was gradually followed by different nations. In 1931, Mexico, a nation with a Roman Catholic tradition but with an anticlerical government, legalized abortion on the grounds of rape. It was the first nation in the world to take this step, which was followed in 1932 by Poland, also Roman Catholic, and even extended the number of legal abortions. However, the acceptance of abortion did not succeed in paving its way and even received serious setbacks in the 1930s. In 1936, in the Soviet Union, Stalin proceeded to invalidate a large part of the abortion legislation, convinced that it was contrary to the national good. Curiously enough, the Popular Front government in Spain, which opposed Stalin's position, legalized abortion in 1937, a step that was reversed by General Franco's victory in 1939. As far as the Soviet Union was concerned, proabortion legislation would not be reintroduced until 1955.

It was precisely during the 1950s—the time when the terrible effects of the Second World War began to be reversed—that the first steps were taken towards the legalization of abortion. In 1959, the American Law Institute (ALI) drafted a model proabortion law that could be adopted by individual states. In 1966, Mississippi became the first state to legalize abortion on the grounds of rape. The following year, the United Kingdom—with the exception of Northern Ireland—legalized abortion, and the states of Carolina, Colorado, and North Carolina did the same based on the ALI model. This was only the beginning, because in 1968, at the same time that Georgia and Maryland were establishing proabortion laws based on the ALI text, President Johnson's Committee on the Status of Women issued a report calling for the repeal of all antiabortion laws. The following year, Arkansas, Delaware, Kansas, New Mexico, and Oregon reformed their legislation according to the ALI's abortion model, while Canada and Australia took similar steps. By the end of the decade, Hawaii, New York, Alaska, and Washington had joined this trend.

However, it was the 1970s, the same years as the Limits to Growth report, that witnessed an extraordinary proabortion momentum. Without a doubt, the U.S. Supreme Court ruling known as Roe *v.* Wade marked a turning point in 1973, but it was preceded by events as important as the Indian Medical Termination of Pregnancy Act of 1971 that changed the moral direction of one of the world's most populous nations and also one of the most opposed to abortion.

The Roe *v.* Wade ruling had an extraordinary projection because it emanated from the most powerful nation on the globe. According to its content, abortion during the first trimester could not be prohibited; its attempt during the second trimester could be regulated, but not prohibited, and that which took place in the third trimester could be prohibited, but only if the limitations did not affect the physical and mental health of the mother. Despite formal inquiries into the subject, it was obvious that the door had been opened for abortion to be performed without restriction, as would indeed happen.

In the following years, different nations joined in the legalization of abortion. This was the case of France in 1975, the FRG in 1976, New Zealand in 1977, Italy in 1978, the Netherlands in 1980, and Spain in 1985. During the following decades, the proabortionist view continued to win one victory after another. Not only were the norms that allowed it becoming more and more lax, but, in addition, there were international aid programs offered to the Third World that were subordinated to the legalization of abortion. But, above all, the view of abortion changed from being considered a lesser evil—the argument used at the beginning of its legalization—to being preached as a right that women cannot be deprived of. In this attempt to legitimize the termination of life, it has been affirmed that before birth, a thirteen-week fetus is a living being, but not a human being.[1] The falsity of this argument becomes apparent when one considers that many

1. https://www.abc.es/sociedad/abci-aido-feto-semanas-vivo-pero-no-humano-200905190300-921017161079_noticia.html.

abortion clinics, such as those run by Planned Parenthood, then sell the remains of the fetus precisely because they are human beings and, as such, can be used for experiments.[2]

During this decades-long process, the loss of human life related to abortion has numbered in the millions of millions, surpassing in mortality the worst wars in the history of the human race. In 2014, 926,240 registered abortions took place in the United States. During the previous decade, the number of abortions had exceeded one million for several years, and just from 1973 to 2011 alone, the number of abortions carried out in the United States had already exceeded 53 million. In other words, more people were legally killed than all those who lost their lives during World War II, including the Jews who perished during the Holocaust. The abortion rate in the United States in 2014 was 18.9% of pregnancies—what kind of a future awaits a nation that exterminates nearly one-fifth of the children it has conceived?—and, on top of that, it wasn't the worst rate in the world. Ahead of the United States were Bulgaria, Cuba, Estonia, Georgia, Kazakhstan, Romania, Russia, Sweden, and Ukraine.

This mass extermination is still being practiced, moreover, under the guise of defending women's rights. That is the main reason why the globalist agenda intends to impose it on all of Latin America, Africa, and Asia. As of today, since the legalization processes of the 1970s, the number of aborted children worldwide exceeds 1.4 billion, which is equivalent to the total population of China.

The alternatives to abortion—giving up for adoption, having the child, etc.—are always presented as more costly from any point of view than simply taking the life of an innocent fetus that cannot defend itself. Even the mother who is willing to give her child away to other parents at the end of her pregnancy knows that she will have gone through a pregnancy that spares the child from abortion. The situation is more difficult when the woman in question decides to raise a child in financial difficulty alone. Let's face it. From the point of view of

2. https://www.elmundo.es/internacional/2015/08/05/55c1946c22601d4e5e8b456c.html.

millions of people, abortion is an ideal method of getting rid of problems—at the cost, of course, of human life and other collateral damage of no small scale. They ignore that they are mere puppets of a globalist agenda determined to drastically reduce the world's population.

Towards the Establishment of Euthanasia

If abortion has proved to be a colossal success in reducing the world's population in accordance with the globalist agenda, something similar is happening with euthanasia, for which more and more social groups are mobilizing for its legalization. If the antecedent for the legalization of abortion was the Soviet legislation of the early 1920s, then that for euthanasia is found directly in Hitler's National Socialism. Although there was a precedent in Uruguay in 1933 that legalized assisted suicide, it was the Aktion-4 program (1933) that permitted the killing of incurable children first, and then quickly extended to the terminally ill and people suffering from mental disabilities or illnesses. Although the program was stopped by churches that protested, the truth is that those precedents of murder by gas were taken up again during the war in carrying out the extermination of the inmates in concentration camps.

Of course, as is customary with all totalitarian projects, the Nazis prepared public opinion to accept the legalization of euthanasia. It is ignored, but the antecedent of the multi-award-winning Spanish film *The Sea Inside* (2004), where the case for euthanasia was made, was the Nazi *Ich Klage An* 1941 ("I Accuse"), an episode, by the way, mentioned in passing in the excellent film *Good* (2008), where the transformation of a "good" man into a collaborator for the Nazi regime is described. In each and every case, something elemental is revealed, but it is often overlooked. The manipulation of certain feelings leads the masses to accept atrocities such as those of legitimizing the extermination of their fellow human beings. However, not everything should be attributed to propaganda. Propaganda gets results because the seeds are planted in already fertilized soil. In this respect, the case for euthanasia could not be clearer.

Perhaps the memory of the horrors of Nazism and the desire to prolong human life delayed the approval of euthanasia for decades. Paradoxically, success in prolonging a person's lifespan and the growth in the number of elderly people drove it. Thus, in 1997, it was legally accepted in Colombia thanks to a decision by the Constitutional Court. However, it was the approval by Belgium, another Roman Catholic nation, in 2002 that opened the way for its extension to other nations. That same year, the Netherlands also legalized euthanasia, followed in 2008 by two other Roman Catholic nations: Luxembourg and Mexico. In 2011, India approved euthanasia.

Not many nations were yet willing to allow the practice of euthanasia within their borders, but the propaganda movement in its favor not only grew increasingly militant, but also began to expand. In 2013, for example, Belgium, a pioneering nation in such unfortunate circumstances, extended euthanasia to children, with the first case taking place in 2016. In that same year, Canada legalized euthanasia, and France passed a rule allowing doctors to keep patients sedated until their death, which resulted in a more formal method of death than actual euthanasia.

That is not the end of the list. In some nations, such as Denmark, euthanasia is not legal, but a 2003 study found that 41% of deaths under medical supervision showed that the doctor decided to end the patient's life. In others, such as Spain or the United States, euthanasia is legal locally. While the statute of autonomy of Catalonia, a region of Spain, was opening the door to euthanasia; at the same time, assisted suicide—a euphemism for euthanasia—was approved in Washington, DC, Colorado, Oregon, Washington, Vermont, California, a county in New Mexico, and, in fact, Montana.

It is true that euthanasia is still illegal in nations like Finland, and attempts this decade to impose it in New Zealand or Norway have failed, but, as in the case of abortion, it finds willing ears in quite a few societies. In their midst, the elderly—those people who, when I was a child, were viewed as members without whom a family could not even be conceived—are regarded by many as just another nuisance. One proof of this is that as houses have been enlarged and improved, and the people who live in them has diminished, for example, because they have fewer children, the elderly, instead of enjoying more space, have been confined to nursing homes. Naturally, that is if they have been lucky, because the most unfortunate ones, whose cases are numerous, have been abandoned at a gas station or in a hospital during the holiday season.

Unfortunately, it must be said that euthanasia is already being practiced in nations such as Spain even before it has been formally legalized. In 2019, a close friend of the author was able to confirm that his father-in-law was being starved to death in a hospital so that he would slowly die of hunger and thirst. Only the fact that my friend had been a hospital floor manager helped him to discover the criminal treatment they were committing against his father-in-law and save his life. It is terrifying to think how many elderly people in Spain are already being subjected to such treatment in a truly genocidal process born of the globalist agenda.

For a society that feels annoyed about the elderly, the legalization of euthanasia is a real blessing. Getting rid of the elderly opens the door to enjoying holidays with little inconvenience, makes the family schedule more fun, and even speeds up the time to collect long-awaited inheritances. The problem—once again—is that all these enjoyments are obtained, as in the case of abortion, at the cost of the death of innocent people.

This drastic reduction in population due to gender ideology, abortion, and euthanasia is not the only demographic experiment driven by gender ideology. Along with the truly genocidal extermination of hundreds of millions of human beings, the globalist agenda is driving a displacement of world populations that will result in the annihilation of national identities—one of its worst enemies—and age-old cultures.

CHAPTER XIV

THE DOGMAS OF THE GLOBALIST AGENDA (IV): The Defense of Illegal Immigration

The Need for Borders

It was A.D. 122 when Emperor Hadrian visited the far reaches of Rome in Britannia. Hadrian was aware that the security of the borders was an indispensable element not only for the well-being but even for the survival of the Roman Empire. Any invasion—be it peaceful or warlike—that violated the borders of the empire and introduced significant masses of population into it could only have negative consequences. For a long time, Rome had granted its citizenship to barbarians, and there were many who, individually or as a group, had ended up integrating into the highest culture of their time. There was, however, another reality. Neither public order, nor economic production, nor the social assistance that provided bread and circuses to the citizens could be maintained by an uncontrolled influx of barbarians. After his inspection of the borders, Hadrian ordered a protective wall to be built from Solway to the River Tyne, that is, from the vicinity of the North Sea to the area of the Atlantic facing the island of Ireland. The work was to be known as *Vallum Hadriani*—Hadrian's Wall—and, tellingly enough, it was not built by slaves, but by Romans who were aware of the importance of that decision. When it was finished, it had barracks placed a certain distance apart with two turrets each occupied by garrisons of between eight and thirty-two men in charge of border defense. Designated in 1987 by UNESCO as a World Heritage Site, Hadrian's Wall was essential to the survival of the Roman Empire for two and a half centuries. In fact, that wall guaranteed peace, security, and stability for Rome on its border with the Britons. However, not all emperors were as clever as Hadrian. In A.D. 376, the Visigoths asked Emperor Valens to let them settle in the southern part of the Danube River. The emperor accepted with dire consequences. Two years later, the Visigoths proved that they could rebel and defeated the Romans at the Battle of Adrianople. Over the course of the following years, the influence of the barbarians on the politics of Rome grew exponentially. In A.D. 476, just as the century was coming to an end from the time when Valens had allowed his massive settlement in the territory of the Roman Empire, one of those barbarian chiefs named Odoacer deposed Romulus Augustus, who would be the last emperor. The Western Roman Empire had just disappeared and, despite attempts, it would never be able to rebuild itself.

What happened to both Adriano and Valens obeys an inexorable historical law, which declares that the State that does not control its borders is condemned to extinction. We find this situation in all cultures. It is not only a question of great building projects such as the Great Wall of China, the only monument that can be seen from space, but one of universal behavior. In the Bible itself, we find many examples. David became a king in every sense of the word when he built the walls of Jerusalem (2 Chronicles 33:14). Solomon showed his stature as a monarch when, among other works, he reinforced the walls of Jerusalem (1 Kings 3:1; 9:15). Israel's actual restoration came when Nehemiah was able to build a wall to defend the people (Nehemiah 3; 4:6; 7:1). Even God is expected to build walls (Psalm 51:18)! In the end, this universal behavior is entirely based on logic and common sense. No one, no matter how hospitable, would let just anyone into his home. On the contrary, we all want to maintain the right of accepting or rejecting anyone in our home. The same is true of nations, but with a specific characteristic, and that is that the well-being not only of one person or family but of millions of people depends on national decisions. The Founding Fathers were no strangers to this way of thinking.

The Founding Fathers and Immigration

Historically, the United States has been a host nation for immigrants. However, that circumstance has never meant that it permitted uncontrolled immigration, that it was open to any type of immigration, and that it was unaware of the danger that could result from not knowing how to manage immigration properly. Already in 1802, Alexander Hamilton, warning against allowing anyone to enter the United States, wrote: "To admit foreigners indiscriminately to the rights of citizens, the moment they put foot in our country, as recommended in the Message, would be nothing less, than to admit the Grecian Horse into the Citadel of our Liberty and Sovereignty."[1] Hamilton's statement could hardly have been clearer. Not all foreigners could receive the benefits of citizenship, and this was because, depending on their cultural background, they could end up becoming an enemy infiltrating the nation—as had happened with the famous Trojan horse—which would have disastrous effects on freedom and sovereignty.

In 1800, writing to John Marshall, a similar view had been expressed when he referred to foreigners wishing to take up public employment, stating: "Among the number of applications..., cannot we find an American capable and worthy of the trust?...Why should we

1. The Examination Number VIII, January 12, 1802, https://founders.archives.gov/documents/Hamilton/01-25-02-0282.

take the bread out of the mouths of our own children and give it to strangers?"[2]

Immigration was acceptable not only if it posed no danger to the freedom or work of American citizens, but also if it brought something really useful to the nation. It would be the first president of the United States, George Washington, writing to John Adams on November 15, 1794, who would say, "My opinion, with respect to emigration, is that except of useful mechanics and some particular descriptions of men or professions, there is no need of encouragement, while the policy or advantage of its taking place in a body (I mean the settling of them in a body) may be much questioned; for, by so doing, they retain the language, habits, and principles (good or bad) which they bring with them).[3] In other words, immigration made sense only if it referred to people who could bring a usefulness to nations and who then learned their language, habits, and principles.

Undoubtedly, the question of assimilation—a concept radically opposed to that of multiculturalism—was enormously relevant to Washington. In that same letter to John Adams, Washington insisted that immigrants "by an intermixture with our people, they, or their descendants, get assimilated to our customs, measures, laws: in a word soon become one people."

Washington's point of view was shared by the rest of the Founding Fathers who were aware of the need for a common national sentiment. In 1802, Alexander Hamilton wrote: "The safety of a republic depends essentially on the energy of a common national sentiment; on a uniformity of principles and habits; on the exemption of the citizens from foreign bias and prejudice; and on that love of country which will almost invariably be found to be closely connected with birth, education, and family."[4] Failure to grasp the importance of that circumstance, according to Hamilton, involved great dangers. In fact, in his words, "the United States have already felt the evils of incorporating

2. https://founders.archives.gov/documents/Adams/99-02-02-4517.
3. https://founders.archives.gov/documents/Washington/05-17-02-0112.
4. https://founders.archives.gov/documents/Hamilton/01-25-02-0282

a large number of foreigners into their national mass; by promoting in different classes different predilections in favor of particular foreign nations, and antipathies against others, it has served very much to divide the community and to distract our councils. It has been often likely to compromise the interests of our own country in favor of another."[5] As Hamilton pointed out in the same text, "The permanent effect of such a policy will be, that in times of great public danger there will be always a numerous body of men, of whom there may be just grounds of distrust; the suspicion alone will weaken the strength of the nation, but their force may be actually employed in assisting an invader." In the end, as Hamilton also indicated, the survival of the American Republic depended on "the preservation of a national spirit and a national character" and in "the recommendation to admit indiscriminately foreign emigrants of every description to the privileges of American citizens on their first entrance into our country, there is an attempt to break down every pale which has been erected for the preservation of a national spirit and a national character."

That an immigration from another culture could have terrible effects for the United States was a reality also contemplated by Benjamin Franklin. In his *Observations Concerning the Increase of Mankind and the Peopling of Countries*, he noted that "the importation of foreigners into a country that has as many inhabitants as the present employments and provisions for subsistence will bear, will be in the end no increase of people, unless the newcomers have more industry and frugality than the natives, and then they will provide more subsistence, and increase in the country; but they will gradually eat the natives out."

A very similar view of immigration was held by James Madison, who, again, pointed out that the only immigrants who should be accepted were those who were worthy and could add to the strength of the nation. Thus, he pointed out: "It is no doubt very desirable that we should hold out as many inducements as possible for the worthy

5. *Idem, Ibidem.*

part of mankind to come and settle amongst us, and throw their fortunes into a common lot with ours. But why is this desirable? Not merely to swell the catalogue of people. No, sir, it is to increase the wealth and strength of the community; and those who acquire the rights of citizenship without adding to the strength or wealth of the community are not the people we are in want of."[6]

It is significant that the Naturalization Act of 1790 required "good character" as a condition for citizenship. Five years later, a new law was passed that, absorbing the spirit of the Founding Fathers, increased the time for naturalization from two to five years and required "good moral character." The requirements for citizenship became even more restricted over the years. The Fourteenth Amendment stated that "all persons born or naturalized in the United States, and subject to the jurisdiction thereof, are citizens of the United States and the State wherein they reside." In fact, Howard, the author of the amendment, noted that "every person born within the limits of the United States, and subject to the jurisdiction thereof, is by virtue of natural law a citizen of the United States," and then added that "this, of course, will not include persons born in the United States who are foreigners, strangers, who belong to the families of foreign ambassadors or foreign officials recognized by the United States government, but will include all other types of persons. This clarifies the question of citizenship in place and removes any doubt about which people are or are not citizens of the United States." This has long been a major desideratum in the jurisprudence and legislation of this country. In other words, those born in the United States were citizens of the United States if, indeed, they were not foreigners belonging to families of foreigners, however high the regard for them might be. This was also the understanding of Democratic Senator Reverdy Johnson, who stated that "the amendment says citizenship may depend on birth, and I know of no better way to give rise to citizenship than the fact of birth within the

6. The Founders' Constitution, Volume 2, Article 1, Section 8, Clause 4 (Citizenship), Document 8. http://press-pubs.uchicago.edu/founders/documents/a1_8_4_citizenships8.html.

territory of the United States, born of parents who at the time were subject to the authority of the United States."

The position of the Founding Fathers could not be clearer. Immigration was acceptable, but only when it came to people who could bring something positive to the nation, who did not come from a culture that could damage American democracy, who did not unbalance the political system, and who ended up integrating as one of the people within the United States. For those seeking citizenship, it would be necessary to have good moral character and wait for five years. Not even later, almost a century later, would it be considered enough having been born in the territory of the United States to be considered an American citizen. To that circumstance, one would have to add the condition of being the child of parents who were citizens.

Whichever way you look at it, this was a fair, balanced, and rational approach to the issue of immigration. However, the globalist agenda has very different plans for the United States and the rest of the world on this issue.

The UN and Immigration

The globalist agenda contains among its dogmas the idea of an immigration—migration, is usually the word used—without State control of any kind. In this respect, its goal may be unknown to most of the world's population, but it has been expressly stated on many occasions. Thus, in 2015, the UN General Assembly approved the so-called Agenda 2030, which set out the goals for the next decade and a half.[7] Under this inspiration, in September 2016, the United Nations General Assembly organized a plenary meeting whose purpose was to address the large displacement of migrants and refugees.[8] It was

7. https://www.un.org/sustainabledevelopment/es/2015/09/la-asamblea-general-adopta-la-agenda-2030-para-el-desarrollo-sostenible/.
8. https://news.un.org/es/story/2016/09/1364511.

the first time that a UN meeting of this kind was entirely devoted to the phenomenon of international immigration. At this meeting, the 193 members of the UN General Assembly adopted the New York Declaration for Refugees and Migrants.

As a result of that declaration, the High Commissioner for Refugees was mandated to propose a Global Agreement on Migrants and Refugees in his annual report to the General Assembly in 2018. The conclusion of the negotiations to reach that agreement took place in July 2018, with the final conference for the adoption of the Agreement scheduled for December 10-11, 2018, in Morocco.

The prospect of what the future pact would be led the United States to withdraw from the negotiations at the end of 2017, and Hungary withdrew as well in 2018. At the same time, and significantly, the Vatican made it known that it was a strong supporter of the agreement.

Finally, the signing took place in Marrakesh. Among the commitments adopted in the agreement were the following: "eliminate all forms of discrimination and counter-pressure," "implement or maintain legislation criminalizing hate crimes," and "promote independent, objective. and quality media communication, including Internet-based information." In other words, the agreement was intended to eliminate all opposition to mass immigration, prevent counterdemonstrations by criminalizing them as hate crimes, and shape society by controlling the media, including the Internet. In addition, every four years, starting in 2022, the Forum will provide a global platform for Member States to discuss and share progress in the implementation of all aspects of the Global Agreement.

A review of those who voted for and against the agreement is revealing. Those nations that did not sign the agreement were mainly those that were keenly aware that illegal immigration could cause them serious dangers. Thus, the United States withdrew from the agreement from the beginning, and Israel, Australia, and even Chile distanced themselves as well. A distancing from the agreement also occurred in the European Union, where the refusal of Hungary was joined by those of Belgium, Austria, Poland, the Czech Republic, Slovakia, Bulgaria, and Italy. Even Germany subordinated its approval to the decision of the Parliament. This was not the case in Spain.

The signing of the UN agreement on immigration carried with it a radical importance that contrasted sharply with the almost total silence of the media when it was approved. As on other occasions, the UN has promoted a plan that will help the globalist agenda, erode national sovereignty, contribute to the annihilation of national cultures, and make the existence of a sense of well-being impossible. The worst-faring nations in the world—that is, most of them—found themselves legitimized to send millions of their people to live at the expense of the most prosperous nations, primarily those in North America, the Pacific Rim, and Western Europe. Such an assault also came accompanied by very specific measures, such as no one could oppose them in the nations receiving immigrants; those who showed their disapproval could be accused of committing hate crimes; the media was controlled so as not to mention the subject or to do so in a positive way; the immense expense of the arrival of millions of immigrants be assumed by the receiving countries; and that there would be spiritual bodies such as the Holy See and Islamic leaders who would support the agreement expressly and enthusiastically. Significantly, the fact that this agreement is linked to the liberalization of abortion does not seem to make the Holy See lose any sleep over it.

It cannot be denied that the agreement on immigration satisfies many. It satisfies the supporters of the globalist agenda who dream of turning the world into a vast herd without any culture or identity and easier to dominate and exploit. It satisfies the Islamic leaders who dream of making Europe a part of the Muslim world. It satisfies the Vatican, which has repeatedly expressed in recent years its willingness to be the spiritual power that stands alongside a world government to govern the destiny of the planet. It satisfies the millions of illegal immigrants who know that they will be able to live at the expense of the welfare systems of advanced nations. It satisfies, finally, the incompetent and corrupt rulers of nations who could be rich and yet are poor because it opens the door to sending millions of their fellow citizens to more prosperous nations.

It can never satisfy those who realize that the arrival of millions of illegal immigrants who will be supported at the expense of State budgets will end up destroying the possibility of maintaining existing social services. Nor can it ever be satisfactory to those who believe in the necessity of defending national sovereignty, to those who love their culture, to those who believe in freedom, and to those who know that independence is based on the control of its own borders. And that was exactly what was happening with the Founding Fathers of the United States.

The Vatican and Immigration

We have already seen in previous pages how Pope Francis and other instances of the Roman Catholic Church have clearly spoken in favor of the absence of border controls and uncontrolled immigration. Michelle Malkin has pointed out in a recent must-read book[9] how the reasons for such behavior are anything but noble and selfless. From the outset, Pope Francis has ignored all the references in the Bible to the walls that are necessary for every State, but above all, he behaves in a deeply hypocritical manner because he does not practice such an open-door policy in the Vatican state and has not opened its doors wide to all foreigners seeking refuge to enter.[10]

His behavior in the case of the United States is motivated, in the first place, by his desire to recover from the decline in membership in the Roman Catholic Church, which lost some three million of "the faithful" between 2007 and 2015. In fact, thirty million Americans define themselves as "former" Roman Catholics, with nearly 30% claiming clergy sex abuse scandals as the cause for

9. Michelle Malkin, *Open Borders Inc. Who's Funding America's Destruction?* (Washington, 2019).
10. Michelle Malkin, *Open Borders Inc*, p. 86.

leaving the Roman Catholic Church. In fact, the number of sexual abuses perpetrated by Roman Catholic clergy has been so colossal that to date the Roman Catholic Church has had to pay four billion dollars in compensation and settlements.[11] The massive influx of illegal immigrants from Roman Catholic sociological nations swells the number of faithful Catholics. As Malkin clearly points out, since 1986, when Ronald Reagan carried out an amnesty for illegal aliens, Roman Catholic leaders have not ceased to act in the United States and abroad to undermine immigration law enforcement and violate legislation.[12]

This behavior, which Malkin rightly calls "unpatriotic perfidy"[13] is also a lucrative business for the Roman Catholic Church. The reunification of children with their relatives alone has provided Roman Catholic organizations with more than $104 million dollars between 2008 and 2018[14] and more than $534 million dollars between 2008 and 2017 in refugee settlement programs.[15] Added to this are the tax benefits and subsidies.[16] The reality is that illegal immigration has become a huge business for the Roman Catholic Church, which is not seeking a spiritual ministry, but rather establishing a political organization, especially in the southwestern states.[17] It is a task designed, according to one of the people who received training, to "create conflict" by exploiting "class envy and race"[18] in pursuit of power. That such entities would receive money from Soros—who donated $1.4 million to the Catholic Legal Immigration Network Inc. (CLINIC) between 2000 and 2014—is understandable. It is less understandable that 96% of the budget of Roman Catholic charities for refugee resettlement comes from federal funds.[19] Not surprisingly, Forbes

11. Michelle Malkin, *Open Borders Inc.*, p. 89.
12. Michelle Malkin, *Open Borders Inc.*, p. 90.
13. Michelle Malkin, *Open Borders Inc.*, p. 91.
14. Michelle Malkin, *Open Borders Inc.*, p. 93.
15. Michelle Malkin, *Open Borders Inc.*, p. 96.
16. Michelle Malkin, *Open Borders Inc.*, p. 95.
17. Michelle Malkin, *Open Borders Inc.*, p. 99.
18. Michelle Malkin, *Open Borders Inc.*, p. 99.
19. Michelle Malkin, *Open Borders Inc.*, p. 106.

estimates the income of Roman Catholic charities in the United States at $3.8 billion.[20]

The Catholic Church' enthusiasm for helping illegal immigrants cannot come as a surprise. This is certainly a very juicy business, but it also allows it to dream of conquering the United States simply by the demographic push of illegal arrivals. This objective of conquering American society is so important that it allows the Roman Catholic Church to maintain the same policy in other nations even if it means losing their positions in favor of Islam there. This is the case, for example, in Spain.

In 2019, the Spanish Episcopal Conference demanded that the government "close the Detention Centers, with clear and legal alternatives." The Detention Centers or CIEs are public buildings that are not prisons but are managed by the police, where people who have entered Spain illegally are detained. If, after sixty days, these illegal immigrants have not been returned to their country of origin—which usually happens with extraordinary frequency—they are released and usually remain in Spain, despite their illegal status. Two-thirds of the people detained during 2018 in the Detention Centers for Foreigners (CIE) came from Morocco and Algeria, according to the Jesuit Service for Migrants-Spain (SJME). According to that report by the aforementioned Jesuit entity, although in the CIEs there are people from 90 different countries, 35.66% are from Morocco and 31.99% from Algeria.

The demand of the Spanish Catholic bishops to close the CIEs was drawn up by the secretary of the Episcopal Commission for Migrations of the CEE, Jesuit José Luis Pinilla, during a press conference on the occasion of the World Day of Migrants and Refugees, held on September 29, 2019. In the quoted passage, the Spanish bishops stated that "concerning immigrants, it is essential that the Spanish government try to eradicate and prevent vulnerable circumstances; the neglect of human rights linked either to administrative irregularities

20. Michelle Malkin, *Open Borders Inc.*, p. 106.

(pregnant women or unaccompanied minors continue to exist in the streets), or the difficulties stemming from our borders; discriminatory laws, and the very painful and harsh confinement conditions in the Detention Centers, for example." The bishops also stated that "for the latter we again ask for their closure with clear and legal alternatives. We request this because the poorest among us are the foreigners without legal documents."

This closure is part of the joint strategy that, for years, has been carried out through the platform Migrants with Rights, which brings together Roman Catholic entities such as Confer, Caritas, Justice and Peace, and the Episcopal Commission for Migrations. In fact, as Luis Quinteiro Fiuza, the Bishop of Tui-Vigo and current president of the Commission, pointed out, "We are convinced that this is an absolute priority."[21] In the message written for the above-mentioned conference, the Spanish Roman Catholic bishops stated that "the bishops cannot close the CIEs, but they can ask for their closure because it offends the dignity of migrants."

When asked about the future government and the possibility of the withdrawal of the wire fences at the border, the bishop of Tui-Vigo asked those who can finally govern to "work together so that migrants can be respected. And the wire fences are not a form of respect." The case of the Spanish Episcopal Conference is by no means an exception.

As we have already pointed out, in the case of illegal immigration, the action of the Vatican has very clear interests at heart. It is, of course, to join the globalist agenda and not remain detached from a very powerful world movement. It is, of course, receiving the colossal economic revenues that the governments of the whole planet spend on receiving illegal immigrants, which amounts to billions of dollars. But, above all, there are geostrategic considerations, such as trying to repair the demographic collapse of the Roman Catholic dioceses in the

21. https://www.religiondigital.org/solidaridad/espanoles-reclaman-CIE-Ofenden-migrantes-refugiados-conferencia-episcopal-menores-solidaridad-centros-internamiento-vox-gobierno_0_2159784018.html.

United States because of the scandals related to the sexual abuse of the clergy and the desire to be able to convert the first world power into a nation with a Roman Catholic majority. That goal, which would entail the risk that the world's first democracy would end up being a nation like those south of the Rio Grande, carries the equal risk that part of Europe will be handed over to Islam, but, from the Vatican's perspective, that would be a minor defeat. However, it is not only the Vatican that benefits economically from illegal immigration.

NGOs and Illegal Immigration

As we mentioned a few pages ago, Michelle Malkin has done a magnificent job exposing the network of NGOs in the United States that take advantage of illegal immigration. Unfortunately, this is not a phenomenon limited to the United States. Nor is it a phenomenon that always stays within limits, which may be hypocritical and immoral, but are legal. It is not uncommon for NGOs that profit from illegal immigration to go beyond the bounds of legality.

This is the case, for example, with ERCI, "A Greek nonprofit organization that provides emergency care and humanitarian aid in times of crisis. ERCI's philosophy is to identify gaps in humanitarian aid and intervene to help in the most efficient and effective manner possible. Currently, ERCI has four active programs to work with refugees in Greece in the areas of Search and Rescue, Medicine, Education, and Coordination in Refugee Camps." On August 28, 2018, thirty members of the Greek NGO Emergency Response Center International (ERCI) were arrested for their involvement in a human trafficking network that has been operating on the island of Lesbos since 2015.[22]

According to a statement issued by the Greek police, which was the result of the investigation leading to the arrests, "The activities

22. https://katehon.com/es/article/otra-banda-criminal-disfrazada-de-ong-erci-una-organizacion-humanitaria-en-grecia-se-dedica.

of an organized crime network that systematically facilitated the illegal entry of foreigners fully came to light." Among the activities discovered were counterfeiting, espionage, and illegal surveillance by the Greek coast guard and the EU's border agency, Frontex, for the purpose of obtaining confidential information on the influx of Turkish refugees. The investigation also led to the discovery of six other Greeks and twenty-four foreign nationals involved in the case. Despite its mission statement and nonprofit profile, ERCI, according to the Greek authorities, has earned considerable amounts of money by serving as a conduit for illegal activities.

ERCI received 2,000 euros from each illegal immigrant it helped to enter Greece. In addition, its members set up a business to "integrate refugees" into Greek society, assuring them 5,000 euros per immigrant from various government programs (in education, housing, and nutrition). ERCI has reportedly been complicit in the illegal entry of 70,000 immigrants into Greece since 2015, which has earned the "nonprofit" organization 500,000 euros per year. This disclosure, however, does not even begin to cover the scope of the illegal activities surrounding the entry of migrants into Greece. In 2017, for example, the Greek authorities arrested 1,399 human traffickers, some of whom were operating under the cover of "humanitarian" operations; and in the first four months of 2018, the authorities arrested 25,594 illegal immigrants.

More disturbing than the exorbitant price paid to human traffickers by the immigrants themselves—or charged by the Greek government in the form of integration assistance—is the toll that the situation is taking on Greek society as a whole. In a society where 10% to 15% of the population are immigrants, the Greek police estimate that more than 40% of serious crimes were committed by illegal immigrants. According to Greek police statistics, there were 75,707 reported robberies and burglaries in 2017. Of these, only 15,048 cases were resolved, and 4,207 were perpetrated by foreigners. The higher percentage of crime among immigrants than among nationals is, unfortunately, not limited to Greece.

Illegal immigration is a serious problem, driven by the globalist agenda and connected to deeply undesirable circumstances. The first is the existence of international mafias that are aware of the business of moving hundreds of thousands of illegal immigrants to Western Europe and the United States and charging them a fee for helping them break the law. The second is the collaboration of some NGOs that may have been humanitarian at one time, but are now servants of the mafias that receive money twice over. Partly, it comes from the nations and international organizations by means of subsidies, and partly from the mafias of human trafficking, which are happy to count on their collaboration that is far from unselfish. In the case of a situation like this, the law can be applied, but NGOs, political parties, trade unions, and the Vatican have been preventing the protection of borders and collaborating objectively with human traffickers for decades. However, the alternative could not be clearer. Either the various nations decide to protect their borders in accordance with their inalienable national powers, or they will be flooded by the actions of the supporters of illegal immigration who support the globalist agenda. That path can bring major or minor benefits in certain instances, but, as history has shown, it involves condemning a nation to its final collapse.

CHAPTER XV

THE DOGMAS OF THE GLOBALIST AGENDA (V): The Nairobi Summit

On November 15, 2019, the Nairobi Summit or International Conference on Population and Development 25 concluded. Its direct precedents were in the announcement, on January 18, 2019, of the observance of the Nairobi Summit to advance the implementation of the Program of Action of the International Conference on Population and Development (ICPD). The Nairobi Summit was to be held in Nairobi, Kenya, from November 13 to 15, 2019. It marked the twenty-fifth anniversary of the 1994 International Conference on Population and Development in Cairo, where 179 nations pledged, for the first time in history, to advance the legalization of abortion and the development of gender ideology. Although the objectives of the Cairo Summit were obvious, it is no less true that the feelings of the vast majority of the populations prevented them, to a greater or lesser extent, from being achieved.

The Nairobi Summit was intended to set the course for achieving the Sustainable Development Goals (SDAs) set for 2030. Thus, from the outset, the summit set itself the goal of "incorporating intersectional and comprehensive interventions on health, mental health, sexual, and reproductive rights into programs, policies, and strategies within the framework of universal health coverage and comprehensive sexuality education (CSE) and legal termination of pregnancy (LTP)."

Although the Nairobi Summit was not an official United Nations Summit and, theoretically, should not have any legal institutional effects, the reality is that its political effects are colossal. In fact, the Nairobi Summit imposed a twelve-point agenda that could not be disputed, which included the legalization and expansion of abortion; the provision of contraceptives to minors; the educational indoctrination of children in gender ideology; and the inclusion in the legal system of the gay lobby's wishes.

Among the entities that supported this agenda were the large abortion multinationals such as the International Planned Parenthood Federation (IPPF), Marie Stopes, IPAS, and Rutges. In each and every case, these were entities that have financed the Nairobi Summit and have been dedicating significant funds for years to impose abortion and gender ideology in Africa and Latin America.

In a very explicit way, practically all the Latin American nations affirmed their commitment to the goals of the Nairobi Summit and, especially, to the abortion agenda and child indoctrination in gender ideology. Thus, Argentina pointed to some twenty goals, among which were the legalization of abortion, masked as women's reproductive rights; the advance of indoctrination in gender ideology, described as comprehensive sex education; and the rights of LGBTTTIQ+ people. In fact, in the case of Argentina, the representatives were Gabriela Agosto, executive secretary of the National Council for the Coordination of Social Policies of the Presidency, and a transsexual who calls herself Camila Fernández and belongs to the organization "Ella decide" ("She decides"). Mexico, in spite of the promises made by its current president during the elections, promised to make abortion free. Similarly, Paraguay—the nation with the lowest percentage of Latin American evangelicals—accepted the abortion agenda despite the majority antiabortion opinion of its population.

The exception to the capitulation to the objectives of the Nairobi Summit was presented by the United States, which denounced the aggressively proabortion agenda of the summit. In Latin America, only Brazil and Haiti supported the United States. In the case of Europe, only Hungary, Belarus, and Poland followed the United States' thesis and opposed the abortion agenda.

The Cairo Summit of a quarter of a century ago marked a true milestone in the history of the control of the human race by a small elite group. Lacking the least moral legitimacy and any political representation, that summit sought—while referring to real problems such as the exploitation of women or the abuse of children as evils to be eradicated—to set in motion a system of mass extermination of the human race through the international spread of the abortion industry.

The agenda of the Cairo Summit advanced without any serious difficulty in Western societies where the effects can be seen today in serious demographic crises and in the more than real possibility of the disappearance of certain cultures in the face of the massive arrival of immigrants. However, such a view hardly made progress in areas of the world such as Africa or Latin America. The fact that the globalist agenda has accelerated in recent years and that, in addition, Latin America is now a battleground on which its independence or its submission to a chilling tyranny will be determined made the Nairobi Summit an absolute must. The idea, once again, was to promote without the least legitimacy a program of world government that involves the mass extermination of hundreds of millions of human beings. In order to understand this, we only have to remember that, in the United States alone, eighteen million African Americans have died in abortions,[1] a figure that is three times that of the Jews who died during the Holocaust, and yet it is never mentioned when it comes to the problems of the black minority in the United States. It is true that there is a movement called *Black Lives Matter*, but, curiously, those eighteen million lives do not seem to matter to anyone.

1. https://abort73.com/abortion/abortion_and_race/.

The consolidation of the goals for 2030 with legalized abortion throughout the planet and gender ideology, especially homosexuality, which by definition is sterile, taught from childhood, would result in a huge reduction of the planet's population. In a significant way, all decisions would be made without any democratic mandate, without most populations knowing what was happening, with little media attention, and with the opposition of a minority of nations, among whom would be the United States. There can be little doubt that the globalist agenda continues to impose its dogmas.

PART IV

A CHANGING WORLD

CHAPTER XVI

THE END OF NATIONAL INDEPENDENCE (I): The European Union

The End of National Independence

The year was 1939, and more specifically March, when the Slovak Republic was established in Eastern Europe. Governed by the Roman Catholic monsignor Josef Tiso, who had carried out important political work while continuing to administer his parish, in theory the new republic was independent and had national sovereignty, with its own president and its own institutions. However, in spite of its institutions, its president, and its proclaimed national sovereignty, the reality is that the Slovak Republic was no more than a protectorate of the Third Reich that decided its foreign policy and a good part of its domestic policy. Both the government of Monsignor Tiso and that of the Third Reich agreed on anti-Semitism, and thus, since the foundation of Slovakia, the intention of converting it into a *Judenfrei* place, that is, free of Jews, was announced. From 1940 onwards, Slovakia proceeded to lock up Jews in ghettos; in 1941, anti-Semitic laws similar to those of Nuremberg were passed, and, at the end of that year, Jews were sent off to camps and settlements. In 1942, Slovakia accepted the deportation of Slovak Jews and even requested, on alleged humanitarian grounds, that entire families be deported, not just individuals destined to work in the East. Significantly, it was a Roman Catholic bishop and member of the Council of Ministers who managed to get the measure accepted against the more moderate members of the cabinet. At the end of that year, the deportations stopped when it leaked that many of the deported Slovak Jews had been victims of mass killings. The deportations resumed in October 1944 when the Red Army approached the borders of Slovakia. By the end of the war, only 5,000 of the 70,000 Slovak Jews had survived. Monsignor Tiso was tried for his crimes and executed. Thus, the existence of the Slovak Republic came to an end. For six years, Slovakia had apparently been an independent nation. In practice, beyond some internal measures, Slovakia had not gone beyond being a political entity subject to the whims of the Third Reich, a true protectorate. That political model is the one that the globalist agenda intends for all the nations of the globe. In theory, they will be sovereign nations, with their own institutions and even with periodic elections. In practice, however, these nations will be no more than mere protectorates obeying the directives emanating from a world government not elected by anyone and devoid of the slightest democratic legitimacy.

The Evolution of Europe

On May 9, 1950, the press was invited to Paris to the Salon de l'Horloge of the French Ministry of Foreign Affairs, on the Quai d'Orsay, at six in the afternoon to announce a "communication of the utmost importance." The text had been written by the Freemason Jean Monnet and was delivered by Robert Schuman, Minister of Foreign Affairs, also a Freemason, Catholic, and currently in the process of beatification. The proposal was to create a supranational European institution, which would be responsible for the joint administration of coal and steel production. Such a step, which would mean the disappearance of the sovereignty of France and Germany in the use of coal and steel, would in theory mean the disappearance of war in Europe, since neither France nor Germany could carry out a rearmament without being discovered. In practice, that process was the first step towards creating a European Union that, initially, seemed to be merely commercial and economic, but which, very soon, headed down the path of political union. Understandably, the date of May 9 became Europe Day, although, quite conspicuously, it is not celebrated by the EU member nations in any special way. Perhaps it is not so strange when one understands how this EU project was actually conceived and how it developed. To understand it, we have to go back a few decades.

In 1921, Count Richard Nicholas von Coundenhove-Kalergit,[1] the son of an Austro-Hungarian nobleman and a Japanese woman, joined Freemasonry, at the Humanitas Lodge in Vienna. Two years later, he published his book *Pan-Europe*,[2] which described a plan for a European Union movement also called Pan-Europe. Three years later, the Jewish banker Louis de Rothschild introduced Coundenhove-Kalergi to fellow Jewish banker Max Warburg, who offered to finance the new movement by giving away sixty thousand gold German marks over the next six years, and who, in turn, connected Coundenhove-Kalergi to other Jewish financiers such as Paul Warburg and Bernard Baruch. That same year, Coundenhove-Kalergi founded the *Paneuropa* publication of which he was the editor and main contributor until 1938. In 1926, the Pan-European movement held its first congress in Vienna. The two thousand delegates elected Coundenhove-Kalergi as president of the central council, a position he held until his death in 1970.

1. An in-depth biography of Coundenhavoe-Kalergi is about to be written. Some hagiographies do exist, such as one by J. M. de Faramiñán Fernández-Fígares, *Coudenhove-Kalergi un ideal para Europa* (Madrid, 2017).

2. There is a Spanish edition of the book by Richard N. Coudenhove-Kalergi, *Pan-Europa* (Madrid, 2010). In a very revealing way, the Spanish edition is published by the Ministry of Foreign Affairs and Cooperation of Spain; we are talking about Europa, the publishing house of the Roman Catholic group Communion and Liberation, and the CEU, a Roman Catholic university. Its prologue is by Otto de Habsburg.

Among the public figures who attended the congress were the likes of Sigmund Freud and Albert Einstein. The following year, the Freemason Aristide Briand was elected honorary president of the Pan-European Movement.

The Pan-Europe project was much more than an attempt to unite European nations. In fact, according to the theses held by Coundenhove-Kalergi, it went much further by including the division of the world into just five States. Thus, the globe would be redrawn into several supranational blocks. The first would be the United States of Europe, which would include the colonial possessions of France and Italy. Then would come the British Commonwealth, which would circle the globe; Russia, which would be situated between Europe and Asia; and the Pan-Asian Union, which would leave control of much of the Pacific in the hands of Japan and China. The division proposed by Coundenhove-Kalergi would inspire George Orwell's story in his novel *1984*, where in a frightening future world only a few large macro-States remain under an oligarchic-socialist system.

The project not only implied that nations would be integrated into large territorial blocks, but they would also be linked to a cultural dissolution into different entities. Thus, in 1925, Coundenhove-Kalergi described in his book *Praktischer Idealismus* (Practical Idealism)[3] the racial future of Europe with the following words: "The man of the future will be of mixed race. The races and classes of today will gradually disappear through the fading of space, time, and prejudice. The Eurasian-black race of the future, similar in appearance to the ancient Egyptians, will replace the diversity of peoples with a diversity of individuals." Strikingly, Coundenhove-Kalergi indicated how within the future Europe, the Jews would represent "a spiritual aristocracy," a statement perhaps related to the financial support he had received very early on for his project. No less significant is that he identified the European spirit with Lucifer.[4]

3. An English translation exists, Coudenhove-Kalergi, *Practical Idealism. Nobility-Technology-Pacifism*, n.d.

4. Coudenhove-Kalergi, *Practical Idealism. Nobility-Technology-Pacifism*, p. 80.

The Second World War logically brought Koundenhove-Kalergi's plans to a halt, but despite the new international order born out of the conflict and despite the Cold War, they did not bring about its end. In 1950, the same year as the Schuman Declaration, in a very significant way, Coundenhove-Kalergi was the first person to be awarded the Charlemagne Prize for those who defended the idea of a united Europe. When he died in 1972, Europe was making great strides towards the guidelines he had devised. Thus, in 1973 and 1974, the Euro-Arab Dialogue was established by virtue of the respective conferences in Copenhagen and Paris.

In 1975, the Strasbourg Resolution formulated within the "Parliamentary Association for Euro-Arab Cooperation" declared: "A medium- and long-term policy must henceforth be formulated through the exchange of European technology for oil and Arab labor reserves...." The declaration voiced its intention "that European governments should provide special measures to safeguard the free movement of Arab workers who will emigrate to Europe as well as respect for their fundamental rights. These rights should be equivalent to those of national citizens." The resolution also included among its objectives: "the need to enable immigrants and their families to practice the religious and cultural life of the Arabs"; "the need to create through the press and other media a climate favorable to immigrants and their families"; and "the need to highlight through the press and the academic world the contribution made by Arab culture to European development." Finally, the resolution stated that "alongside the inalienable right to practice their religion and maintain close ties with their countries of origin, immigrants will also have the right to export their culture to Europe. In other words, the right to propagate and spread it." The European continent was opening up itself by leaps and bounds to massive immigration of Islamic origin.

In 1983, the Symposium for European-Arab Dialogue was held in Hamburg, where it was also pointed out that "the rights of Muslim immigrants had to be equal to those of the citizens who welcomed them," and included among its objectives that "they should publish and create newspapers, radio, and TV stations in Arabic and call for measures to increase their presence in unions, local governments, and universities."

In 1991, in the course of the European Union Parliamentary Assembly, during the Symposium entitled "Contribution of Islamic Civilization to European Culture," it was pointed out among its findings that "the Enlightenment had its origin in Islam, and that Islam is one of the most extraordinary political and moral forces in the world today," and so a mandate was formulated "to withdraw school texts that do not emphasize the participation of Islam in European culture, to establish chairs in the faculties of law, philosophy, theology, and history for the study of the Koran." These theses became Recommendation 1162 on the contribution of Islamic civilization to European culture. However, the historical reality is that Islam has never had any contact with the Enlightenment, in which even openly critical figures of Muhammad stood out, as is the case with Voltaire, who even openly mocked him in one of his works.[5] It seems that the execution of the plan could not be stopped simply because it clashed with history.

The twenty-first century was a clear confirmation of this line of development. In 2003, during the Sixth Conference of Euro-Mediterranean Foreign Ministers, in order to strengthen and advance their partnership, they established the "gradual integration into the enlarged European internal market and ultimately the possibility of achieving the four fundamental freedoms of the EU: free movement of goods, services, capital, and people." In other words, Muslim immigrants would eventually enter and circulate on EU territory without restriction.

In 2004, the Euro-Mediterranean Parliamentary Assembly was created, composed of 120 members of the European Union countries, who are members of national Parliaments or the European Parliament, and an equal number of representatives of the Parliaments of Islamic countries.

5. Voltaire, *El fanatismo o Mahoma el profeta*, Oviedo (2016).

All these concessions to Islam within nations that were never Muslim or which, as in the case of Spain, expelled the Islamic invaders after a centuries-long struggle, were carried out by the European Parliament without the populations of the various European nations generally being aware of it. In other words, Europe was preparing to be assaulted by huge masses of Muslims, and it was she herself who opened up the doors, granting them important academic, economic, social, and media power. Was this perhaps the hidden agenda of the European Union?

To be fair, it must be pointed out that the so-called process of rebuilding Europe initiated after the First World War has had results that can only be described as positive. The fact that there has not been a war that has affected most of Europe in more than half a century, that economic borders have disappeared, that courts of justice have been set up that can correct the mistakes of national courts, that a human rights charter has been made universal, and that a strong common currency has been created are all aspects that deserve a positive judgment in general terms.

However, not all aspects relating to the EU can be seen in the same positive light. To begin with, the EU was conceived before its creation as a project of cultural and national dissolution. Its purpose was not so much the salvation of Europe as such, but rather its mutation into a pot where different races and identities alien to those of European origin could be melded. In that sense, it is not surprising that Koundenhove-Kalergi was a mestizo, nor that he received financing from international banks.

Obstructed during a period between the wars that was strongly marked by nationalist responses to communist internationalism, the Paneuropean Movement advanced after the war on the basis of circumstances such as the horror of the Second World War; the drive for Freemasonry that was often linked, in a very revealing way, to Roman Catholic Christian democracy; the Cold War; and economic and financial interests that were not always transparent.

For many nations, such as the Spain, which did not accept the Marshall Plan, or those that came out of the communist dictatorships at the end of the twentieth century, the EU has been seen as a kind of paradisiacal goal that, supposedly, would solve all the ills they had been unable to solve for themselves over the centuries. This was a hopeful, naive view, and today it must be pointed out that it is far from the truth. On many occasions, the EU, along with positive aspects, has included others that are very difficult to point out as such, such as the loss of economic sovereignty, the absence of control over the movement of foreigners, or the submission to policies such as those concerning non-European Muslims who come to Europe by the millions.

Whether we like it or not, the undeniable reality is that, in a very significant way, the EU may be contributing, perhaps in a decisive way, to the destruction of Europe's cultures and identities in order to replace them with a dreadful future that entails the extinction of Europeans who, in 1900, represented one hundred per cent of the European population and who, in some nations, will become a minority in the coming years. Perhaps for a mestizo such as Koundenhove-Kalergi such an end is desirable, the disappearance of a centuries-old Europe that will be replaced by a mestizo race that is more easily controlled, but it would not be out of place for Europeans to know this and to reflect on it.

Resistance in Europe

It is not only a question of replacing the European population with others that are mainly Muslim, but also of the disappearance of the last shreds of national sovereignty. Such a situation has not escaped various social groups within the European Union who have expressed their opposition to this national dissolution in various ways. One example has been the opposition to the signing of the Free Trade Agreement with the United States or TTIP. Despite the secrecy with which the negotiations were conducted, the fact that European courts eventually lost their jurisdiction in favor of arbitration courts dependent on the transnationals, the imposition of much more lax rules on medicines and food from the United States, and the departure of the Obama presidency ended up preventing the TTIP from becoming a reality.[6] It is more than possible that this cession of sovereignty—and the triumph of the globalist agenda—would have advanced had Hillary Clinton, a fiery supporter of the globalist agenda, reached the White House.

Another episode of resistance to this loss of sovereignty that is particularly relevant has been that of the so-called Brexit or exit of the United Kingdom from the European Union. On December 13, 2019, after years of discussion and a referendum that was won, the British citizens gave an absolute majority—363 of the 650 seats in the House of Commons—to the conservative Boris Johnson. In doing so, they made it clear that they persisted in their intention to leave the European Union.

In June 2016, a referendum had been held in which 51.9% of the British people expressed their willingness to leave the EU. The government was then forced to announce in March 2017 that it was leaving the EU, initiating a process that should be completed by January 21, 2020. Attempts to reverse the result of the referendum were certainly made, but in the end, at the beginning of 2020, everything indicates that the UK will leave the EU. What led the British to vote in favor of leaving the EU? Fundamentally, and although they were not entirely aware of it, it was the strong desire to oppose the globalist agenda. The British were tired of having no control over their borders, of receiving unwanted immigration, and of subjecting their economy to supranational dictates. Whether they will finally succeed in preserving their independence is unknown. It is obvious that the rest of the European nations—of which very few are resisting—are walking towards the end of their sovereignty, replaced by the will of

6. https://www.theguardian.com/commentisfree/2016/sep/06/transatlantic-trade-partnership-ttip-canada-eu; https://www.globaljustice.org.uk/sites/default/files/files/resources/wdm-ttip-briefing.pdf.

undemocratic, nonrepresentative entities, not elected by the people and submitted to a globalist agenda that will determine their end as a culture thanks to massive influxes of Islamic and non-European immigrants.[7] Without doubt, this is a future desired by certain institutions, but one that is frightening for millions of Europeans.

7. On the reasons for Brexit, see: https://www.youtube.com/watch?v=xsev9DP10f8; https://www.youtube.com/watch?v=gVzL1J47IrM; https://www.youtube.com/watch?v=NhKIqt_SIFg; https://www.youtube.com/watch?v=hqTrQ-Co81s.

CHAPTER XVII

THE END OF NATIONAL INDEPENDENCE (II): Latin America

The Antidemocratic Origins of Latin America

The year was 1819 when Simón Bolívar proposed the creation of a political system for Spanish America emancipated from the Spanish empire. During the middle of the constituent convention held in Angostura, Bolívar promoted the idea of a framework that was not at all democratic, but one that would have a lifetime president and a chamber of hereditary senators formed by the generals of independence. With this idea, which repeated his proposal from four years earlier that was contained in the letter from Jamaica, Bolívar was advocating a system that hardly differed from the Spanish one, except that the king was called president for life and the aristocracy were the senators, all of which lacked any historical roots. Both the Angostura and Cúcuta Conventions rejected the system for Venezuela and New Granada, but Bolívar was determined to impose it and personally drafted a constitution with those characteristics, which was later approved for Peru. Faced with criticism that it was not legal to apply it in Greater Colombia, Bolívar insisted that it might not be legal, but it was popular and that made it democratic.

Certainly, Bolívar was an exceptional character despite his poor formal education. He traveled more kilometers than Vasco de Gama or Colón, fighting in often terrible conditions, without giving up and acquiring resources from the most unsuspected places. Defeated in 1810 and 1813 in his attempt to secure independence for Venezuela, he returned from exile in 1816 and three years later had liberated Venezuela and Colombia (then called New Granada) and created a republic that included those two countries plus Ecuador, which was still in Spanish hands. In 1822, he liberated Ecuador, eclipsing the extraordinary José de San Martín, and two years later, Bolívar went on to complete the liberation of Peru before sealing Bolivia's independence the following year. By this time, his taste for dictatorial powers in Caracas in 1813, in Angostura in 1817, in Lima in 1824, and finally in Bogotá in 1828 had become evident.

In each and every case, Bolívar made it clear that, unlike leaders like Washington, Jefferson, or Adams, he was a direct result of the Hispanic-Catholic culture that arrived in 1492. The fruits of that view are undeniable as we have already mentioned a few pages ago. By 1830, Colombia, Peru, and Ecuador had separated; the Bolivarian attempt to create an Andean confederation ended in a war between several nations; and the Congress of Panama that was conceived as the first step towards a federation that would encompass the entire hemisphere collapsed shortly after it was inaugurated in 1826. Along with his absolute inability to create free societies, Bolívar demonstrated a clear desire to create a system similar to that of the Spanish conquistadors consisting of a noble elite that would control the emancipated Americas, a system, incidentally, to which the Freemasonry to which Bolivar belonged also aspired and which he ended up repudiating and outlawing.

Likewise, Bolivar always preserved the typical racism of the Hispanic conquest. He may have been a liberal in bed, but he was a staunch believer in the idea of racial cleansing. In fact, he always had a dreadful fear of the possibility that Indians, mestizos, and blacks might rise up against white rule. No less clear was his rejection of the supremacy of the law, a principle that does not exist in the nations marked by the Counter-Reformation. If factors derived directly from the Hispanic-Catholic culture are added to the above, such as the very low level of literacy, the view of work as divine punishment, welfare, clientelist corruption, or the absence of economic culture (all of which are characteristics of the Counter-Reformation), then Bolívar's failure to create free and equal citizen societies comes as no surprise, nor his final bitterness, the internal struggles of the Spanish American republics, or, above all, the fact that almost two centuries later those failures have not been eradicated. To tell the truth, those failures cannot be avoided because the cultural basis remains the same. In addition to this certainly ominous panorama of more than two centuries, there is now a practically generalized institutional crisis derived from the globalist agenda and the attempt to convert the nations of Latin America into mere protectorates of supranational powers.

The Current Crisis in Latin America

Even a cursory inspection of today's Latin America reveals an immense institutional, economic, political, and social crisis. To the north, Mexico is on the verge of becoming a failed State from not addressing the necessary reforms to end corruption, drug trafficking, and institutional distortions. Suffice it to say that, today, around 90% of the crimes perpetrated in Mexico go unpunished.[1] In fact, one must wonder if, despite its immense wealth, Mexico would not be at serious risk of going bankrupt if it did not receive the money transfers that millions of Mexican immigrants in the United States send back to their home country.

1. https://www.animalpolitico.com/2019/08/delitos-denuncia-impunidad-mexico-justicia/; https://aristeguinoticias.com/1008/mexico/mexico-primer-lugar-del-continente-por-delitos-no-denunciados-ethos/.

In the rest of Central America the situation is no better. Nicaragua is still under a Sandinista dictatorship that is barely concealed and that does not hesitate to resort to the most brutal violence to repress dissidents. Honduras and El Salvador are vying for the sad role of being the nation with the highest percentage of murders in the world while becoming, increasingly, bases for drug trafficking. Guatemala has suffered a brazen intervention on its sovereignty thanks to the International Commission against Impunity in Guatemala (CICIG) created on December 12, 2006, which was not dissolved until September 3, 2019. Added to this is the possible explosion of an indigenous rebellion—again, the case of the indigenous population being used as a battering ram to weaken national sovereignty—as the Indians, for the first time since the arrival of the Spanish, once again now make up more than half the population. Only Panama—hard hit by the scandal of the so-called Panama Papers; Costa Rica, subjected, however, to the dictates of gender ideology; and Belize, which is not Hispanic—escape, in part, this bleak Central American panorama.

In Cuba, the new president, who is not a member of the Castro family, persists in maintaining a dictatorship that is ineffective and totalitarian, and which, by the way, unlike all the others in Latin America, has failed to bring down the opposition in more than sixty years. Aware of where the wind of history is blowing, the Castroists have reformed the constitution to allow homosexual marriage, and Raul Castro's own daughter is the flag bearer for the LGTBI lobby.[2] The Cuban tyranny is very well aware that international public opinion, conveniently shaped by different organizations, does not tolerate opposition to the dictatorship of gender ideology, even if it is condescending toward the reality of political prisoners, torture, and the assassination of dissidents. Although it may seem surprising to many who remain trapped in the extinct dynamics of the Cold War, the truth is that the Castro approach to the globalist agenda has been an

2. https://www.dailymotion.com/video/x48unz3; https://www.elmundo.es/loc/2016/05/18/573b31c0268e3ed8638b463d.html.

indisputable reality since the 1990s and has a solid logic, which is that of a tyranny that seeks, fundamentally, to perpetuate itself.

In the Dominican Republic, steps continue to be taken towards unification with Haiti, a situation that would have dire consequences for Dominicans, but which, once again, is on the globalist agenda, as is the imposition of gender legislation over challenges such as educational backwardness.

In Venezuela, Juan Guaidó, as the author of these lines has pointed out from the beginning,[3] has failed miserably to displace the Bolivarian Maduro from power. While it is clear that Guaidó, a socialist and Freemason, has given in to the globalist agenda and there are disturbing signs of corruption in his administration,[4] it is a frightening spectacle that thousands of the more than four million Venezuelans who fled their country prefer to return home rather than face the bad conditions and even hostility they have found beyond their borders. To tell the truth, with increasing dollarization, Venezuela's economic situation improved slightly in 2019 and the regime ended the year strengthened.

In Colombia, instability has increased with a faction of the FARC deciding to rearm themselves and with an assault on power by left-wing forces surrendered to globalism that are fierce defenders of gender ideology.[5] As elsewhere, the Left has become the "useful fool" of the globalist agenda.

In Peru, in late 2019, a coup d'état was staged by the president to prevent the legislature, which has a conservative majority, from appointing members of the constitutional court, thus preventing the advancement of gender ideology. The next elections that were held were done in a dubious legal manner.[6]

3. https://www.youtube.com/watch?v=gGY2F2njq6I; https://www.youtube.com/watch?v=jQgY5vT3rvk; https://www.youtube.com/watch?v=-M0dI2WAvhg.

4. https://www.abc.es/internacional/abci-destitucion-embajador-guaido-colombia-agita-aguas-oposicion-maduro-201911300208_noticia.html.

5. https://www.vanitatis.elconfidencial.com/famosos/2019-12-17/claudia-lopez-alcaldesa-bogota-lesbiana-123_2302760/.

6. https://cesarvidal.com/la-voz/la-entrevista/entrevista-a-christian-rosas-golpe-de-estado-globalista-en-peru-04-10-19.

In Ecuador, the president's attempts to realign the battered economy have provoked a backlash because of indigenous people being exploited. As happened in Bolivia, and will probably happen in Peru or Guatemala, it is obvious that indigenous people will be used as a violent force in the conquest for power. Significantly, the first day of demonstrations left 35 people injured, including 21 police officers, and 277 detained.

In the Southern Cone, Chile is the object of a real coup d'état that we will describe in a few pages, while in Argentina, a deep institutional and economic crisis is looming after the return of a corrupt and ineffective Kirshnerism to power. As a measure of absolute submission to the globalist agenda, the new government rushed to guarantee, in a dubious legal way, the practice of abortion.[7]

In Paraguay, the country has already entered a recession, and the economic outlook looks difficult due to an unbearable public debt. An indigenous reaction cannot be ruled out either, despite the capitulation to the agenda of the Nairobi conference.

At the beginning of 2020, there are only three exceptions to this general trend—Brazil, Bolivia, Uruguay—the general trend of a cast of nations losing, piece by piece, their sovereignty and being subjected to the globalist agenda. The first is Brazil, where President Bolsonaro has achieved some economic and public order successes, but is the target of a savage media campaign against him for his opposition to gender ideology and the attempt to control his country from abroad. Both Macron[8] and Pope Francis[9] seem more than determined to deprive Brazil of its sovereignty in the Amazon in order to place this part of the world under international control. This is an immoral action, but very much in line with the globalist agenda.

7. https://elpais.com/sociedad/2019/12/13/actualidad/1576240534_342282.html.

8. https://cnnespanol.cnn.com/2019/08/22/nuestra-casa-esta-en-llamas-macron-se-une-a-la-protesta-por-los-incendios-del-amazonas-y-dice-que-el-g7-lo-discutira/;https://www.elmundo.es/ciencia-y-salud/ciencia/2019/08/23/5d5fffd5fdddff93b08b45bb.html.

9. https://www.religiondigital.org/luis_miguel_modino-_misionero_en_brasil/Oscar-Beozzo-Francisco-Sinodo-Iglesia_7_2156554326.html.

In Bolivia, the armed forces refused to keep Evo Morales in power after a new voting fraud. Evo Morales was forced to flee.[10] This fact has made it clear that, contrary to what many think, Cuba and Venezuela have little more strength than their bravado and have certainly not been able to keep Morales in power. Little by little, the drug-trafficking plot has come to light on which Morales relied, and even the way in which this plot has served to favor people linked to characters from the PSOE and Podemos, the two forces that form the current Spanish government. It is not without significance that José Luis Rodríguez Zapatero, the socialist president who promoted gender ideology in Spain, is one of the people who has come to light in the investigation of people financed by the narco-regime of Evo Morales. Rodríguez Zapatero refused to go to Bolivia to answer to the administration of justice, and as an argument for the refusal he gave, he said that he had seen the Bolivian government performing evangelical prayer rites. It is significant that, like others, Rodríguez Zapatero saw evangelicals as adversaries of leftist tyrannies and enemies of the globalist agenda that the Spanish socialist has so unquestioningly followed for decades.

In Uruguay, the center-right displaced from power a left-wing government that was unquestioningly submissive to the globalist agenda. Whether it will be able to deal with it or not is a question that will soon be seen.

In practically all the countries of Latin America there has been a fierce offensive to enforce the globalist agenda at any cost, especially in areas such as gender ideology, global warming, and uncontrolled immigration. As we have already seen, the Amazon Synod has organized, in this respect, a gigantic pagan ceremony to integrate elements such as the intervention of the Vatican, the action of the indigenous people, and the globalist agenda in joint projects.

Whichever way you look at it, the current situation in Latin America is truly disturbing. Appeals by some for the United States,

10. https://es.theepochtimes.com/crisis-en-bolivia-el-expresidente-evo-morales-huye-a-mexico_556594.html.

which are constantly being insulted, to intervene in different nations to change the situation and appeals by others to use indigenous people or any sector of the subsidized population to stay in power or overturn the government are not only pathetic but also highlight societies that, unfortunately, have not fully matured in political and social terms. Following the line taken by Spain itself, these nations, with their particular nuances and exceptions, have enormous difficulties in analyzing the roots of their failure, in recognizing their own responsibilities, and in not blaming others for the events that are the result of their own behavior. Thus, the Venezuelans blame the Cubans, the Cubans blame the Americans, the Argentines blame the English and the Yankees, the Mexicans blame the United States and the Central Americans, the Colombians blame the Venezuelans, and so a long chain is created that, if true, would force the conclusion that none of the countries are responsible for what is happening, but that it is someone else's fault.

The reality, of course, is quite different and has roots going back centuries. First of all, the Spanish conquest brought a Roman Catholic worldview that created, by means of the blood cleansing statute, a separation from indigenous people as well as the establishment of mestizo societies, but deeply racist societies where there is no work ethic; education and science have a very limited role, the supremacy of the law is unknown, and corruption is rampant; lies and theft are considered to be venial sins; an absurd welfare system is advocated, and politicians gain power to distribute it among their own people as Cortés, Pizarro, or Almagro did in the past.[11] To top it all off, the mental schemes of the Roman Catholic Church, the one and true Church, outside of which there is no salvation, have created psychological patterns in which dialogue, agreement, and simply listening to another takes place, where everything has to be imposed dogmatically, resorting to violence if necessary. This model with its terrible consequences was perpetuated, with few variations, by the

11. For an analysis of all these aspects, see C. Vidal, El legado de la Reforma (Tyler, 2016), pp. 257-345.

emancipators, in many cases, brave and brilliant characters—as the Spanish conquerors had been—but absolutely incapable of creating democratic societies as the Protestants did in the north of the continent. To make matters worse, in many cases, these emancipators began in Freemasonry, another entity not characterized by transparency or democratic character but by an elitist worldview of social control exercised from the shadows.

At the end of the day, Latin America—like Spain—suffers from secular ills that it refuses to address, that it blames others for, and that periodically subjects the various nations to a succession of painful and not infrequently bloody crises. When disaster strikes, it is enough to blame others or to shout "black legend" (biased propaganda), which changes absolutely nothing. And so it will continue as long as Latin America continues to travel the tortuous roads into which it was introduced more than five centuries ago. The proof of the veracity of what we say can be seen in the persistence of certain historical icons or in the fragility of the apparently more stable nations like Chile. The following pages are dedicated to these aspects.

The Permanent Irrationality of the Che Cult

It was 1967, and more specifically on Sunday, October 8, when Félix Ismael Rodríguez, a Cuban exile who served in the CIA and was stationed in Bolivia, received the news that a guerrilla fighter had been captured in the La Higuera area. The next day, after informing his superiors in Langley, Virginia, Rodriguez went to meet the most famous guerrilla fighter of the moment, the Argentinian Ernesto "Che" Guevara. The CIA wanted to keep him alive and proceed to interrogate him, but the Bolivian authorities had made the decision to execute him. The death of Che took place in this way, together with the dubious fate of his body, about which there is no less controversy than that caused by the remains of Christopher Columbus.

To die young is a tragic circumstance, but history rewards it on many occasions with the halo of martyrdom and even the veil of innocence. For fifty years, Ernesto Guevara has been immortalized as a point of reference for the Left on T-shirts, mugs, and books. Che has even been compared to Jesus of Nazareth, also supposedly revolutionary, young, and executed by the empire. The truth is that the historical reality of Guevara is not so positive or flattering.

His fellow guerrilla fighters called him Che because of his Argentinian origin, but also the Pig because of his lack of interest in personal hygiene. His adversaries did not hesitate to call him the Jackal because of the pleasure he felt—recognized by Guevara himself—when executing his enemies. It was logical, because as he himself would say on December 11, 1964, before the United Nations General Assembly: "We must say here something that is a well-known truth and that we have always asserted before the whole world: executions? Yes, we have executed people; we are executing people and shall continue to execute people as long as it is necessary. We know what the result of a losing battle would be and the worms also have to know what the result of the lost battle is today in Cuba...".

However, nothing initially foreshadowed such a bloodthirsty course. Born into an upper-middle class family, sick with asthma and an undergraduate student of medicine, from a very young age he was possessed by an adventurous streak that led him to tour a part of Latin America on a motorcycle. From that chapter of his life would emerge a bad book and an acceptable film,[12] but, above all, legends like those of the Indians who still claim that decades ago a young Guevara cured them at Machu Pichu. In Peru, Ernesto Guevara met the Trostkyst Hilda Gadea who, older than him, indoctrinated him in the most radical Marxism and gave him a daughter. Guevara would point out that he only had sexual relations with her because "my asthma was very serious..." and then he would say "it's too bad she's so ugly."

12. We refer, of course, to *Diarios de motocicleta*.

The next milestone in his life would be Guatemala, where he supported the reformist Arbenz, whose greatest misfortune was to damage the business of a multinational business whose lawyer was the brother of the CIA director. Whether Arbenz was a Marxist will be debated further—there are reasons to doubt it[13]—but Guevara was already committed at that point to the violent spread of communism. It must also be said, with an air of moral superiority, which is typical of the communist nomenlatura, that, in his case, he did not hesitate to spew out a flood of scandalous racism. Regarding the indigenous people, he would write that they were a "stinking and lousy flock" that "gave off a powerful but warm stench." Nor would he hold back when it came to claiming that Bolivian peasants were "like little animals." Of the blacks, he would not hesitate to point out that they were "magnificent specimens of the African race that have maintained their racial purity thanks to their lack of interest in bathing," an assertion that was at least striking coming from the fact that he was almost allergic to bathing.

While taking refuge in Mexico after the fall of Arbenz, Guevara met the Cuban Fidel Castro there and joined the July 26th Movement. By that time, some of his comrades had already begun to look at him with displeasure given his blatant racism. On December 2, 1956, the group of revolutionaries landed on Las Coloradas beach, in the south of Oriente province, near Sierra Maestra. The operation was a complete disaster, but Castro and a small group managed to survive and escape into the mountains. His total submission to Castro resulted in Guevara—who constantly suffered from asthma attacks—being appointed commander over other guerrilla fighters with more merits than him.

At that time, Guevara formed a team with the future Cuban dictator who, among other purposes, sought to remove from relevant positions other insurgents whose inspiration was much more democratic. A black darkness characterized those times when Frank País

13. We have addressed the issue in *El águila y el quetzal* (México, 2016).

was betrayed for following Fidel Castro's instructions[14]—which led to his death—or the revolutionaries from Santiago who ended up having to integrate with Castro's Sierra Maestra guerrillas. Guevara made no secret of the fact that he patterned his revolutionary model from the countries of Eastern Europe, which he called the Iron Curtain, following an expression very typical of Latin America. As he would say in December 1957 to René Ramos Latour, the national coordinator of the July 26th Movement: "Because of my ideological background, I belong to those who believe that the solution to the world's problems lies behind the so-called Iron Curtain." René Ramos Latour's response was that he saw no point in ridding himself "of harmful U.S. domination through no less harmful Soviet domination."

By the time the guerrillas were about to begin their invasion of the western Cuban provinces, military command was in the hands of Guevara and Camilo Cienfuegos. It is significant that, instead of what is supported by myth, Che managed to advance by clever means of bribing corrupt leaders of Batista's forces, such as Colonel Dueñas. By this time, Guevara's totalitarian reputation had preceded him. Thus, when they arrived at the province of Las Villas, the anti-Batista guerrillas refused to recognize his command, and the same thing happened with the Second National Front of El Escambray. Even the famous episode of the capture of the armored train, which has been told so many times, is only a myth, since the merit of the action did not correspond to Guevara, but to the men of the Revolutionary Directorate.

Batista's escape and Fidel Castro's seizure of power gave Guevara an immense capacity for repression, which he took advantage of to the hilt. Appointed military chief of the La Cabaña Fortress, Guevara personally assassinated Lieutenant Castaño, Chief of the BRAC (Repressive Bureau of Communist Activities) in his office and ordered hundreds of documented deaths. The cold blood with which he carried out the crimes only finds parallels between the most bloodthirsty

14. https://www.elnuevoherald.com/noticias/sur-de-la-florida/article69769897.html; https://cubahoracero.wordpress.com/2015/07/30/el-doble-asesinato-de-frank-pais/.

Che followers in the Soviet Union or the Spanish Civil War and the commanders of the Nazi death camps.

It is not surprising, however, that such conduct flowed directly from Che's worldview. As José Vilasuso, who belonged to the organization in charge of the judicial processes in La Cabaña, would relate, Che's instructions had been: "Do not delay the causes, this is a revolution, do not use bourgeois legal methods; the world is changing, the evidence is secondary. We must proceed by conviction. We know why we are here. These are a gang of criminals, murderers, henchmen... I would line them all up on the wall and execute them with fifty ratatatat..."

In the following years, Guevara would serve as president of the National Bank of Cuba and as the Minister of Industries. However, his popularity stemmed from a propaganda that presented him as the "new man" of Cuban communism and his own claims in which he boasted that he would continue to execute mercilessly indefinitely, and that his intention was to create many Vietnams to destroy the United States. He would even travel through Spain repeating his fiery speeches—where a department store had to be opened on a holiday for him to pontificate in front of the cashiers.

Che did not hide how far he would have been willing to go had he been able to do so. In an interview granted to Sam Russell, from the *London Daily Worker*, collected by *Time* magazine on December 21, 1962, Che stated in regards to the missile crisis: "If the missiles had remained in Cuba, we would have used them against the very heart of the United States, including New York City." This was not just an idle boast. In 1968, in *Tactics and Strategy of the Cuban Revolution*, published in *Verde Olivo*, he stated: "The peaceful path is eliminated and violence is inevitable. In order to achieve socialist regimes, rivers of blood will have to flow, and the path to liberation must go on, even if it is at the cost of millions of atomic victims." Fortunately, the Soviet leaders—who regarded Castro and Guevara as madmen if not fools—were not prepared to follow this tactic.[15]

15. César Reynel Aguilera, El sóviet caribeño. *La otra Historia de la revolución cubana* (Columbia, 2018), pp. 318ff.

Guevara was never a military genius and did not even reach the level of discreet tactician. No matter how much he wrote a book on guerrilla warfare, he put his scandalous incompetence on record time after time. Far from being the stubborn, Lawrence of Arabia or Chapayev, he was no more than an unscrupulous communist, chauvinist, and racist fanatic when it came to shedding blood. It is not surprising that he failed in the Congo in his attempt to prop up a leftist dictatorship, and that the same thing happened in Bolivia.

It will be long disputed whether the Bolivian expedition was Fidel Castro's idea to get rid of Che's proximity. It is not easy to know. What is obvious is the society he intended to set up because he spoke about it repeatedly. In that new society, there would be no freedom of expression because, as he said, "You have to put an end to all newspapers, because you cannot have a revolution with freedom of the press. Newspapers are instruments of the oligarchy." In this new society, the workers would not enjoy labor rights either, since, as he indicated on television on June 26, 1961, when he was Minister of Industries, "Cuban workers have to get used to living in a regime of collectivism and in no way can they go on strike." In that new society, not even the leaders could feel safe from the dictatorship. As he would affirm in a letter published in March 1965 in the Uruguayan weekly *Marcha*: "To build communism, simultaneously with the material base, it is necessary to create a new man (...) It is the dictatorship of the proletariat exercising itself not only over the defeated class, but also individually, over the victorious class."

At this point the countries that he called the Iron Curtain viewed him with growing skepticism. It is often said that it was because of his pro-Chinese wanderings. In reality, it was more due to the fact that as a propaganda trick, he could hold a certain interest, but in any other respect he was a total and complete nullity. The idea of trying to spread the revolution in Bolivia was not as far-fetched as has often been insisted. In fact, Bolivia could be a good base for injecting subversion into almost half a dozen nations. A separate question is what Che gave of himself as a soldier, which was close to nothing. He did not have a large army to lead, but the arrest of his friend, fellow traveler Regis Debray, was enough to make his entire strategy, if it can be called that, fall apart. As a high military official would say, it was decided to execute him in the belief that "this will teach them that they cannot come to Bolivia to screw around."[16]

This is how the bloodthirsty communist died and the legend was reaffirmed. The most terrible thing is that this legend, woven with threads of romanticism, social justice, and the desire of the people for liberation, hardly corresponds to historical reality. A few months before his death, in an article published on April 16, 1967, in a special supplement of the *Tricontinental* magazine, Che literally stated: "Hatred is an element of struggle, intransigent hatred of the enemy, which drives him beyond the natural limitations of a human being and turns him into an effective, violent, selective, and cold killing machine. Our soldiers have to be like that; a people without hate cannot triumph over a brutal enemy (...) We have to take the war as far as the enemy takes it: to his home, to his places of entertainment; make it total."

This was a total declaration of principles not only in favor of war, but also of terrorism coming from a terrible guerrilla who would die in Bolivia. Very possibly, his death prevented untold evils to the human race, but only the knowledge of the historical reality can prevent the continued honoring of a person who was characterized by contempt towards other races, a rude disdain towards women, the longing to impose a dictatorship without recognition of individual rights, hatred as the driving force of politics, the bloodthirsty use of violence, and even the lack of personal hygiene. It is truly shocking to think that his image—which today can only be explained by evil, ignorance, or stupidity—appears in public demonstrations taking place in Western Europe or the United States and is paraded mainly by foreigners, who are often illegal, and by young people. This is because such a model can only lead to hatred, misery, and violence. The truth is, however,

16. Personal conversation of the author with Carlos Sánchez Berzaín.

that the Soviet Union disappeared decades ago; that China, another communist dictatorship, has no intention of exporting its model, which it considers to be totally unexportable; and that if certain left-wing dictatorships are perpetuated, it is essentially due to transnational interests that do not understand democracy or dictatorship but rather domination and profit. Venezuela is one such case.

The Survival of the Dictatorship in Venezuela

In 1917, the Bolsheviks staged a coup d'état in Russia that would lead to the creation of the first totalitarian State in history. Practically all the governments on the planet refused to recognize the communist dictatorship that had taken over Russia, not only because it had murdered Tsar Nicholas II and his family, but also because it constituted a real danger for the extension of the revolution and, in fact, had tried to do so with a few days of success in Germany and Hungary. However, despite the international repudiation, numerous companies, especially from the United States and Great Britain, traded with the Bolsheviks and gave them substantial economic loans. In this apparently unnatural alliance between communism and capitalism, one circumstance weighed heavily: the possibility of taking over Russia's mineral wealth.[17] A good part of the hardest and most combative sectors of European and American capitalism amassed great fortunes with the wealth of Russia and, at the same time, saved the communist regime that had raised the flag for the end of capitalism. Such actions could be described as serious mistakes, but in reality they were nothing more than measures taken to ensure control of essential raw materials regardless of the government's ideology. To tell the truth, a leftist dictatorship was much easier to exploit than a democratic system that seeks to defend national interests. The combination of government control of the economy with absolute political power provides an

17. Regarding this subject, see: A. C. Sutton, *Wall Street and the Bolshevik Revolution* (Forest Row, 2011). Especially, pp. 154ff. and 169ff.

excellent channel for plundering national wealth. This model, although hidden, is what explains the survival of Chavism in Venezuela.

The figure of Hugo Rafael Chávez Frías (1954-2013) is one of the most controversial in recent Latin American history.[18] A career military man, Chavez was one of millions of Venezuelans disenchanted with the national political system. It is impossible to deny that such a system led to enormous economic advances in the decades prior to Chávez's arrival in power, and that it was also brimming with scandalous corruption. It was this corruption of a system turned into pure demagogy where politics were reduced to flattering the people, to use the Greek term, for the benefit of oligarchies that, in the end, lifted Chávez to power. In fact, his march to the presidency was long and bumpy. In 1980, he founded the clandestine Revolutionary Bolivarian Movement-200 (MBR-200), but his real leap into politics took place in 1992 when he led the MBR-200 in a failed coup against the Social Democratic Action government of President Carlos Andrés Pérez, which was frighteningly corrupt. The coup failed and Chavez was jailed, but two years later he was released after President Rafael Caldera was dismissed and founded the political party The Fifth Republic Movement.

In 1998, Chavez came to power not because of Cuba's intervention—as is repeatedly and interestingly stated—but through the ballot box and based on the desire of most Venezuelans to see political change. At this point, as much as one would like to deny it, Chávez was extraordinarily popular, a popularity he took advantage of to follow a model of State decentralization, which was typical of Mussolini's fascism but not the Soviet or Cuban models. That model can be seen in the way he achieved without particular difficulty the approval of the 1999 Constitution and triggered the so-called "Bolivarian Revolution," which, despite being described as a socialist revolution, came closer to the fascist model of the 1920s and 1930s of the twentieth century. Taking advantage of record oil revenues during

18. Regarding Hugo Chávez, see: *A. Barrera Tyszka and C. Marcano, Hugo Chávez sin uniforme* (México, 2007) and especially, M. Collon, *Los 7 pecados de Hugo Chávez* (Barcelona, 2014).

the first decade of the twenty-first century, Chavez created a huge clientele favored by subsidies and by entities such as the Bolivarian Missions and shepherded by State propaganda. This very expensive policy of subsidies impoverished members of the middle classes, but it improved the situation of many of the lower classes from 2003 to 2007. It also opened the door to the emergence of billionaires from the corruption of the regime. It is really no surprise that he won the elections again in 2002. Even a coup d'état unleashed against him that same year ended in resounding failure. Following the 2004 presidential referendum, Chavez was reelected in the 2006 elections, where he won more than 60% of the vote, and he revalidated his success in the October 2012 elections. By that time, the dictatorship had become an almost perfect mechanism because, in order to stay in power, he did not have to suppress the electoral mechanism, the press, or the opposing parties, so he could claim that democracy was still standing and even deepening. Again, the differences with the Soviet or Cuban model were evident.

In his political success, not only did Venezuelan wealth weigh in, especially oil, which allowed him to obtain the grateful vote of millions of subsidized people, but also a message that he called anti-imperialist, with which he sought to avoid the influence of the United States in Latin America and through which he drew up a clear alliance, more or less solid, with governments such as those controlled by the Castros in Cuba; Evo Morales in Bolivia; Rafael Correa in Ecuador; Tabaré Vázquez and Pepe Mujica in Uruguay; Lula da Silva in Brazil; Nestor Kirchner and Cristina Fernández in Argentina; and Daniel Ortega in Nicaragua. Far from being a puppet of Cuba—whose dictatorship he helped economically in a more than relevant way—the truth is that Chavez developed his own initiatives, such as the creation of the Union of South American Nations (UNASUR), the Community of Latin American and Caribbean States, the Bolivarian Alliance for the Peoples of Our America, the Bank of the South, and the regional television network TeleSUR, all initiatives that had never been carried out by Fidel Castro. For the Left, not only of Latin Americans, but a good part of the European Left as well, Chavez was not only not a dictator, but a model of how to come to power through elections and then create the mechanisms with sufficient clientele to remain in power indefinitely. It is not surprising that he had a very close relationship with the Spanish Prime Minister, the Socialist José Luis Rodríguez Zapatero,[19] nor that he financially helped Podemos, a Spanish communist party,[20] which was currently in power.

However, as with all clientelist systems, Chavism went into crisis. At the end of Chávez's presidency, corruption and uncontrollable spending to maintain welfare policies logically led to poverty, inflation, and increased crime, especially violent crime. The collapse of Chavismo ran parallel to that of Chávez's own health, who, suffering from cancer, in 2011, died on March 5, 2013, at the age of fifty-eight.

Chávez's death aroused optimism in the opposition, which thought it could dislodge Chavism from power. On the other hand, his successor, Nicolás Maduro, did not seem to have sufficient charisma or intelligence to stay in power. The truth, however, is that the errors of the opposition decisively contributed to the preservation of Chavism. His determination to identify Chavism with Castroism (a huge mistake, since it was a much more sophisticated system than the Cuban one); in copying the strategy of the Cuban opposition (the only dictatorship that has not come to an end in all of Spanish America); from forming other entities due to Personalism; to not seeing the roots of Chávez's triumph; and in ignoring what happened in Venezuela has nothing to do with the Cold War, but rather with a changing world, have all had fatal results. The spectacular failure of Juan Guaidó, an interim president with claims of replacing Nicolás Maduro, has been only one of its consequences, but, quite possibly, more serious is that he did not know how to take advantage of the immense blow to the Venezuelan economy and the survival of Chavism that the pact between President Obama and the King of Saudi Arabia to lower the price of oil in

19. https://www.elmundo.es/internacional/2018/09/16/5b9e3d83468aeb66618b4679.html.

20. https://www.elconfidencial.com/espana/2016-01-14/la-dea-de-eeuu-revela-que-venezuela-e-iran-pactaron-financiar-a-podemos-con-hispantv_1135373/; https://es.panampost.com/sabrina-martin/2019/12/19/pablo-iglesias-dinero-venezuela/.

2015 meant. Since more than 90% of Venezuela's exports were then reduced to crude oil, the impact would have been colossal in a nation with a competent and honest administration. Directed against an incompetent and corrupt government, the consequences were horrific. However, Maduro, the successor to Chávez, knew how to react in a way that went unnoticed by most of the media, determined to continue analyzing the international situation from the obsolete perspective of the Cold War.

Faced with a scenario in which the price of crude oil had dropped by 22%, in 2016, Maduro decided to activate the Orinoco Mining Arc (AMO), as a National Strategic Development Zone. This territory is an area extraordinarily rich in mineral resources that began to be exploited in 2017. Among its reserves are raw materials such as gold, copper, diamonds, coltan, iron, and bauxite. In fact, it doubles the size of the Orinoco Oil Belt.

That same year, the head of the Central Bank of Venezuela (BCV), Nelson Merentes, said that in one month they hoped to establish the joint ventures signed with Canadian, American, and German companies. Among those companies was the Canadian Gold Reserve, whose investments in Venezuela were confiscated by President Hugo Chávez, but which from then on would once again enjoy licenses from the Chávez government.

In August 2016, in the "Gastón Parra Luzardo" hall of the BCV, Maduro greeted what he called "friends of the world" who were businessmen and ambassadors from Canada, China, the United States, Germany, South Africa, and India, among other countries, mostly with democratic governments. He then went on to outline how the project would be developed. In November 2016, four agreements were signed with transnational companies, specifically with the following companies: China Camc Engineering Co. Ltd.; Yakuang Group from China; Afridiam from the Republic of Congo; and the Canadian Gold Reserve for the exploitation of the Orinoco Mining Arc. Over time, nearly forty nations have been represented in these agreements, most of which have democratic governments.

In addition to these licenses to foreign companies, there are also those concentrated in the Orinoco Belt where four joint ventures between PDVSA and international oil companies currently operate: Petrocedeño, where Total from France and Statoil from Norway participate; Petropiar (Chevron from the United States), Petromonagas (Rosneft) and Sinovensa with the CPCH. Petrocedeño, Petropiar, Petromonagas, and Sinovensa produce 200,000, 250,000, 160,000, and 140,000 barrels per day of heavy crude oil, respectively, which is processed in upgrading plants to make it light, a crude oil whose price is high in international markets.

In a very significant way and in spite of President Trumps' anti-Chávez policy, the North American company Chevron is the transnational oil company with the most business in Venezuela, because in addition to the Belt, where it is the company that extracts the most crude oil, it produces 30,000 and 15,000 barrels per day of heavy oil and natural gas in the Boscán (Zulia) and Quiriquire (Monagas) fields.

The Orinoco Belt is the only oil area in the country that has increased its production due to the activity of combined companies, which currently pump between 1.2 million and 1.5 million barrels a day. The prosperity of the Belt contrasts with the collapse of the Venezuelan production system. In fact, the Spanish Socialist Rodríguez Zapatero was accused of having a license in the coastal Belt for some Spanish businessmen whose last name was Cortina.[21] If that were the case, Rodríguez Zapatero would not be a "imbecile," as Almagro,[22] the secretary general of the OAS, called him. Rather, he would be someone much worse.

The press and the Venezuelan opposition may claim that Russia and China are maintaining Chavism. That is not the case. Undeniably, if anyone has kept Maduro's regime afloat since 2016 during the large demonstrations against it, it has been the action of large transnationals with the United States and China at the head.

21. https://www.elmundo.es/internacional/2018/10/16/5bc52a0a46163f4b1f8b45c7.html.

22. https://www.abc.es/internacional/abci-almagro-aconseja-zapatero-no-imbecil-hablar-sobre-venezuela-201809221234_noticia.html; https://www.youtube.com/watch?v=wEiKm7-7ne4.

If Chavism has begun to deteriorate, it is due to the artificial drop in the price of oil provoked by Obama in alliance with the King of Saudi Arabia. If Maduro, in spite of everything, including the collapse of the Chavista clientelist system, has remained in power, it has been thanks to having kept in his control the system of repression and the sale of Venezuela's natural resources in the hands of companies from mostly democratic nations. The fact that the condemnation of Maduro by dozens of nations has not had devastating consequences for the Chavista regime depends fundamentally on the fact that the multinational companies—which we insist come from mostly democratic nations—continue to pay. For the future, there are numerous indications that either Venezuela will continue to be subjected to a ruthless Chavista dictatorship, or the socialists, of which Guaidó is part of in coalition with the anti-Maduro Chavistas, will gain power and, predictably, implement the globalist agenda of government that will include gender ideology. In either case, Venezuela's wealth will be exploited by supranational entities, and it fearful that it will not be for the benefit of the majority of Venezuelans. After all, we live in a changing world that is no longer what it used to be, but is close to the one that a small minority designed a few decades ago. In Latin America, Chavista Venezuela has not escaped from this interventionism eager to turn nations into submissive protectorates, but neither has the country that was considered by many as an oasis: Chile.

The End of the Chilean Oasis

In 2015, Chile's Energy Minister, Socialist Máximo Pacheco, met with George Soros[23] in New York. A friend for several decades, George Soros was helping Pacheco to get investors, and Pacheco paid tribute to him as the man who had helped not only him but also his father, a former minister and diplomat of the Christian Democratic Party.

23. http://www.economiaynegocios.cl/noticias/noticias.asp?id=186894; https://www.elmostrador.cl/noticias/pais/2016/11/28/george-soros-la-conexion-de-lagos-y-hillary-con-wall-street/.

Pacheco—who addressed Soros several times as Dear George—pointed out how the magnate had played a key role in the Chilean plebiscite of October 5, 1988. Pacheco also stated that Soros had been essential in achieving international support for the socialist Ricardo Lagos in the course of the 2000 elections. This was undoubtedly a remarkable fact, but it far from revealed all of Soros' interference in the Spanish-American country.

Thus, in 2017, the DCLeaks made it clear that Giorgio Jackson, one of the leaders of the Frente Amplio, had received money from Soros when he led the Democratic Revolution (RED), a political party born out of student mobilizations in Chile that has been integrated into the Frente Amplio (Broad Front). Giorgio Jackson has acknowledged that he received a sum of 12 million pesos, but the real figure would have been close to 50 million.[24] According to this document, the 50 million pesos given by Soros would have been provided in three stages. The first phase, from August 1, 2012 to August 1, 2013, was characterized by financing an activist strategy among students in the amount of $24,990. The second phase, from November 1, 2013 to April 1, 2014, would have financed student activism again, seeking to establish a new education system in the amount of $24,990. Finally, the third phase, from November 1, 2014 to December 1, 2015, also in the amount of $24,900, would have insisted on a reform for Chilean education and the consolidation of the RED political party. The sum of the donations is $74,790, which is the equivalent of $49,266,416 pesos, and involved the financing of leftist activism among the students. In fact, that funding has involved Soros' direct intervention in Chilean student settings from 2012 to 2015. Not everything came down to funding. Thus, in February 2014, in line with this line of action, Giorgio Jackson was interviewed by one of Soros' Open Society publications regarding education and the student movement.

If, on the one hand, Soros was clearly involved with the Left; on the other, Pope Francis, the second great icon of the globalist agenda,

24. https://elminuto.cl/george-soros-de-filantropo-a-terrorista-domestico/.

did not feel any sympathy for the Chilean Right either. In January 2018, Pope Francis visited Chile. The papal visit was a scandalous failure related to the Karadima case of sexual abuse by Roman Catholic clergy. In fact, the trip was described as the worst visit of the pope.[25] In October 2018, President Piñera visited Pope Francis. Various sources suggest that the pontiff did not hide his displeasure with the Chilean president as he had previously done with Argentine President Macri.[26]

In October 2019, Soros announced in an interview broadcast by France Press, among other media, that the wave was again moving in favor of "globalists" like him and that this process would be undeniable in 2020.[27] Soros' statements came after Chile failed to support the UN's Global Compact for Migration, a decision made by President Sebastian Piñera that was in direct contradiction to the open-door policy on immigration promoted in different forums by George Soros.

From that moment on, one of the objectives of the globalist agenda was a constitutional change that would pave the way for its objectives. In the case of Chile, the aim was to empty the executive branch of its powers in relation to international treaties by handing them over to the legislature, where it would be easier for them to count on the complicity of politicians subject to their directives. Significantly, the Democratic Revolution Party presented a bill to this effect at the end of 2018, which was supported by different legislators from different parties, including some from Renovación Nacional (National Renewal), one of the parties that are part of the electoral coalition supporting the current President Piñera. The bill included the reform of article 54 of the Chilean Constitution in this sense.

In the midst of this tension between President Piñera's action and the objectives of the globalist agenda on immigration, on October 18, 2019, the increase in subway fares took place in Chile. The issue had been previously studied by experts and, in objective terms, it should

25. https://www.france24.com/es/20180121-conclusiones-visita-papa-francisco-chile; https://www.clarin.com/mundo/gira-chile-papa-convierte-peor-anos-pontificado_0_Hy0QNT0EM.html.

26. https://diariocorreo.pe/politica/papa-francisco-hace-desaire-ante-el-saludo-de-sebastian-pinera-798195/; https://www.latercera.com/voces/la-frialdad-papal-pinera/.

27. https://www.servimat.info/2019/11/george-soros-advierte-rebelion-global.html.

be noted that it was moderate. However, despite this circumstance, there was an immediate outbreak of violence, mainly by students, who not only destroyed, first, subway stations, but immediately resulted in riots and even deaths.

In response to the situation, the government decreed a state of emergency and a curfew with restrictions on movement and meetings at certain times. While trying to restore order, the executive branch announced measures to try to calm the situation, which were also carried out in different regions. Overwhelmed even by the violent explosion in which young students played a more than prominent role, President Piñera apologized and even opened the way for constitutional reform. This was precisely what a group of deputies had been aiming for for a year and what would pave the way for George Soros' globalist plans.

At the same time, during the riots, churches, mostly evangelical, were attacked and burned down, gay exhibits were held where demonstrators put a dildo in their anus next to anti-Christian posters, and violence broke out at the university. In a highly revealing way, the apostolic administrator of Santiago de Chile, Celestino Aós, publicly stated that "there is no doubt that we must change the Constitution"[28] and called for churches to be opened for use by incumbents of the Church. In other words, the Roman Catholic Church was joining in the goals of a subversion that sought to end the constitutional order and open the way to surrender to the globalist agenda. After a few days of unrest, the revolt in Chile numbered more than 4,000 arrested; 1,600 civilians injured; 1,000 law enforcement officials wounded; several dead; and an approximate cost of 12.6 billion pesos (about $16 million dollars) for damage to the public infrastructure in the Metropolitan region alone. All this while there was not the slightest indication that the nation would calm down in the coming days.

In objective terms, nothing justifies the situation of unleashed violence that Chile began to suffer at the end of 2019. In fact, when the

28. https://www.latercera.com/nacional/noticia/celestino-aos-indudable-cambiar-la-constitucion/892559/.

subversion broke out, Chile had the highest GDP per capita, the highest social mobility, the best education, the lowest levels of poverty, and the third best human development index in the region. Even in terms of inequality, Chile's situation was among the best. Measured by the Gini coefficient, inequality in Chile was 0.45 compared to a Latin American average of 0.47. In fact, of the 18 countries in the region, Chile was ranked eleventh in terms of inequality. If that index is broken down by age, inequality is even lower in all generations born after 1970. Finally, the percentage of citizens whose income is less than 50% of the average wage was also the lowest in all of Latin America: 14.1% as opposed to 18.8% for the region as a whole. With these facts, it is not surprising that any analyst, at the end of 2019, thought that Chile deserved to be called an oasis in the midst of the instability suffered by Latin America.

In fact, after decades, Chile's macroeconomic and social categories only began to decline during the government of socialist Michelle Bachelet from 2014 to 2018, when Sebastián Piñera came to power. The process had, however, been normal. Socialist Bachelet's legislative initiatives on tax and labor issues had led to a decrease in growth of 1.7%, and Chileans had voted for an alternative in the center-right. The measures taken by Piñera to counteract that situation had optimal and immediate results. In fact, Chile closed 2018 with a 4% increase in GDP compared to 1.5% in 2017, the highest in the last six years. It must be recognized that there was no reason to think about a social outburst. And suddenly, everything exploded, everything was in question, everything pointed to a worsening of the social and political situation. How could this whole process have happened?

Those who have not yet learned that the Cold War ended no less than thirty years ago tried to fit a totally different reality into those parameters. This was a huge mistake. The world is no longer divided into the Western bloc and the democratic bloc. Today's world is changing and is increasingly divided between globalists and patriots, and while the latter are only gradually waking up, the former continue to use all means to advance their agenda, an agenda that involves emptying nations of their substance by subjecting them to the designs of an international elite, promoting gender ideology as a way of doing away with the institution of the family, and eliminating any opposition that Christianity might pose to this new scale of values.

The examples in the area had been very clear in the weeks before. In Peru, the president had staged a coup d'état to prevent the legislature from appointing a constitutional court that could block the globalist agenda and pushed for a new constitution that would include NGOs, such as those led by George Soros. In Ecuador, social unrest erupted for a cause as debatable as in Chile, but tellingly after the legislature prevented the legalization of abortion. In Chile, the explosion occurred after Pope Francis, one of the biggest promoters of the globalist agenda, expressed his discontent with the election of Piñera and, above all, after the Chilean president refused to join the UN migration pact that has been so warmly defended by George Soros and Pope Francis. As on so many occasions and in ways that are hard to believe happened by chance, the spark ignited in environments that had been influenced for years by Soros' economic aid, in this case, those directed at the student sector.

President Piñera himself accepted the thesis of a new constitution, and after a few days, the political parties drafted a pact in this regard. Does this mean that Chile will be free of the problems caused by subversion? It is doubtful. In fact, quite significantly, according to a recent survey—carried out by "Chilecracy"—the idea of a new constitution ranks ninety-ninth among Chileans' concerns.[29] Indeed, Chileans are far more concerned about issues such as employment, health, education, citizen insecurity, and immigration. But the new Chilean constitution does not respond to the popular will or to a democratic impulse. In fact, there are ample indications that the basis for the new constitution will not come from Chileans but from foreign guidelines.

In that regard, it should be remembered that the program of the socialist Bachelet to which the Piñera government had already

29. https://www.youtube.com/watch?v=9cRJ0DWOCwo.

indicated that it would adopt was based on the work of ecclesiastical councils carried out during Bachelet's own term. These meetings lacked any democratic legitimacy because only a small number of Chileans participated in them and, moreover, not even their proposals were the ones finally accepted. In fact, the process of including specific aspects in Chile's new constitution was carried out by the UN. At present, there is one person in charge of supervising Chile from the UN, and that is Silvia Rucks.[30] This UN supervision is so clear that Chile's ministries are subject to the supervision of around twenty UN agencies.

Thus, the United Nations Program for Sustainable Development (UNDP) provided the keys for the new constitution. In this way, the UN Committee on Economic, Social and Cultural Rights asked Chile to guarantee economic, social, and cultural rights in the new constitution, emphasizing that there are profound levels of inequality in Chile. The way in which this was done fit in completely with the globalist agenda. The political discourse focused on the fight against inequality, a cause driven by the globalist agenda and the Left, as well as gender laws. Silvia Rucks has insisted on going down that road now, or it will take two hundred years to attain equality.[31] In an interview, she even pointed out that the most urgent issues are the approval of gender violence laws, a quota law in the private sector, and the revision of all curricula to incorporate equality and inclusion. In addition, there is a general push for abortion, since the new constitution will no longer protect unborn children.

Contrary to those who have insisted on seeing the involvement of Cuba and Venezuela—two nations that have been unable to keep the Bolivian Evo Morales in power—behind the Chilean crisis, the reality is that there are abundant indications to confirm that what the Spanish American nation is suffering, which in another time had been prosperous and calm, is, essentially, a coup d'état that intends to convert Chile into a simple protectorate of the globalist programs.

30. https://www.youtube.com/watch?v=VHmQ0XMtg6g.

31. https://www.latercera.com/nacional/noticia/silvia-rucks-coordinadora-onu-chile-no-se-realizan-nuevas-acciones-requerir-200-anos-llegar-la-equidad/560049/.

Unfortunately, everything seems to indicate that neither freedom or prosperity or equality will emerge from the new Chilean constitution unless such equality is understood as equality in misery. What will emerge, predictably, will become a slave nation subject to the guidelines of the globalist agenda on issues such as abortion, gender ideology, education, or gay marriage. To top it all off, its economy will become an economy lacking freedom that will be subject to bureaucrats who will never bring wealth, as they have not done anywhere in the world. Like it or not, Chile is at serious risk of becoming a protectorate at the service of a globalist agenda.

Colombia, Subversion Predicted

Hardly a few weeks since the beginning of the subversion in Chile, the writer of these lines predicted that another subversive process was going to be unleashed in Colombia in the streets as well in service to the globalist agency and with the Left acting as a "useful fool."[32] There were plenty of reasons to predict everything.

At the beginning of this century, Colombian President Alvaro Uribe launched his Democratic Security policy to fight, once and for all, the guerrillas and the Peasant Self-Defense Forces or paramilitaries. Previously, the government of Andrés Pastrana had failed in the Caguán talks, which, by handing over territory to the narco-terrorist group known as the FARC, allowed the latter to extend its military power in many areas of the country. Uribe's policy expelled the narco-terrorists from areas they previously controlled, wiped out their main leaders (Raúl Reyes, Mono Jojoy, Alfonso Cano), and decimated the FARC, who realized that they would not be able to gain power through armed violence. It is possible that Uribe believed that the narco-terrorist group would eventually give up its weapons in exchange for only eight years in prison for the crimes committed. He also seems to

32. https://cesarvidal.com/la-voz/editorial/editorial-colombia-hacia-el-golpe-de-estado-esta-semana-18-11-19.

have been convinced that this goal would be achieved not by him, but by Juan Manuel Santos, his defense minister, who, by the way, managed to win the 2010 presidential elections thanks to Uribe's support. That was not the case.

Contrary to expectations, President Santos distanced himself from Uribe's policies from the outset and, instead, approached Venezuela's Hugo Chávez to the point of calling him his "new best friend."[33] At the same time, he stopped harassing the FARC and began secret talks with the narco-terrorist group that Chávez had convinced could come to power through the electoral process, as had happened with him. To achieve his objectives, Santos did not take into consideration that the FARC had committed horrible crimes that included, in addition to hundreds of thousands of deaths, 27,000 kidnappings, 25,000 missing persons, and six million displaced persons. Similarly, Santos overlooked that the FARC had become the world's third-largest drug trafficking cartel, with revenues of $600 million a year. Instead, Santos chose as intermediaries in this negotiation process the governments of Cuba and Venezuela, which were ideologically aligned with the FARC's narco-terrorists.

After four years of negotiations, the final agreement included cessions such as criminal impunity, since the narco-terrorists would not even pay for the so-called crimes against humanity. On the contrary, they would have a temporary restriction of freedom in previously agreed areas where they would carry out «repair and restoration works or activities, environmental protection programs, rural development, waste disposal or infrastructure repair." It should be noted that, unlike the dealings that Santos agreed to with the drug traffickers, many of the military personnel who fought them and were being investigated or had already been convicted (many of them unjustly) remain in military detention centers.

In addition, the transitional justice—a concept that should increasingly arouse suspicion—agreed upon with the narco-terrorists under

33. https://www.semana.com/mundo/articulo/santos-dice-chavez-su-nuevo-mejor-amigo/124284-3.

the name of Special Jurisdiction for Peace would be made up of foreign bodies and would have powers that would go beyond those of the country's own courts. In fact, the Attorney General's Office, the Public Prosecutor's Office, and the Treasury Inspector's Office would lose their powers over criminal matters, and their decisions could even be reviewed and even annulled. As if all of the above were not enough, and in a clear capitulation of the judiciary to the will of the narco-terrorists, in addition, the rulings of the Special Peace Jurisdiction would not permit the right to appeal.

Taken together, these concessions turned the narco-terrorists into a true legislative power that controlled the judiciary with the complacency of the executive. Unfortunately, the Havana agreements did not end there. As if all this were not enough, drug trafficking was considered nothing more than a crime of rebellion and could continue to be practiced as an immense source of resources for the FARC, which had been transformed into a political party. In fact, the decision of the Santos government to suspend glyphosate spraying of the FARC's extensive coca crops led to a considerable increase in these crops over the previous two years. Today, they cover no less than 170,000 hectares. At the height of the mockery, and despite the monetary resources of the drug, the FARC, of course, said that they lacked resources and would not repair the damage caused to their victims. And that was not the end of it...

The agreement also included the handing over of ten constituency seats to the narco-terrorists for eight years and without the necessary support in votes. In addition, there would be another sixteen in the House of Representatives from the special peace constituencies located in areas where the FARC enjoys a dominant presence. In addition, the future political party that emerged from the FARC would receive 10% of the resources that the State allocates to all the parties. It would also enjoy an additional 5% to finance better dissemination of its ideological platform and would have access to thirty-one radio stations and a new television channel. In this way, narco-terrorists would receive benefits never before granted to any political party in the history of Colombia. In addition, there would be benefits derived from the so-called integral rural reform, which would create a fund of free and permanent land distribution to be controlled by the drug traffickers.

One does not have to be particularly sharp to see that the terms of the agreement totally violated the Colombian legal system and furthermore—an aspect to which they have stubbornly closed their eyes—opened the door to the Chavista assault on power, all with the money of the citizens and the support of the president himself! To be honest, Santos was not the only one interested. The agreement had the express backing of the Latin American dictatorships, the terrorist group ETA, or the Spanish Podemos party, but—let's not fool ourselves—also of the Holy See. Pope Francis expressly announced his intention to travel to Colombia as soon as it was approved in a referendum by the U.S. State Department and Spanish diplomacy, among others. The agreement was also supported by the gay lobby, which insisted during the campaign that supporting it meant that gender ideology would be included in education and even in Colombia's constitution.

As if all this were not enough, the project was accompanied by more than questionable propaganda from a moral perspective that equated capitulation to narco-terrorists with peace, while the defense of integrity, justice, and victims was equated with warmongering. Add to that numerous legal irregularities or pressure on officials to vote in the direction desired by President Santos. And then the unthinkable happened.

In spite of the unanimous "yes" vote from the opinion polls, the people voted no. Then something typical of Hispanic-Catholic culture occurred: the powers-that-be did not respect the will of the people. While in Great Britain, the result of the Brexit referendum was respected by all institutions; in Colombia, President Santos maintained the agreement with the FARC, which was rejected by the people, including all aspects related to gender ideology. In the end, the will of the people did not matter at all, and Santos was even awarded the Nobel Peace Prize, which, by the way, has also been received by, among others, some deceitful natives, some unscrupulous nuns, as well as former terrorists and repeat bombers.

To what extent this mockery of the will expressed by the people, together with the implementation of gender ideology, is intolerable can be seen if we stop to reflect on some of the crimes perpetrated by the FARC. Because in addition to numerous war crimes such as the kidnapping, torture, and murder of civilians, the FARC has added acts of sexual violence against minors on a massive scale. According to data provided by the National Observatory of Memory and Conflict of the National Center of Historical Memory (CNMH), girls and adolescents were the population group that suffered most from sexual violence during the armed conflict.[34] Children and adolescents not only suffered these atrocities directly, but also as witnesses of this violence against their mothers, sisters, and family members in charge of their care. Of the total of 15,076 people who were victims of sexual violence in the armed conflict since 1958, at least 5,013 were girls and adolescents. Of these 5,013 victims, 2,094 were children between the ages of 10 and 14. The largest number of female victims was in the 15-19 age range, with 2,865 cases.

This data, contained in the national report: "The war inscribed on the body," by the CNMH,[35] coincides with the analysis of the seven sentences issued by Justice and Peace on paramilitary action. Thus, of 57 cases of sexual violence, 24 were committed against girls and adolescents between the ages of 9 and 17, i.e., 42%. What is frightening is that all the armed perpetrators, legal and illegal, had a fixation with the virginity of girls and adolescents.

As the report acknowledges, not even boys were exempt from such violence, who were raped as a way of humiliation and blackmail, which increased the guilt and stigmatization of those attacked. Boys were raped especially during childhood and adolescence. According to

34. http://www.centrodememoriahistorica.gov.co/noticias/noticias-cmh/262-197-muertos-dejo-el-conflicto-armado.

35. https://www.elpais.com.co/elpais/archivos/bastaya.pdf; http://www.centrodememoriahistorica.gov.co/informes-2017/la-guerra-inscrita-en-el-cuerpo.

the report, "Between the ages of 10 and 14, the highest number of male victims is listed with 137 records, followed by the range of 15 to 19 years old with 132." This was the case, for example, of Rogelio, who was raped when he was five years old, in the municipality of San Carlos, in eastern Antioquia, in 1992. He was intercepted by two men from the FARC when he was leaving school. One raped him, while the other kept watch. Rogelio did not talk about it with his family, because he was threatened and because he felt ashamed.

As a result, children and adolescents of both sexes in places such as Norte de Santander, Tolima, Magdalena, Bolívar, Sucre, Valle del Cauca, Arauca, Córdoba, Nariño, and Antioquia have been in a state of continuous fear of being raped. Indeed, such sexual violence continues to exist in the poorest territories and areas in the lives and bodies of minors, without the State avoiding, preventing, or punishing it. Thus, according to the Coalition against the Involvement of Children and Young People in the Armed Conflict in Colombia (Coalico), there is a form of sexual exploitation known as "mobile lovers," which consists of taking children of both sexes from village to village so that the armed perpetrators can rape them. Likewise, in Medellín, to give another example from the report, the sexual exploitation of girls and adolescents "... has become a strong form of financing for armed groups, which have even gone so far as to auction off, via the Internet, the virginity of girls who have been captured, either through seductive economic promises or through threats and intimidation." Despite the dreadful situation, Lorena Murcia, president of the Rosa Blanca Corporation, which represents various victims of the former FARC, said that in the Special Jurisdiction for Peace, they have not wanted to receive their complaints about sexual crimes. The fact that such atrocities went unpunished due to the will of Santos and the promoters of the globalist agenda forces us to reflect.

In August 2018, Iván Duque won the presidential elections in Colombia. Although Iván Duque is located in the center-right, the fact that his positions have been less favorable to President Santos' policy of concessions placed him from the beginning in the spotlight of the Left, but also of all entities that were in favor of the FARC narco-terrorists and the advancement of gender ideology. Since coming to power, Duque has faced fierce opposition because of security policy focused on combating drug trafficking and illegal crops, in addition to his attempt to modify the agreement made with the FARC, the most powerful terrorist group in the Americas. That opposition was further radicalized by the announcement of a sector of the FARC that it was returning to the armed struggle, and by the electoral victory of the Left in the recent municipal elections, where, for example, a lesbian, a fierce defender of gender ideology and the globalist agenda, took over the mayor's office in Bogotá.

It was not difficult to foresee that Colombia would soon be subjected to a process of subversion similar to that which Chile was already suffering, and using exactly the same methodology. Thus, a so-called national strike was called for November 21, which attempted to justify itself by referring to social demands and the bombing of a FARC camp by army forces, during which minors used by narco-terrorists for their actions died.

The protest, organized since last October by the General Confederation of Workers, the Confederation of Workers of Colombia, and the workers' unions, was also supported by different student movements, trade unions, social and political organizations as well as people linked to the media and the world of entertainment. Similarly, the FARC, the political arm of the narco-terrorist group FARC, supported the strike. However, it would have been very wrong to hold the left-wing forces exclusively responsible for the subversion. As had happened in Chile a few weeks earlier, the Colombian Bishops' Conference also joined the call for a national protest in a gesture that surprised many, but it fit in with the very line drawn by the Vatican.[36] In fact, in its document on the subject, the Colombian Episcopal Conference appealed directly to Pope Francis.

36. https://www.semana.com/nacion/articulo/paro-nacional-21-de-noviembre-la-iglesia-catolica-se-pronuncia/640284.

The National School of Trade Unions pointed out ten points that, in theory, would be the cause for calling a national strike, and which included going against the labor and pension reform, against the reform that would allow the auditing of state funds by an external entity, against privatization of the electricity sector, against corruption, against the increase in energy tariffs, and against the tax reform that would result in a lowering of taxes for companies. Along with the program that was against the alleged reforms, the national strike made the minimum wage, the organizations of civil servants, students, indigenous people, and the extension of the legal limits of social protest their rallying cry. The President of the Republic, Iván Duque Márquez, tried for weeks to show the public that many of the flags waved by the organizers of the national strike did not correspond to reality. However, it was useless for him to point out that there was no government plan to lower the minimum wage, but that he had tried to agree to an increase and that he did not defend delaying retirement age or the increase in the workers' contributions either.

As in other Latin American nations, in Colombia, there is also an attempt to advance the globalist agenda by weakening the position of the current president through a combination of leftist, indigenous, and student organizations. This project, barely concealed by the coup, began with a major national strike supported even by the Colombian Episcopal Conference. In this way, Colombia was becoming the next piece to fall by means of illegal and subversive action, which obey the globalist agenda, and dresses itself with a supposed social legitimacy that is nothing more than demagogy that enjoys the support of the bishops. If the result is going to be the surrender of Duque alone or the seizure of power by forces of a different nature that are willing to push the globalist agenda, that is something that cannot be determined at the moment. That one of the objectives may be a constitutional change is more than possible.

What would happen if the globalist agenda finally succeeds in Latin America? It is not difficult to imagine the more than possible scenario. We would find ourselves with a group of nations devoid of sovereignty, similar to eggshells from which the yolk and white have been extracted. Formally democratic institutions might even continue to exist within them, but each and every nation would in fact be no more than a protectorate subject to a supranational power that would govern them at will. Imagination excess? Absolutely. In fact, this situation has existed for years in another part of the world.

CHAPTER XVIII

THE END OF NATIONAL INDEPENDENCE (III): Africa

Genocides Are Not a Thing of the Past

If the European Union finds itself on a dangerous path of cultural dissolution driven by organizations that lack democratic legitimacy, and if Latin America runs the risk of becoming a string of protectorates subject to the globalist agenda, a large part of Africa already shows us the panorama towards which the world situation could be evolving. The media seldom refer to this continent, and ordinary citizens would have trouble distinguishing the majority of their countries on a blank map, and yet in Africa, where more than a billion people live and where the planet's indispensable wealth is concentrated, there is no democracy, no freedom, and no respect for human rights. The place of all those circumstances has been filled with civil wars, coups d'état, neocolonialism, and even genocide. In the following pages, we will stop at three simple examples to show the condition Africa is in, despite the fact that an almost complete silence has descended on the continent, and despite the fact that it is only mentioned in the media when someone wants to justify an invasion, and despite the fact that millions of people suffer and die without almost anyone on the other continents even seeming to care, and, above all, without realizing that this may be their fate tomorrow.

In 2019, it was the twenty-fifth anniversary of some terrible events. Rwanda is a nation that was fundamentally divided into two ethnic groups in 1994. The Hutu majority formed 80% of the population, and the Tutsi minority barely reached 20%. Despite their minority status, the Tutsis had ambitions to seize power in Rwanda and even extend it to other nations in the Great Lakes region of Africa. On August 4, 1993, the French government managed to get Hutus and Tutsis to sign an agreement that forced them to share power. However, one Tutsi party, the Rwandan Patriotic Front (RPF), was determined to seize absolute power despite representing only the Tutsi minority. To that end, on April 6, 1994, the Rwandan Patriotic Front, acting in exile, carried out the assassination of the Rwandan President who was a Hutu by shooting down his plane. At the same time, the RPF set up a radio station called Radio Muhabura and sowed hatred against the Hutus. In reaction to this radio, the Thousand Hills Radio was created, which called for the assassination of the Tutsi.

The RPF knew that the assassination would provoke reprisals, but they decided to carry it out thinking that the Hutus would kill a few hundred Tutsis so that the RPF would have an excuse to invade Rwanda and take over the government. The reaction of a Hutu minority exceeded the RPF's prediction, and over the course of a hundred days, the Tutsis that were killed grew into the hundreds of thousands and reached 75% of those living in Rwanda. However, the massacre was not limited to the Tutsis, and thousands of Hutus were also killed, which were not added to the crimes that had been committed. As if that were not enough, the genocide perpetrated against the Tutsis opened the door for them to invade the country under Kagame's command, subjugate the Hutu majority, and establish a dictatorship that continues to this day.

In fact, the massacres of Hutus and their oppression by the Tutsi minority have been commonplace for the last quarter of a century, although the media and the chancelleries have silenced them. Thus, if France supported the Hutu majority in the Rwandan government, the United States has subsequently supported the bloody rule of the Tutsi minority.

A key role in the crimes was played by the Roman Catholic Church, which did not hesitate to support the killings in not a few cases when you consider Hutu clergymen were exterminating Tutsis or by allowing mass killings to take place even inside churches. This was the case, for example, of the five thousand killed in the Catholic Church in Ntarama on August 15, 1994. The site is now considered one of the six largest memorials in Rwanda.

There were also genocidal clerics such as Father Athanase Seromba who ordered his church to be bulldozed while 2,000 Tutsis took refuge inside. It was also the case of Father Wenceslas Munyeshyaka,[1] who drew up lists of people to be exterminated and raped several young women as established before the UN tribunal of international criminals.

These execrable actions stemmed from the marriage of the Roman Catholic Church with the regime, since Archbishop Vincent Nsengiyumva was part of the central committee of the ruling party for almost fifteen years, at a time when policies discriminating against Tutsis were being approved.[2] Archbishop Nsengiyumva not only did nothing to stop the killings, but also refused to consider them a genocide and managed to have several Tutsi priests, monks, and a nun killed.

The Roman Catholic Church in Rwanda itself acknowledged that members of its clergy had planned, assisted, and perpetrated the genocide and refused to acknowledge their complicity in the crimes. Understandably, the Organization of African Unity noted that the Roman Catholic Church had provided "indispensable support" to

1. https://www.newtimes.co.rw/section/read/193499; https://www.theguardian.com/world/2014/apr/07/rwanda-genocide-20-years-priests-catholic-church.

2. https://www.theguardian.com/world/2002/apr/05/chrismcgreal.

the Hutu regime during the killings and that Catholic Church leaders played an "outrageously significant role" in the genocide. This behavior, according to the OAU, resulted in many Roman Catholics deciding to support the genocide.

As with the Nazis and other war criminals at the end of World War II, the Roman Catholic Church created a network to help the *genocidaires* flee. This was the case with Father Munyeshyaka, who was entrusted with the care of a parish in Gisor, France, or with Father Seromba, who became a parish priest in Florence and was eventually sentenced to life imprisonment.[3]

After two decades in which the Vatican denied the role of the Roman Catholic Church in the genocide, Pope Francis himself acknowledged, after a meeting with Rwandan President Tutsi Paul Kagame, "failures" of the Church and its members, a certainly mild term for genocide.[4]

It is quite significant that a quarter of a century before 2019, Rwanda had more than 90% of its citizens who were members of a Christian religious denomination, 50% of whom were Roman Catholics and 50% Protestants, and then after the genocide a large number of Roman Catholics have left their church to become members of an evangelical church.

The Rwandan genocide allowed the RPF to present itself as a liberator, to establish a dictatorship that lasts until today, and to proceed with the murder of more than two hundred thousand Hutus that nobody talks about. To this day, Rwanda remains under a Tutsi minority dictatorship, and crimes and systematic human rights violations continue to be perpetrated, even though the media does not say a word about it.

The Rwandan genocide has been one of the most horrific and manipulated episodes in recent decades. The official version has been to place all the blame on the Hutus and on the passivity of the UN.

3. https://www.protestinfo.ch/200803174617/4617-condamnation-a-perpetuite-du-pretre-rwandais-athanase-seromba-pour-sa-participation-au-genocide.html;https://www.liberation.fr/planete/2001/07/18/un-pretre-rwandais-cache-en-italie_371878.

4. https://www.milenio.com/internacional/papa-disculpa-pecados-iglesia-genocidio-ruanda.

What is extraordinary is that it has been claimed that France, as a dominant Western power, also had a responsibility in what happened. This has been enshrined in films, documentaries, television series, and books. The reality is much broader, terrible, and enduring.

To begin with, the outbreak of violence came from a conscious act by Tutsi forces abroad who murdered the Rwandan Hutu president to provoke a reaction against the Tutsis that would justify their invasion of the territory. The terrorist act was to be the way that would allow the Tutsis abroad to hide their crimes and present themselves as liberators. The reality, however, is that without that perverse Tutsi plan, there would have been no Tutsi killings and no chain of drama that continues to this day. Secondly, the responsibility affects the Hutus who allowed themselves to be dragged into the campaign of hatred unleashed by the Tutsi attacks and who sought to exterminate them en masse. Thirdly, there was a clear responsibility on the part of France and the UN, who did not want to intervene in the conflict in the first case because it meant keeping the Hutu majority in power with whom they had good relations, and in the second case because of the irresponsibility of thinking that everything would be under control. Fourthly, there was a terrible responsibility on the part of the Roman Catholic Church, which, as usual, acted not according to moral principles, but according to their interests, and whose ministers, including bishops, not only did not contain the genocide but encouraged it and participated in it in a massive and bloody way, even though it involved the murder of Roman Catholic clergymen who were Tutsis. As is customary in the Catholic Church, she helped priests flee and protected clergy who were criminals, and, to this day, although it has regretted what happened, it has never asked for forgiveness. Fifthly, there is no denying the role of the United States, which favored the invasion of Rwanda by Tutsis living abroad and which has supported the dictatorial, minority Tutsi government of Kagame.

Finally, there is no denying the responsibility of the media, which has shelved the past genocide in order to forget and hide the terrible misfortune of the Hutu majority, which has been subjected to the

Tutsi minority for a quarter of a century. That drama has also cost hundreds of thousands of lives and is still linked to the sufferings of hundreds of thousands of refugees, but there is no indication that there will be films, books, or documentaries to narrate it.

The tragedy of Rwanda, which began more than twenty-five years ago, is not over and highlights the terrible nature of an international policy that is never told. It is about the behavior of political forces that think only of the annihilation of their adversary even if this means the death of their own; of neocolonial powers that act only at the behest of their desire for power and the theft of raw materials; of a Roman Catholic Church that is always allied with those who think they will prevail even if the assessment of the situation goes wrong; of a distressing ineffectiveness of international organizations; and of media that are ready to keep silent in the face of horror. Genocide continues to exist in nations that are included on the list of democracies only because several parties exist and elections are held, when, in reality, they are no more than protectorates where mass slaughter can break out. Such protectorates sometimes even make up colonial empires.

Françafrique[5]

For many, Africa, apart from being a distant and unknown continent, is a place where, after the Second World War, all the colonial powers eventually disappeared. Such a view of Africa is, at best, a half-truth because the continent, with its peculiar nuances and exceptions,

5. J-P. Bat, "Le rôle de la France après les indépendances" in *Afrique Contemporaine*, Cairn.Info, March 11, 2011, https://www.cairn.info/revue-afrique-contemporaine-2010-3-page-43.htm; J-L. Borloo, "Les relations entre la France et l'Afrique" in *Geoéconomie, Cairn.Info*, September 23, 2013, https://www.cairn.info/revue-geoeconomie-2013-3-page-7.htm; T. Chanda, "Défense: Que Fait l'armée Française En Afrique?—RFI," *RFI Afrique*, November 15, 2018, rfi.fr/afrique/20181115-evolution-presence-militaire-francaise-afrique-depuis-1960-base-opex-alliance; J-P. Chrétien, "Indépendances de l'Afrique Francophone," FranceArchives, 2010; P. Hugon, "La Politique économique de la France en Afrique la fin des rentes coloniales?," Cairn.Info, November 15, 2012, https://www.cairn.info/revue-politique-africaine-2007-1-page-54.htm?try_download=1; D. Servenay, "Les Accords Secrets Avec l'Afrique: Encore d'époque?" *L'Obs*, July 26, 2007, https://www.nouvelobs.com/rue89/rue89-politique/20070726.RUE1127/les-accords-secrets-avec-l-afrique-encore-d-epoque.html.

is largely subject to a neocolonial regime in which the new nations are no more than protectorates. This is the case of the so-called Françafrique or France-Africa. General de Gaulle, President of France, while developing the process of decolonization, knew how to take steps to continue governing African politics and even appoint the presidents of the new nations. He put Jacques Foccart, a veteran of the secret services, at the head of the effort. Foccart appointed Maurice Robert, who headed the African service of the SDECE, the French equivalent of the CIA. Immediately, African presidents were appointed by France. This was certainly the case for Houphouët-Boigny, the first president of the Ivory Coast, and Léopold Senghor, the first president of Senegal. In both cases, they were submissive leaders willing to accept France's leading role behind the scenes. The result of this appointment of presidents speaks for itself. In Gabon, Omar Bongo, who succeeded President Léon M'ba in 1967 under the leadership of France, remained in power until 2007. He was succeeded by his son Ali Bongo. In Congo-Brazzaville, Denis Sasson-Nguesso remained president from 1979 to 1992, returning to power in 1997 after a coup d'état. In Cameroon, Paul Biya has been in power since 1982. In Equatorial Guinea—a former Spanish colony—Teodoro Obiang Nguema came to power in 1979 and has always won elections with no less than 95% of the votes. Of course, some presidents did not submit to France, as was the case with Silvanus Olimpio, the first president of Togo. In those cases, they were assassinated.

This frightening—and unknown—reality should not come as a surprise. Through agreements that were often signed in secret, the new African nations subjected their economy, their currency, their culture, their legal system, and their armed forces to France. In fact, French remained the language of the former colonies, and the CFA franc became their currency. The so-called advisory role of France, in areas such as public order or the armed forces, allowed the European power to subdue the supposedly independent nations. Right after the declaration of independence, France signed agreements with Cameroon, the Central African Republic,[6] the Comoros, the Ivory Coast, Djibouti, Gabon, Senegal, and Togo, which made these nations protectorates. Instead of independence, what took place was the replacement of the old colonialism by a new colonialism.

Certainly, France has spent various sums on development aid in these decades. However, after more than half a century, all these nations are still dependent and extremely poor. The fundamental reason is that the money taken from the French middle classes through taxes does not go to the miserable Africans but to the corrupt political castes. Whether we like it or not, the forced taxation of the northern middle classes does not solve any problem except that of increasing the fortunes of the corrupt oligarchies of the Third World.

The situation did not change with the end of the Cold War, with the enlargement of the European Union, or with globalization. France is now the second largest European exporter to Africa, after Germany. In fact, one-third of French exports are destined for the African continent. A nation like the Ivory Coast accounted for 32% of French exports to West Africa in 2018. Not surprisingly, Business France, a French public agency, organizes export missions every year called Ambition Afrique. In the end, France's surplus to each and every one of these African nations is truly spectacular.

In 2017, there were more than two thousand French subsidiaries in Africa. The influence in African economies is truly colossal to the point that it can be said that not a single one of them could survive without the French presence. In the field of energy, the dependence of the above-mentioned African nations on France is total. The influence is also huge in the area of transport with Air France; the industry with Lafarge; construction with Bouygues and Sogea-Satom; services with BNP Paribas and Bolloré; mass distribution with CFAO; agro-industry with Bel; telecommunications with Orange—more than 100 million African customers in 19 countries—and France Telecom. Three

6. On the intervention in this immensely rich and no less immensely unknown place, see: Louisa Lombard, *State of Rebellion, Violence and Intervention in the Central African Republic* (London, 2016).

French banks—Banque National de Paris, Société Générale, and Crédit Lyonnais—control 70% of the banking activity in the CFA franc zone. The CFA franc has an exchange rate of 655 per euro and allows France to control the economy of these African nations.

The African Financial Community or Franco Cooperation (CFA Franc) created in 1945 by De Gaulle is the last operating colonial currency and allows CEMAC (Central Bank of African States) and UEMOA (Central Bank of West African states) to also exercise the right to veto economic decisions at the behest of the Bank of France. As if that were not bad enough, nations in the CFA Franc area are required to deposit 50% of their foreign exchange surpluses in a French trading account. To cap it all off, the protectorates of France in Africa cannot devalue currency, nor create it according to their interests, and they also have to buy in euros, which is a stronger currency than the dollar in which they sell. Under this colonial control, it is not surprising that the Democratic Republic of the Congo,[7] which has cobalt, gold, and diamonds, or Niger, which has uranium, are among the ten poorest countries in the world. All this without taking into account the immense impact of corruption, the damage caused by industries such as uranium, or the continued military presence of France.

Since the 1960s, France has launched no less than sixty military operations in Africa. To understand the influence of French armed interventionism, suffice it to say that of its Opex forces—supposedly destined to keep the peace—45% are deployed in Africa. Of its forces permanently deployed outside France, there are bases in Djibouti, Senegal, Gabon, and the Ivory Coast. Such a presence, however, did not prevent the Rwandan genocide, nor has it been particularly useful in other parts of the continent.

It should come as no surprise that this neocolonial rule is not viewed well by Africans. To tell the truth, most people take a better view of the Chinese presence, and there is a real risk that Françafrique could be replaced by a China-Africa, because the conditions that China

7. On foreign interference in the Congo, see: J. K. Stearns, *Dancing in the Glory of Monsters. The Collapse of the Congo and the Great War of Africa* (New York, 2011).

offers to African countries are better and are not linked to ambitions of colonial rule. Meanwhile, Africa is, in no small measure, a chain of protectorates in which neither freedom nor democracy is conceivable. In fact, even in those nations where it has been insisted that a better tomorrow has dawned, the reality is very different. The South African Republic is one of the most obvious cases.

The Failure of the South African Republic

On May 8, 2019, elections were held in the Republic of South Africa. The results received no special media coverage, perhaps because South Africa is one of the most colossal failures of Western politics on the African continent and a resounding example of the results of Western self-deception. To understand everything, one must go back more than a century, to 1912, when the African National Congress was founded in South Africa. It was a nationalist party with strong links to the Communist Party and whose most prominent leader was Nelson Mandela. The African National Congress chose to carry out terrorist acts as an appropriate strategy to end the apartheid regime, which led to Mandela and some of his comrades being imprisoned in 1964. Mandela himself would be imprisoned for this cause for twenty-six years.[8] But international pressure eventually led to the demise of the apartheid regime, and in 1990 the African National Congress ceased to be an underground party and began an uninterrupted take-over of power in South Africa, which was largely based on Mandela's transformation into an international icon.

In 2019, the ANC won South Africa's elections for the sixth time in a row, albeit by a smaller margin than on previous occasions. The ANC's victory was supported by 56% of voters, up from 62% in previous elections. However, this percentage was sufficient to maintain the majority of the 400 seats in the National Assembly (lower house),

8. Of particular interest is David James Smith, *Young Mandela. The Revolutionary Years* (New York, 2010).

which was then to appoint the country's president, the current president Cyril Ramaphosa.

Whichever way you look at it, it is quite significant that only the ANC has won an election in decades—since 1994—and that it does so at a time when Cyril Ramaphosa's presidency has been marked, among other calamities, by high crime rates in the country and youth unemployment. Furthermore, the economic situation in South Africa can only be described as disastrous, and several studies indicate that its deterioration is proving to be more rapid than that suffered by some nations at war. Thus, it is common for companies to suffer constant power outages throughout the country and for foreign investors to leave. As if all this were not enough, the ANC intends to reform the constitution to take land away from the white population without any financial compensation,[9] an outrageously racist action that is not reported as such in the media.

As if all this were not enough, the only significant opposition force to the ANC is the Democratic Alliance, whose leader, Mmusi Maimane, head of the opposition, has been involved in cases of corruption, money laundering, and tax evasion.

The Boer minority is made up of whites of Dutch origin who, in many cases, arrived in the territory of South Africa before some black ethnic groups that currently inhabit it, such as the Zulus. This minority sees the possibility of secession as the only way out in the future and in light of the prospects of plundering raised by the current president.

The case of South Africa has been one of the most subject to media manipulation over the last decades. For years, the figure of Nelson Mandela—ultimately imprisoned for committing terrorist acts—was shrouded in an aura of legend that eventually led to his release, his glorification, and the awarding of the Nobel Peace Prize and two hundred and fifty other honorary prizes. The fact that he publicly acknowledged his links with dictators such as Fidel Castro was hidden or minimized, since he had been turned into a media

9. https://www.bbc.com/news/world-africa-45026931; https://www.bloomberg.com/news/articles/2018-11-23/south-africa-s-path-to-land-reform-is-riddled-with-pitfalls.

figure.[10] No less heinous were his wife Winnie's criminal activities that were hidden, including torture and murder, which were carried out with total impunity, although these were some of the reasons that prompted Mandela's divorce. Even less did they want to see the subsequent development of South Africa. Certainly, the apartheid regime was unacceptable, but what has followed is not the journey of a free, prosperous nation without racial conflict. In fact, despite Mandela's best wishes, South Africa has gone from being an extraordinarily prosperous nation, possibly the only one south of the Sahara that deserves that description, to a country in ruins, with a shocking crime rate and appalling insecurity that affects the white population in particular.

The rampant corruption of the ANC, the continuous assaults against domestic and foreign targets, the economic deterioration accompanied by constant power outages, the flight of foreign investors, and now the announcement of the widespread plundering of white people's lands make South Africa one of the worst countries in the world and certainly one of the most insecure and violent. However, no one seems to want to talk about it. Mandela has been so praised in the past, the struggle against apartheid has been so mythologized, and public opinion has been turned into a cause much more blurred than it seemed at first sight that no one, absolutely no one, will ever acknowledge his mistake.

To tell the truth, it does not seem likely that feminist organizations will say a single word against the astronomical number of rapes of white women. It does not seem likely that those who censored the white government would issue a single censorship against a black government that oppresses whites and is willing to deprive them of everything they have. It does not seem likely that those who economically boycotted the former South Africa will utter a single word of complaint against the present one. It does not seem likely that those who cried out against the old repression are now crying out for the victims

10. https://www.youtube.com/watch?v=mtGh5VqsBI0; https://www.youtube.com/watch?v=0Abqg7iNab8; https://www.nytimes.com/2016/11/30/opinion/fidel-castro-a-south-african-hero.html?ref=nyt-es&mcid=nyt-es&subid=article.

of the ANC regime. It does not seem likely that those who accused governments like President Reagan's for maintaining diplomatic relations with South Africa will now complain about the ties of people like Mandela with dictators like Castro, or move a finger to avoid the great catastrophe that is coming. In the end, the myth must be kept alive and worshipped as an idol even if the cost is that freedom, prosperity, and democracy will never take root in the African continent...despite the clues of what may happen in other parts of the world if the globalist agenda succeeds.

PART V

RESISTANCE TO THE GLOBALIST AGENDA

CHAPTER XIX

THE PATRIOTIC AND DEMOCRATIC MOVEMENTS

Viktor Orbán or the Resistance in the European Union

The globalist agenda, imposed by all means, including law fraud and coup d'états, has ended up provoking reactions. In some cases, these have been massive citizen responses against gender ideology and the legalization of abortion. In others, it has been the emergence of politicians who, to a greater or lesser extent, oppose the globalist agenda from a patriotic perspective. As President Trump once noted,[1] the political confrontation today is between globalists and patriots. To ignore this reality and to insist on maintaining the division of the Cold War or of the Right and Left—a concept that dates back to the last decade of the eighteenth century—is to fail to understand our changing world. In the following pages, we will focus on three politicians—in the European Union, Latin America, and the United

1. https://www.passblue.com/2019/09/24/globalists-and-patriots-at-the-un-a-great-fracture-revealed/; https://www.whitehouse.gov/briefings-statements/remarks-president-trump-74th-session-united-nations-general-assembly/

States—who embody this confrontation between patriots and globalists and who, in turn, respect the democratic system.

The first example is Viktor Orbán, the current Prime Minister of Hungary. Although the media—in an easily understandable way—usually attacks Orbán by calling him an extreme right-wing politician, the reality is that the extreme Right has a low representation in the Hungarian Parliament where Orbán has a two-thirds majority of the seats. Orbán may have been attacked by Hillary Clinton, Angela Merkel, and European Commission presidents José Manuel Barroso and Jean-Claude Juncker, but an overwhelming majority of the Hungarian people support him.

Interestingly, Orbán—who is an evangelical—received a student grant from the Soros Foundation, of which subsequently he has been very critical. In 1988, Orbán was one of the founders of the Fidesz party (*Fiatal Demokraták Szövetsége,* Hungarian Civic Union). In 1989, Orbán demanded free elections and the withdrawal of Soviet troops. This was a step that gave him a very important role in the transition from a communist dictatorship to a democratic regime in Hungary. In 1998, Orbán became Prime Minister after rallying right-wing forces.

The economic achievements of Orbán's government have been more than remarkable. The creator of a multifaceted centralized economy, he is committed to reducing the public deficit and lowering taxes, and inflation, which in 1998 was 15%, had fallen to 7.8% by 2001. At the same time, in 1999, Hungary joined NATO along with Poland and the Czech Republic and began negotiations to join the European Union. In a decision that caused enormous controversy, Orbán's government extended health, work, and education rights to Magyars who did not have Hungarian citizenship and lived in the neighboring nations of Romania, Slovakia, Serbia, Montenegro, Croatia, Slovenia, and Ukraine.

In 2002, the Socialists, amid rumors of electoral fraud, returned to power and Orbán went over to the opposition. At that time, Orbán took a stand against illegal immigration—one of the dogmas of the globalist agenda—which would result in the building of protective fences on the borders of Serbia and Croatia. In 2010, Orbán obtained 52.73% of the votes, achieving a two-thirds majority in Parliament. The constitution was then reformed in a way that was totally contrary to the globalist agenda. The constitutional text appealed to Hungary's Christian background, defined marriage as the "union between a man and a woman," and expressed itself as antiabortion by defending the protection of the fetus "from the moment of fertilization." Significantly, Orbán initiated a policy to avoid creating political patronage. It is not difficult to understand why Orbán was to become a "black beast" for globalist media and politics. In 2014, Orbán won the elections resoundingly—133 seats out of 199—a success that was repeated in 2018.

That same year, the European Parliament sanctioned his government. This is not surprising, because in Hungary in 2013, sleeping on the streets was banned, a ruling that was tightened in 2018; in 2015 a law was pushed through that incarcerates those who help illegal immigrants to apply for asylum; and in 2017, the expulsion of illegal Syrians took place. Orbán has repeatedly stated his refusal to receive Muslims in Hungary and his steadfastness in defending national borders against what he considers an invasion. To top it all off, in search of increased employment, in 2018 he carried out a labor reform that reduced the role of trade unions and gave priority to making employment contracts more flexible.

Orbán's policy is essentially patriotic and places national interests above the globalist agenda. He has outright refused to assume any of the globalist dogmas and has policies that are profamily, prolife, and against immigration, which is out of control. All this has been endorsed, time and again, by huge electoral victories and, of course, by ruthless attacks from the media, institutions, and politicians committed to the globalist agenda.

Jair Bolsonaro or the Resistance in Latin America

On January 1, 2019, Jair Messias Bolsonaro, a politician and military man who had already served seven terms in the chamber of deputies, became president of Brazil. In 2014, Bolsonaro had become the most voted for federal deputy in the state of Rio de Janeiro, and three years later, he was considered by the FSB institute to be the most relevant legislator on social networks. As in Orbán's case, Bolsonaro has been the object of a ruthless media and political campaign in which he has been harshly branded as a figure of the extreme Right. The reality is that Bolsonaro defines himself as center-right, and there is no reason to deny it.

After a military career as a paratrooper, in which he defended the increase of military salaries, in 1988 he entered politics as a councilman of the city of Rio de Janeiro. From the beginning, Bolsonaro became known for his opposition to communism and the Left. In 2014, he became the most voted for congressman in the state of Rio de Janeiro. By this time, his opposition to the globalist agenda was obvious. In relation to gender ideology, Bolsonaro is against homosexual marriage, adoption of children by homosexual couples, and the alteration of the civil registry for transsexuals. Likewise, Bolsonaro opposes the legalization of drugs and the approval of legal privileges for blacks or browns. In addition, he advocates that rural landowners should have weapons to defend themselves against land occupations by leftist forces.

On October 7, 2018, he was confirmed as a candidate for the second round of the presidential elections after winning the first round and obtaining 46.03% of the votes counted. He was up against Fernando Haddad from the Workers Party, who had obtained 29.28% of the votes. The second round of elections took place on the twenty-eighth of the same month, and Bolsonaro was elected president with 55.13% of the votes. At that time, he had been the target of an attack during the election campaign[2] and of many demonstrations against him in different countries organized by feminist and gay groups.[3] It is not surprising that in the midst of these circumstances, his electoral victory was

2. https://www.economist.com/the-americas/2018/09/08/jair-bolsonaro-is-stabbed-at-a-rally.
3. https://www.theatlantic.com/international/archive/2018/11/brazil-women-bolsonaro-haddad-election/574792/.

directly related to the support of Brazilian evangelicals for his prolife and profamily positions. His wife is also an evangelical, and he himself was baptized in the Jordan river by an evangelical pastor and attends an evangelical church. Nothing seems to indicate that they were disappointed with Bolsonaro's first year in office.

Apart from keeping his election promises, Bolsonaro, in economic terms, has followed an economic policy very similar to that of President Ronald Reagan. There has also been no lack of initiatives such as those aimed at facilitating the possession of weapons and discovering the teachers who are engaged in indoctrinating students. In foreign policy, Bolsonaro has been very close to the United States and Israel and clearly opposed to China despite the fact that Brazil has a surplus in trade with China. He also was the force behind the departure of Cuban doctors from Brazil. On top of that, Bolsonaro has openly demonstrated his opposition to the removal of the Amazon from Brazilian sovereignty to be governed by a supranational entity as intended by French President Macron and the final document of the Amazon Synod. Time and again, Bolsonaro has appeared as one of the democratic opponents to the globalist agenda.

Not surprisingly, defending the family and life, refusing to accept the gender ideology, the control of the national territory by supranational entities, the uncontrolled immigration, and the creation of a political patronage, Bolsonaro is abhorred and receives a markedly negative treatment from the media.

Donald Trump or the Resistance in the United States

On November 8, 2016, Democratic candidate Hillary Clinton and Republican candidate Donald Trump faced each other in the U.S. presidential election. By all appearance, Hillary was the only one who could win in that electoral contest. Not only did almost all the media in the United States and abroad announce a comfortable victory for Hillary, but Trump, who had not been supported by a large part of his own party's elites, had been portrayed in the worst light. In fact, only the deeply democratic nature of the primary had allowed Trump to become the Republican candidate. However, one thing was what the media claimed, and another, which was very different, was what the American people thought. In September 2016, the writer of these lines announced in the European media that Trump could win the election. I repeated it in the American media in the following weeks.[4] And that is what happened. On January 20, 2017, Trump became the fiftieth president of the United States.

The reasons for his victory resulted, for many reasons, from the horror inspired in millions of American citizens by the politics, openly supportive of the globalist agenda, that Hillary Clinton planned to carry out. Of course, a large part of the Democratic Party was not prepared to accept the electoral defeat, and during that same month of January 2017, the author of these lines was able to hear from a relevant member of the party how they would try to have Trump impeached before the middle of his term in office. It must be recognized that Trump's challenges to the globalist agenda were clear and forceful from day one. Determined to defend US borders, the new president banned citizens of several Muslim-majority countries from traveling to the United States for security reasons and insisted on the need to build—or rather expand—the border fence between Mexico and the United States. Not convinced of the veracity of the global warming advocates' theses, he withdrew the United States from the Paris Agreement on climate change. Eager to maintain national sovereignty in the area of the economy, Trump also pulled the nation out of the Trans-Pacific Economic Cooperation Agreement and imposed import tariffs on various products from China, Canada, Mexico, and the European Union. In addition, Trump defined himself as prolife during the election campaign and has cut subsidies to Planned Parenthood, a virtual abortion industry. A supporter of natural marriage, he has not hesitated, however, to send greetings to the gay community in the United States.

4. https://cesarvidal.com/blog/actualidad/votar-a-trump.

In other aspects of international policy, such as the withdrawal from the intermediate-range nuclear forces treaty or the agreement on Iran's nuclear program, Trump has not been particularly original, and Republican and even Democratic presidents could have done exactly the same. Something similar can be said of the abandonment of his firm position towards Saudi Arabia. He has proved to be more daring on issues such as the recognition of Jerusalem as the capital of Israel or the annexation of the Syrian Golan Heights by Israel, since both positions are in conflict with international law and were therefore avoided by previous presidents. In fact, that has been the position of the vast majority of the international community.

However, the fact that Trump has nonetheless distanced himself from the globalist agenda in areas such as illegal immigration, the right to life, and the theses of the global warming advocates, combined with the Democratic Party's inability to accept the electoral defeat of 2016, has resulted in a harassment against Trump that has no legal basis.

Thus, the investigations to prove that there was Russian interference in the presidential elections and that Trump agreed to such a circumstance came to nothing. At no time was it possible to prove that Trump had reached any kind of agreement with the Russians,[5] but even in the case of the Russians, the alleged interference did not go beyond the opposing position of some Russian media to Hillary Clinton and the suspicion that even certain leaks were made by the Democratic Party in an attempt to do damage control.[6] Such a setback has not prevented the Democratic Party from initiating impeachment proceedings against Donald Trump in late 2019. This revealing step began shortly after the failure of the so-called Russian plot—Russiagate—and after it came to light more explicitly, because of the fact that it had been going on for years, Joe Biden, the Democratic Party's leading candidate for the presidency, succeeded in removing the Ukrainian

5. https://www.nytimes.com/2019/03/24/us/politics/mueller-report-summary.html; https://theintercept.com/2019/04/18/robert-mueller-did-not-merely-reject-the-trumprussia-conspiracy-theories-he-obliterated-them/.

6. https://www.forbes.com/sites/paulroderickgregory/2017/06/19/is-russiagate-really-hillarygate/#26acacd55cf6.

attorney general from office who was investigating the alleged corruption of Joe Biden's son Hunter Biden in this Eastern European country characterized by precisely that kind of shameful practices.

If we have to look at the issue from a purely functional perspective, it is imperative to point out that the impeachment proceedings against Trump have virtually no chance of success. In fact, Article I, Section 3 of the United States Constitution requires that in order to achieve impeachment or presidential removal there must be a two-thirds majority vote of the Senate, which today would be 67 votes out of 100 senators.

Even if, on the other hand, the 45 Democratic senators were to vote against Trump, they would have to be joined by 22 Republican senators and two independent senators to achieve that goal. It is hard to believe that this is possible, and even more so when 12 Democratic senators have already indicated that they will not vote for Trump's impeachment, which, apart from demonstrating their common sense, means that the number of Republicans—and independents—who would have to vote against Trump would have to increase to 34. It does not seem very likely that such an eventuality will arise.

Precisely when one analyses data so simple and evident that they point to the almost absolute impossibility of the effort's success, it is more striking that Nancy Pelosi did not call for a vote prior to the decision to promote the impeachment, that she did not identify a single crime that Trump is alleged to have committed, and even that she did not wait to read the transcript of the conversation between Trump and Ukrainian President Zelensky, which, by the way, forces the Democratic Party's theses to be discarded outright.

To tell the truth, Pelosi's behavior contrasts sharply to that of her counterpart, the Republican Newt Gingrich, who waited four years of investigation before initiating impeachment proceedings against Clinton, proceedings that were much more solidly based than Trump's, and yet nevertheless failed.

Initially, it was thought that the crime that the Democrats would charge Trump with would be 50 USC 30121, a type under the heading of "Contributions and Donations by Foreign Nationals," which states that a foreigner cannot donate or contribute money or "a thing of value" to a federal or state election, nor can an American "solicit" such a "contribution or donation" from a foreigner. From this perspective, by allegedly asking Ukrainian President Zelensky to investigate Joe Biden and his son Hunter for corruption, Donald Trump would have been requesting assistance for the 2020 election campaign in violation of 50 USC 30121 and committed an abuse of power.

However, the Democrats' argument is legally and factually very weak, as it implies, for example, that the "thing of value" would be the investigation that, incidentally, would be legally legitimate, since it would be related to an alleged criminal action by American citizens.

Indeed, the fact that Bill Clinton once lied about his sexual relations with Monica Lewinsky had no legitimate objective, since he was only trying to save his career for political reasons. However, if Trump had asked for an investigation into Biden's actions—something that is far from being established—he would have legal backing to do so, since Ukraine receives millions in aid from the United States, and it is not legal for taxpayers' money to go into the pockets of corrupt foreigners. In fact, Article II of the Constitution empowers Trump, as head of the executive branch, to encourage such actions.

In fact, as Peter Schweizer reported in his very interesting book *Secret Empires*,[7] Hunter Biden, son of then Vice President Joe Biden, accepted a job for which he earned $50,000 a month as a consultant for Burisma Holdings, a Ukrainian natural gas company. Whichever way you look at it, it is absolutely undeniable that the fact that then Vice President Joe Biden was in charge of the investigation into corruption in Ukraine, including the company where his son worked, created an undeniable conflict of interest, a conflict of interests that had to be avoided.

7. P. Schweizer, Secret Empires: *How the American Political Class Hides Corruption and Enriches Family and Friends* (2019).

This conflict of interests was even more evident when one considers that Hunter Biden did not have the slightest professional competence to carry out such lucrative work. The Ukrainians may have discovered a hidden pearl of energetic wisdom within themselves, but it is hard not to think that the position was a payoff to reconcile with Joe Biden's actions, and even more so in a nation like Ukraine, where, as one politician has testified, there are even specific amounts stipulated to bribe members of their Parliament or Duma when it comes to voting.[8]

Indeed, the conflict of interest was so evident that it led John Kerry's stepson, Chris Heinz, to terminate his business partnership with Hunter Biden. Heinz, despite not holding public office, made it clear that he had a greater sensitivity to this issue than Vice President Biden.

As if all this were not enough, in the course of his videotaped speech at a panel held in January 2018 at the Council on Foreign Relations, Joe Biden boasted that he had succeeded in getting Ukrainian prosecutor Viktor Shokin removed from office.[9] The prosecutor, incidentally, was investigating the company that was paying Hunter Biden so well, and Biden was able to secure his removal by blocking $1 billion in aid that the US was to give to Ukraine.[10]

At this point in the story, it is not surprising that the deposed Ukrainian prosecutor Viktor Shokin has signed an affidavit for legal proceedings currently underway in Austria claiming that Joe Biden succeeded in getting him removed because he was conducting a "wide" investigation into the Burisma company whose board of directors included Hunter Biden.

Unfortunately, the Bidens' evidence of corruption is not confined to the very corrupt Ukraine. In fact, one of the most interesting chapters relates to deals with China by Joe Biden and his son Hunter. In that particular case, we would be talking about a figure in excess of one and a half billion dollars.

8. https://cesarvidal.com/la-voz/candilejas-teatro-y-espectaculo/entrevista-a-alexander-onischenko-ucrania-o-la-dictadura-ucraniana-29-03-19.

9. https://www.youtube.com/watch?v=UXA--dj2-CY.

10. https://www.foxnews.com/politics/ukraine-prosecutor-biden-burisma-back-off-state-department-files.

With these facts in hand, it is obvious that, in the case of impeachment against Trump, the prosecutor would have to prove that Joe Biden and his son Hunter did not act corruptly, because if they did, and there are strong indications of this, any move by Trump to move forward with his prosecution would be legally legitimate and even mandatory. But the case does not end there.

It should be noted—and this is another circumstance that makes Democrat Pelosi's initiative a dangerous step—that the transcript of the call between Trump and Zelensky shows not that Trump requested help for his campaign, but that Zelensky raised the issue of the need to clean up corruption and that Trump responded by not mentioning the Bidens, but CrowdStrike, the company that served as support for Russiagate, which was later found to be in the hands of Ukrainian nationalists.[11]

It is precisely at the mention of CrowdStrike that Zelensky pointed out that he knew Rudolf Giuliani, Trump's personal lawyer, was investigating Biden's pressure to have Shokin removed. Only then did Trump say, "I heard that you had a prosecutor...Biden was bragging that he had stopped the investigation, so if you can look at him. Sounds awful to me." At which point Zelensky assured Trump that all investigations would be "open and honest."

However much the transcript is spun, Trump does not address the issue, much less condition the investigation of Biden on the delivery of aid. In fact, Zelensky has already stated publicly that he did not feel pressured by Trump at any time, and in fact references to U.S. aid were not mentioned at that point in the conversation, but at the beginning. These realities became even more apparent when the Democrats finally made public the reasons for the impeachment in a document entitled "Constitutional Grounds for Presidential Impeachment."

According to the document, the first reason for the impeachment is the alleged abuse of power by Trump in pressuring Ukraine

11. For a transcription of these conversations, see: https://www.lawfareblog.com/transcript-first-conversation-between-trump-and-zelensky-april.

to investigate the corruption of Joe Biden on behalf of his son who worked for a company under investigation for corruption. The second reason is the alleged obstruction of Congress. Strikingly, the text lacks legal and factual basis, but it abounds in considerably debatable historical interpretations. On page 32, for example, the document refers to the fact that "many officials were dismissed for noncriminal wrongdoing against the British system of government." The text then mentions "*the Duke of Buckingham (1626), the Earl of Strafford (1640), the Lord Mayor of London (1642), the Earl of Oxford, and the Governor General Warren Hastings (1787).*" This argument is at least striking because it refers to English precedents from the seventeenth and eighteenth centuries and also precedents that do not involve the commission of a crime. In other words, the Democrats intend to remove a president without having taken any illegal action simply on the basis of the dismissal of seventeenth- and eighteenth-century English officials. The Democrats' attempt to remove Trump without a legal basis is substantiated in a quote from Supreme Court Justice Joseph Story, who died in 1845, who is quoted several times and is reproduced twice here: offenses deserving of impeachment "are so varied and complex in character, so profoundly impossible to define or classify, that the task of positive legislation would be impracticable, if it were not almost absurd to attempt it." Judge Story's quote is followed by the statement that "Congress has never, in any investigation or impeachment proceeding, adopted a definition of 'serious crimes and offenses' or a catalogue of offenses that are worthy of impeachment."

The wording of the Democratic document might give the impression that impeachment proceedings are very common, but the reality is that over the centuries they have been followed only twice, first against Andrew Johnson in the nineteenth century and second against Bill Clinton in the twentieth century, and neither case was successful. Nixon, on the other hand, resigned before the impeachment proceedings began.

In its attempt to justify an impeachment without any crime and with a more than debatable factual basis, the document goes on to state that "although President Nixon resigned before Congress could consider the articles of impeachment against him, the allegations of the judicial committee included many noncriminal acts."

Added to this lack of legal basis for initiating Trump's impeachment is a set of citations that do not support such conduct, but allegedly justify it. Alexander Hamilton is quoted as saying that while "the King of Great Britain is sacred and inviolable, the president of the United States can be impeached, tried, and on the basis of a conviction...removed from office." This is an acceptable statement, but it does not by any means imply that Trump is in that position.

This absence of a legal basis for the prosecution of Trump and the attempt to hide it through history reaches a real climax when it is told that King Louis XVI of France wanted to give the American ambassador Benjamin Franklin a snuff box containing 408 diamonds, which led Congress to adopt the Foreign Emoluments Clause, which prohibits presidents and other federal officers from accepting any gift, remuneration, office, or title of any kind from any foreign king, prince, or State without the consent of the Congress." The story of Louis XVI, a late eighteenth-century French monarch, certainly has its historical interest, but beyond the Democrats' insistence on presenting Trump as a monarch, it makes no sense here.

No less striking is that the Democrats' document quotes American lawyer William Rawle, who in 1829 wrote that impeachment should be reserved for men who can "bring about the most serious disasters," which makes one wonder whether, in Trump's case, the disaster feared by the Democrats is simply that he will win reelection next year.

At the same time as the document was being presented, the mother of Tab Biden's son, Joe Biden, has publicly demanded that Biden reveal the money he was receiving from a Chinese company and from Burisma, the Ukrainian company under investigation for corruption.[12]

12. https://www.foxbusiness.com/money/hunter-biden-joe-biden-baby-mother-under-oath-finances; https://www.breitbart.com/politics/2019/12/24/report-hunter-biden-love-childs-mother-paid-by-company-sharing-his-hollywood-hills-address/.

Finally, congressional Democrats have brought charges against President Trump to secure his impeachment, and the result has been deeply disappointing. On the one hand, they point out that Trump abused his power by putting pressure on the president of Ukraine to investigate Biden's corruption, and on the other hand, they indicate that he obstructed the work of Congress. Both allegations have no factual or legal basis. First, the Ukrainian authorities themselves have publicly denied that such pressure existed from Trump, but the fact is that the president, using his executive power, could have urged them to investigate the allegedly corrupt conduct of an American citizen. Second, to call it obstruction of Congress by not taking part in the Democrats' manipulations could be seen as real sarcasm.

The reality is that there is not the slightest legal basis for the impeachment procedure, and the Democrats seem to be aware of this to such an extent that much of their report attempts to justify it with arguments as flimsy as Louis XVI's gift to Benjamin Franklin or the idea that any action, even if not illegal, can serve as a basis. Whichever way you look at it, such reasoning is totally unacceptable and is in direct conflict with the spirit and the contents of the United States Constitution.

To top it all off, the reality remains that Joe Biden, vice president under Obama, by his own admission, did force the dismissal of the Ukrainian prosecutor who was investigating the corrupt company where his son worked and, moreover, has allegedly been involved in a similar episode also involving his son, but located in China. It is no small inconvenience for the only Democratic candidate who would have a minimal chance of facing off with Trump in the election.

In the end, it is hard not to think that what the Democratic Party is after is not justice or that institutions work, but covering up its own corruption and avoiding, at any cost, an electoral defeat next year. As these lines are being written, the Democratic Party has not yet begun the procedures for the Senate to initiate the impeachment procedure.

No matter how you look at it, the initiative to start an impeachment process against Donald Trump seems totally out of place from a legal and factual perspective, but there must surely be reasons. Among them, very possibly, is the inability of a good part of the Democrats to digest the defeat of Hillary Clinton, a defeat that seemed totally impossible judging by what the immense majority of the media was saying, and that constitutes a very powerful reason to submit to a critical analysis what the media is disclosing.

This inability to accept the defeat dragged the Democratic Party into the absurdity of the so-called Russiagate that concluded that Trump never received or agreed to receive help from Russian agents to win the elections, which has also ended up bringing to light the unexemplary conduct of some officials and the fact that the company that provided the data is owned by two Ukrainian nationalists, who are more than interested, of course, in souring relations between the United States and Russia. From that situation, a sector of the Democratic Party—many of them already disillusioned before—came to the conclusion that the path of impeachment was absurd, but what is even more striking about Pelosi's motion is the way in which it was done.

In the case of impeachment, there are two more reasons of enormous gravity. The first is the more than likely desire to prevent an investigation from being opened into Joe Biden, whose alleged corruption, previously reported, would put the entire Obama era under the worst possible light. The fact that Biden was at the time the best candidate situated to win the Democratic nomination for the presidential race added to the gravity of the matter. Not only could Trump compete with someone less influential than Biden—and win the election—but all the propaganda of the Obama era could come crashing down like a house of cards.

The second reason is much more important and, from the point of view of the author of these lines, decisive. I am referring to the very serious drift of the Democratic Party towards socialist positions. With a Right wing, the blue dogs, who remember much of what the Democratic Party has been in other decades, and a Left wing in which figures such as Bernie Sanders or the four women of the Squad stand out, the center of the Democratic Party has shown itself time and again to be incapable of maintaining a balance, recovering the historical positions of the party founded by Jefferson, and eluding the socialist threat. Finally, Nancy Pelosi has not known how, has not been able, or has not wanted to resist the pressures of the socialist sector, and has decided to go towards an impeachment procedure that is practically impossible to win, but which, moreover, contains enormous dangers. For example, the opening of the investigation implies a certain risk of a direct investigation of the activities not only of Joe and Hunter Biden, but also of Hillary Clinton on issues such as the unfortunate episode of Benghazi and of Obama himself. Trying to avoid, therefore, the discovery of the alleged corruption of the vice president, the whole Obama era could be brought into the public light as it never has been. Some may think that even if the impeachment fails, Trump's image will be so muddled that his chances of victory will be diminished. Perhaps, but history shows that Clinton, who went through such a bitter spell, came out, revealingly, prevailing, and the same seems to be happening with Trump. In the end, the next election will surely be determined by something as prosaic and necessary as the economy. If Trump manages to maintain the growth and employment figures—truly exceptional—obtained during his term of office, he will spend eight years in the White House. If the economic crisis shatters in his hands, we may see overwhelming situations.

In the previous lines, we have shown three examples of how there are patriotic politicians who are determined, to a greater or lesser extent, to prevent the advancement of the globalist agenda and who remain within democratic orthodoxy. In the following pages, we will be able to see how other nations have also taken sides in favor of patriotism and against the globalist agenda even if their regimes are not liberal democracies.

CHAPTER XX

RESISTANCE TO THE GLOBALIST AGENDA (I): Russia

A Long and Unknown History

One of the most deplorable manifestations of political and historical ignorance that is easy to encounter is the belief that today's Russia is similar to the former Soviet Union. Such a concept is not only a grave mistake, but a pitiful sign that people have not understood, in the least, that we live in a changing world, one in which the huge division has ceased from passing through the arena of the Left and the Right (Russia is mostly a conservative nation) to establish itself among the globalists. Russia belongs to this second group, so far.

The history of Russia begins relatively late if we compare it with other European nations such as Spain or France, although it is an old nation when compared with those that make up the American continent, not to mention the African ones. That journey was also due to certain circumstances. As Alexander Kérensky,[1] who died in exile

1. A. Kérensky, *Memorias* (Barcelona, 1967), p. 54.

in the United States, would well remember, Russia was, from the beginning, the victim of continuous attacks. Having as its first capital, Stavraya Ladoga, as second—Novgorod—where Prince Rurik reigned, who is considered the founder of the Russian State—and as third, Kiev—the current capital of Ukraine—where the son of Rurik reigned after the death of the founder, Russia resisted the nomads of Asia and then later the aggressors from Lithuania, the Germanic Teutonic Order, Poland, Sweden, and Turkey. She survived all these aggressions thanks to a vigorous sense of national independence, her victory in the great work of liberation against the Tartars, and her formation around a church. If the Tatars are exchanged for the Muslims, and the Orthodox Church for the Catholic Church, the parallel with a nation like Spain is obvious. Another parallel between the two nations lies in the fact that Russia failed to develop a sense of law, and many intellectuals found themselves against State authority and formal law.[2]

That Russia—located in the middle of borders that began in the Barents Sea, which loomed large next to the lands occupied by the Finns, the Baltics, the Poles and the Tartars, and which ended in the Adriatic, in the middle of the fifteenth century—began to emerge from two centuries of servitude under the Mongols and the Turks, precisely at the moment when the Byzantine Empire was disappearing in the face of the Mongols' and Turks' advances. The annihilation of Byzantium in 1453, the heir to the Roman Empire and the quintessential Orthodox power, was of momentous importance to Russian history. It is no coincidence that Ivan III (1462-1505), the first Moscow prince to take the title of Tsar (literally, *tsar*, the Russian form of Caesar), did so shortly after that event. In 1480 Ivan III formalized Moscow's independence from the Golden Horde of the Mongols. As would be repeated time and again, from then on, the first Rome had fallen (476), as well as the second Constantinople (1453), but Moscow had become a third Rome that would not disappear.

2. *Idem, Ibidem.*

In 1533, Ivan IV, who would be called the Terrible, ascended to the throne. Russia would not only begin to trade with England and the Netherlands, but in 1581, it would begin expansion into Siberia, and in 1584, it would open its first port in Arkhangelsk. Russia had survived terrible onslaughts, and with Ivan IV it became an empire, but the death of the tsar was the starting point for the nation to be plunged into anarchy. It is often thought that Russia has been a permanent aggressor against Poland. The reality is that this historical confrontation between the two nations began when Poland decided to subdue Russia by dragging it into submission to the pope. In 1601, Poland was encroaching on Russian territory and supporting an illegitimate claimant to the throne, whom it presented as Dmitri, the son of Ivan IV, who had been murdered years earlier. In 1605, Polish troops occupied Moscow. In 1611, Poland annexed the Russian city of Smolensk with the aim of seizing the Russian crown. Perhaps Russia would have been condemned to be the political and religious servant of Roman Catholic Poland had there not been a popular uprising that began in 1612 and was led by the merchant Minin and Prince Pozharskiy. Both Russian patriots have a monument in Moscow's Red Square.[3] Mikhail III Romanov was forced to accept the loss of Russian territories to Poland and the retreat in areas such as the Baltic and present-day Finland, but, in spite of everything, not only did Russia maintain its independence, but, in addition, it consolidated a dynasty that would remain on the throne for just over three centuries.

Throughout the seventeenth century, Russia expanded considerably into Siberia and began to eliminate the power of the Tartars who had oppressed it. Only the Crimean Tartars, protected by the Turkish Empire, managed to maintain their independence until the end of the eighteenth century, when Crimea became part of Russia. After making peace with the Chinese Empire in 1689, Russia set out to explore the north and eventually annexed the territory on both sides of the Bering Strait, including Alaska. However, the

3. An excellent cinematic portrayal of the moment in the film *1612* directed by Vladimir Jotinenko.

most important thing for Russia would surely not be the continuous territorial expansion, but the modernizing attempts of Peter I, rightly called the Great. Poland, the fierce enemy, had been neutralized in 1667, and Peter was aware of the need to "open a window on Europe." Convinced of the benefits of Protestant culture—it has even been speculated that he joined the Quakers on one of his trips to England—Peter I strove to drag Russia into a social model similar to that of the nations where the Reformation had triumphed. The Protestant culture of work, open education for all, the incorporation of scientific advances, all the aspects that characterized Protestant societies since the sixteenth century and that had so much influence in the solidifying of the United States, were considered by Peter I as goals for whose attainment he relied, not surprisingly, on Germans, Swiss, Scots, and English. On his death, Peter I would leave behind clear victories over Sweden (1721) and Persia (1723), and a new capital with his name—St. Petersburg—which would mean an outlet to the sea in the Gulf of Finland.

After a period of instability and during the reign of Catherine II (1762-96), the southern borders of Russia were secured, and Tartar attacks ceased. By the end of the eighteenth century, Russia controlled all the territories inhabited by the East Slavs and had also managed to retaliate against the aggressions launched by Poland and suffered in the previous century. In fact, Poland ended up being torn apart by Austria, Prussia, and Russia.

Russia, of course, was affected by the French Revolution and the Napoleonic Empire that followed it. Emperor Napoleon threatened Russia's international situation by supporting the creation of an independent Poland since 1807. Russia tried to make a pact with Napoleon regarding the respective affected zones in the Treaty of Tilsit, but she could not prevent the French invasion of 1812. In that war, Russia, under Alexander I, became, together with Spain, the only continental power that managed to defeat the French emperor on its soil. Thanks to the victory over Napoleon, Russia secured its control over Poland, Finland, Bessarabia, and much of the Caucasus.

Nicholas I, the successor to Alexander I, solidified an autocratic system based directly on the Orthodox Church which, for that very reason, sought to grant its protection to peoples of the same faith. Such a view would end up in a clash with Turkey, an Islamic power, which ruled not only the former territories of the Byzantine Empire but also its Christian populations. In 1853, Russia had to confront France and England, who were determined to defend Turkey even if it did not guarantee the freedom of worship for Christians living in the territory of the Muslim empire. While in the Mediterranean, France and England were shoring up an Islamic empire to stop possible Russian expansion; in Central Asia, Britain was doing its best to win in what would become known as the Great Game, i.e., the rivalry with Russia over areas of Asia such as Afghanistan. Great Britain was not confronting Russia on ideological grounds, but out of a desire to maintain or extend its imperial rule in Asia.

From the Reforms of Alexander II to the Revolution

At the end of the nineteenth century, Russia occupied one sixth of the globe, within its borders lived one hundred and thirty million subjects of the czar made up of ethnic groups such as Russians and Jews, Germans and Armenians, Uzbeks and Georgians. It was undoubtedly a great power, but its backward structures forced it to undertake a thorough modernization. This challenge was taken up by Tsar Alexander II,[4] who would go down in history, especially thanks to the abolition of serfdom,[5] which at that time weighed down on 44.5% of the Russian population. On March 3 (February 19, according to the Gregorian calendar) in 1861, Alexander II signed the manifesto for

4. On Alejandro II, see: E. Belyakova, *Detsvo i iunost imperatora Aleksandra II: Ocherk* (Saint Petersberg, 1911); N. Golubev, *Vospominanya o tsare-osovoboditele Aleksandre II* (Pskov, 1882); V. A. Kovalev, *Zalozhniki zabluzhdenya: Istorya pokushenyi na Aleksandra II* (Moscow, 1995); E. Radzinsky, *Alexander II. The Last Great Tsar* (New York, 2005).

5. On this matter, see especially: P. A. Zaionchkovskii, *The Abolition of Serfdom in Russia, Gulf Breeze, 1978* and *Idem, The Russian Autocracy in Crisis, 1878-1882* (Gulf Breeze, 1976).

the emancipation of the serfs. This came before Abraham Lincoln's Emancipation decree in favor of American slaves and also adopted much stronger measures such as returning the land to the serfs. Three years after the abolition of serfdom, in January 1864, a modernization also took place, not without democratic overtones, of local government through the establishment of the *zemstvo* (a system of elected councils to administer local affairs), which, until its abolition in 1917, enabled truly extraordinary progress to be made in areas such as education and health, to the extent that it provided Russia with a socialized medical service, with all the details one could want, well before that of other European countries. At the end of that same year, the legal system was reformed. Fundamentally focused on making judges an independent branch of the administration and inserting the principles of freedom of the press and speech into the process, it can hardly be denied that it served to turn the Russian judicial system—until then one of the most backward in Europe—into one of the most advanced in the world. Significantly, the Russian courts were very lenient towards political prisoners—even if they were terrorists—and did not allow themselves to be pressured even by popular animosity towards the accused. This zealous judicial independence was of enormous importance before the revolution. It is revealing that when Tolstoy wanted to write his great drama about judicial injustice, the novel *Resurrection*, he attributed the misfortune to a technical error of the jury, but not to the institution nor the judges.

Alexander II was also aware of the need for changes in the financial field, which had, among other consequences, the establishment of a single public treasury, the publication of an annual budget, and in 1866 the creation of a State bank whose mission was to centralize and facilitate credit and finance. Alexander II's reforms were of paramount importance and involved genuine giant steps forward in areas that had remained unchanged for centuries. In fact, at the beginning of the twentieth century, many nations still lack institutions as modern as those promoted by Alexander II. However, it is no less true that they emerged at a time of particular tension between generations, a tragic social evolution that derived from a terrorist-focused populism. In 1876, Land and Liberty was founded for that purpose, and three years later it was split into two groups called Total Distribution of Land and People's Will. The members of the People's Will had concluded that, given the centralized nature of the empire, a certain number of murders would lead to its collapse. Of course, the ideal victim was the Tsar himself, who was the target of a serious hunt until he was successfully assassinated on March 13, 1881. Together with Alexander II, the terrorists of the People' Will killed any possibility of political reform that could have been undertaken by the sovereign's immediate successors. Modernization would continue, but it would henceforth be autocratic.[6]

The new tsar, Alexander III, in his manifesto on May 11, 1881, stated that his priorities were to suppress the revolution and put an end to terrorism. He succeeded, but at the same time he opted for a policy of Russification and the predominance of the Orthodox Church, which had disastrous results for Protestants, Catholics, nationalities (especially Polish), and Jews. From 1887, quotas for Jewish students were also established.[7]

From 1881, pogroms became common within the Russian empire, especially in areas such as Poland, the Ukraine, and the Crimea, where the number of Russians was smaller and the influence of the Roman Catholic Church was particularly strong. In fact, the accusation of ritual crime was unknown in the Orthodox Church—as well as in the Protestant Church—but it played a significant role in the Roman Catholic Church, where alleged victims of Jewish ritual killings are venerated even today. Discouraged at first, and

6. Apart from the above-mentioned more advanced works for specific aspects, on industrialization, see: W. L. Blackwell, *The Beginnings of Russian Industrialization, 1800-1860* (Princeton, 1968); A. Gerschenkron, "Agrarian Policies and Industrialization, Russia 1861-1917" en *Cambridge Economic History*, 6, parte 2 (Cambridge, 1966); *Idem*, *Economic Backwardness in Historical Perspective* (Cambridge, MA, 1962); L. Lih, *Bread and Authority in Russia, 1914-1921* (Berkeley, 1990); J. P. McKay, *Pioneers for Profit: Foreign Entrepreneurship and Russian Industrialization, 1885-1913* (Chicago, 1970); M. I. Tugan-Baranowsky, *The Russian Factory in the 19th Century* (Homewood, 19700; T. H. Von Laue, *Sergei Witte and the Industrialization of Russia* (New York, 1963).

7. These were a maximum of ten percent of the students in the confinement area, a maximum of five percent in other provinces, and a maximum of three percent in Moscow and St. Petersburg.

then condemned by the Orthodox Church authorities, they were very often linked to episodes of subversion whose reprisals did not fall on the Jews alone. For example, the Kishiniov pogrom in 1903 took place in a town where there were fifty thousand Jews, fifty thousand Moldovans, and eight thousand Russians, most of whom were Ukrainians. The protagonists of the pogrom were actually the Moldovans. In fact, it was the Moldovan Pavel Krushevan who was responsible not only for stirring up the masses, but also for writing the first version of the *Protocols of the Wise Men of Zion*, the anti-Semitic pamphlet. The fact was widely known to the Jews living in Russia at the time.[8] Nevertheless, the Russian justice system acted with great seriousness in the face of the terrible episode. The number of arrests was close to one thousand, and 664 people were brought to justice for the crimes committed.

At the same time, the process of industrialization began to receive direct support from the State.[9] In 1894, when Alexander III died and his son, Nicholas II, succeeded him, the main policies of his reign—autocracy and industrialization—were indelibly and irrevocably set in place. The advance in the field of communications was truly extraordinary both in economic[10] and military[11] terms. Sergey Yulievich Vitte played a decisive role in the development of this czarist policy. Appointed in 1892 as Minister of Communications and shortly after the Treasury, he developed a fiscal policy in line with his development goals and demonstrated considerable ability to manage a growing public debt. In addition, he founded schools for training engineers and maritime personnel, reformed corporate law, founded a weights and measures office, achieved the convertibility of the

8. S. J. Zipperstein, *Pogrom. Kishinev and the Tilt of History* (New York, 2018).

9. By way of example, before the outbreak of the First World War, Russia produced, for example, four million metric tons of iron and steel, forty million metric tons of coal, and ten million metric tons of oil.

10. The train lines linking the Volga and Ukraine to the Baltic were intended, for example, to facilitate grain exports; in other cases, such as those around Moscow, the Urals and Ukraine, the aim was to boost new industrial centers. The Trans-Siberian itself was intended, among other things, to facilitate mining in Siberia.

11. The most obvious cases were, for example, the St. Petersburg-Warsaw or Moscow-Brest.Litovsk-Warsaw train lines, which were intended to facilitate military transport in the West. The Trans-Siberian was also partly intended for this purpose at a time when Japan was becoming a threat in the East and China was in a thorough process of disintegration.

ruble, promoted savings banks, and, especially, restructured the State Bank so that it could grant loans for industrial purposes. Naturally, a policy of this magnitude could hardly be carried out in the midst of political turbulence and international tension, so Vitte, aware of this, became a pragmatic pacifist. Thus, in 1899 he enthusiastically supported the First Peace Conference held in The Hague. Born of this Russian initiative, it established some of the first rules of humanitarian law of war and, above all, the International Court of Justice was established in The Hague.

Vitte believed strongly in the expansion of Russian influence in the international arena, but he considered that these goals had to be achieved using financial rather than military instruments. Along with industry and economic expansion, Russia experienced spectacular demographic growth at the same time. In 1867, the Russian population was 63 million; by the outbreak of World War I the figure had reached 122 million.

Russian companies copied, in part, the European pattern of acquiring a large amount of capital. However, there was also a rapid increase in small businesses. Similarly, in 1882, the first workers' legislation was passed, and child labor under the age of twelve was banned and their working hours limited. However, it should be noted that on the eve of World War I, the industrial proletariat was limited to 5% of the population.[12] It was on that portion of the population that the social democrats[13] acted, not as the present non-Marxist socialists, but precisely those who followed Marx. They advocated giving a political priority role to the proletariat and, in 1903, founded a party whose aim was to bring about socialism. Since the majority of the nation was agrarian, the social democrats lacked unity of action and even the ability

12. R. W. Goldsmiths, "Economic Growth of Tsarist Russia 1860-1913" in *Economic Development and Cultural Change*, 9, p. 442.

13. On the social democrats, see: S.H. Baron, *Plekhanov: The Father of Russian Marxism* (Stanford, 1963); I. Getzler, *Martov : A Political biography of a Russian Social Democrat* (New York, 1967); L. H. Haimson, *The Russian Marxists and the Origins of Bolchevism* (Cambridge, MA, 1955); J. L. H. Keep, *The Rise of Social Democracy in Russia* (Oxford, 1963); D. W. Treadgold, *Lenin and His Rivals: The Struggle for Russia's Future, 1898-1906* (New York, 1955); A. B. Ulam, *The Bolsheviks* (New York, 1965); A. Wildman, *The Making of a Workers' Revolution: Russian Social Democracy, 1899-1903* (Chicago and London, 1967).

to formulate new ideas. Far from expecting the evolution of society according to Marxist orthodoxy, Vladimir Ilyich Ulyanov, alias Lenin, was in favor of creating an organization of revolutionaries that would, in a professional way, accelerate the process of revolution and socialism. Lenin's position was severely criticized by the rest of the social democrats who were orthodox Marxists. This led to the division between Lenin's Bolsheviks (majority) and Mensheviks (minority). In the end, Lenin's heterodox pragmatism would eventually impose itself on the orthodoxy of the Mensheviks in a country with a hundred million peasants.

In 1896, the first general strike in Russian history broke out. It ended with the workers' defeat, but, the following year, the second one took place, and this time the government was forced to reduce the working day to eleven and a half hours.[14] Russia was advancing, without the slightest doubt, but progress was affecting its inhabitants unevenly. This could be seen during the great famine of 1891. In the course of this famine, the peasants literally began to die of hunger. In 1898-1899 there was another famine, this time in the Volga region, and in 1901 and 1902 the peasants' hunger of Poltava and Kharkov ended up triggering violent uprisings. It is easy to understand why the agrarian revolts took place in areas where land was scarce due to a variety of circumstances ranging from population growth (out of step with production) to the decrease of rental land by its owners for more lucrative purposes such as sugar beet cultivation. It is not surprising, therefore, that in the late nineteenth and early twentieth centuries there was an increasing migration to Siberia as the only way to escape debt and hunger in the countryside or exploitation and misery in the city.[15] However, the life of Russian peasants was no more difficult, for example, than that of their contemporaries in Spain or Italy as well as in much of Eastern Europe. Their biggest problem, in fact, was their population growth. On the eve of the revolution, the peasants already

14. For an interesting study, see: *V. Sviatlovsky, Professionalnoye Dvizhenie v Rossii* (St. Petersberg, 1907), pp. 18ff.

15. In the same vein, see: F.X. Coquin, "Faim et Migrations Paysannes en Russie au XIX Siècle" in *Revue d'Histoire Moderne et Contemporaine*, 11 (1964).

possessed as much land as the lords and merchants, but they wanted the Tsar to carry out a national distribution that would give the communes the land that was still out of their control and in private hands. The peasantry also experienced extraordinary advances in the field of education during the last years of the nineteenth century. While in 1868 the number of illiterates was well over 90% of the peasantry, in 1897 half of those under twenty years of age could read and write, and the number of farmers with a high school diploma had tripled.[16]

Embedded in a policy of forced modernization that was not without enormous social costs, Russia was not going to easily obtain the success that it expected. Industry had certainly made huge strides. However, it lacked a large enough domestic market and still needed a continuous influx of foreign loans and State aid. The latter were secure, but the former posed problems. For example, Britain was opposed to the development of a power with which it competed in the Mediterranean and Central Asia. In the United States, moreover, some Jewish bankers like Jacob Schiff insisted that no loans be granted to Russia. Schiff[17] would later help the Russian revolutionaries.[18]

As the turn of the century approached, despite its undeniable economic and social advances, a growing detachment of the population of the Russian empire from its institutions had begun. Ethnic minorities—especially Jews and Poles—felt alienated if not oppressed. The peasantry, which formed the largest segment of the population, did not seem particularly grateful for the liberation of the serfs and wanted concessions that the tsar could hardly give them. Finally, in spite of its very minority character, a large part of the proletariat did not see in a positive light the economic advance, of which it formed a substantial part. The main cause of this dissatisfaction was the *intelligentsia*, which, in general terms, did not expect a reform that would

16. C. A. Anderson, "A Footnote to the Social History of Modern Russia - The Literacy and Education Census of 1897" in *Genus*, 12, 1-4, 1956.

17. Regarding Schiff, the work of Cyrus Adler is indispensable, *Jacob H. Schiff. His Life and Letters*, 2 vols. (New York, 1928).

18. A. C. Sutton, *Wall Street and the Bolshevik Revolution* (Forest Row, 2013), pp. 186ff.

change the monarchy in a liberal sense, but simply its disappearance. A person with a legal background and a Christian base, as was the case with Alexander Kérensky, had already reached the conviction in 1905 that terrorism was "unavoidable."[19] A rereading of the literature of the time is enough to see that, far from assimilating the positive changes, the *intelliguentsia* only saw Russia as a society to be annihilated from top to bottom.

In 1894, Nicolas II ascended to the throne of the Russian Empire.[20] Only two years later, the Fundamental Law of the empire had been promulgated, whose first article stated that the Tsar had "unlimited power" and that this originated from "the same God" who ordered that he be obeyed "both out of conscience and out of fear." Far from being a feudal regime—as is often inaccurately repeated—Russia was subject to a patrimonialist view of power close to certain forms of oriental government. Nicholas II might have been a good constitutional monarch if he had been educated to do so. He lacked the skills to be an autocrat. In 1905, Russia suffered a defeat at the hands of the Japanese, which led to a revolution. It was aborted, but the Tsar did not know how to run the country's life despite making some liberal concessions.

In 1906, the Tsar appointed Piotr Arkadievich Stolypin—a man who had demonstrated an extraordinary ability to control the situation from his position as governor during 1905—as president of the government and dissolved the Duma, the Parliament established after the revolution. Stolypin was not only to follow the path of modernization, but also to put an end to the violence of popular insurrections and terrorist attacks.[21] During 1906 alone, the number of officials killed, despite the strong antiterrorist measures articulated

19. A. Kérensky, OC, p. 80.

20. Regarding Nicolás II, see: S. Harcave, *Years of the Golden Cockerel: The Last Romanov Tsars, 1814-1917* (New York, 1968); R. K. Massie, *Nicholas and Alexandra* (New York, 1967).

21. Regarding the subject, see: A. Geifman, *Thou Shalt Kill: Revolutionary Terrorism in Russia 1894-1917* (Princeton, 1993); D. Hardy, *Land and Freedom: The Origins of Russian Terrorism* (Westport, 1987); A. Platonov, *Stranichka iz istorii eserovskoi konttrevoliutsii* (Mosow, 1923); A. Spiridovitch, *Histoire du terrorisme russe, 1886-1917* (Paris, 1930).

by Stolypin, was close to four thousand.[22] This is undoubtedly an overwhelming figure, which indicates, on the one hand, the violently radical nature of a significant part of the opposition and, on the other, that the tsarist repression, despite all that has been written, was far from being as harsh and as effective as that of the Bolsheviks a few years later.

It was in this atmosphere of revolutionary violence and response by the tsarist authorities that the second Duma was convened, with the date of its inauguration set for February 20, 1907. Significantly, the Second Duma had an even more left-wing structure than the First Duma. Its failure would be similar to that of the first and the third and fourth that followed it. Whatever one thinks, the Parliamentary regime did not seem to work in Russia.

At the same time, in macroeconomic terms, no one can deny that Stolypin achieved enormous successes. Increasingly, monopolies appeared in Russia[23] under the direct influence of Russian banks and foreign capital, especially French capital.[24] In the countryside, Stolypin tried to create a class of average farmers to serve as a defense against a possible peasant revolution. The results, however, were apparently encouraging. In fact, if in 1907 the number of riots in agriculture reached 1,337, by 1915, already in the middle of the World War, it had been reduced to 96.[25]

On the eve of World War I, the Russian empire was going through a long phase of economic growth, industrial development, military might, and social stability. No one could have denied—because it was an unquestionable reality—that Russia had never been larger or stronger or richer. One could even point out that Stolypin had begun to take steps to solve problems such as the discrimination suffered by the Jews. The truth, however, is that the reality was more

22. L. I. Strajovsky, "The Statemanship of Peter Stolypin" en SEER, 37, 1959, n. 89, p. 356.

23. V. I. Boyvkin, I. F. Guindin, K. G. Tarnovsky, "Gosudartsvernii monopoliticheskii Kapitalizm v Rossii" en Istoriya SSSR, n. 3, 1959, p. 92.

24. F.X. Coquin, "Aperçus sur l'economie tsariste avant 1914" in *Revue d'Histoire Moderne*, n. 7, 1960, p. 68.

25. Dubrovsky, *Stolypinskaya Zemelnyaya Reforma* (Moscow 1963), p. 518.

diverse and, above all, more dangerous. Stolypin was murdered—after seven previous attempts—by a Jewish terrorist named Bogrov in September 1911. Significantly, Bogrov was the son of a bourgeois who was bent on destroying the world in which his father had managed to prosper.

On June 28, 1914, Austrian Archduke Franz Ferdinand and his wife were murdered by a Serbian independence fighter. When Austria-Hungary declared war on Serbia, Germany was the guarantor of the former and Russia of the latter. At the time the tsar ordered the mobilization, Germany interpreted this as an act of hostility and declared war on him and his ally France. In response, Britain made the same decision regarding Germany. Such steps unleashed an explosion of joy in the governments and people that did not exclude even the socialist parties,[26] which up to this time had been defined as internationalist and pacifist. Being able to choose between their nation and their proletarian brothers and sisters in other countries, the overwhelming majority of socialists opted for the former. In Russia, at the Duma session of July 26, 1914, the deputies were unanimous in their support for the war, with the exception of the six Mensheviks, the five Bolsheviks and the Trudoviki or Labor Party.[27]

At the same time, the enemies of the regime continued to advance their positions. On the eve of World War I, the Bolsheviks had taken control of most of the trade unions in St. Petersburg and Moscow.[28] This was a process that would culminate in the St. Petersburg general strike of July 1914.[29] There, the workers continued to fight in the streets until July 15, just the day before Russia entered World War I.[30]

26. In this regard, see: B. Tuchman, *Oc*, pp. 474ff.

27. As on so many other occasions, Lenin took a very personal stance. According to this position, the war should not be prevented, but should be transformed into a civil war against the bourgeoisie, even if this meant the loss of all Russian borderlands for the time being. In the same sense, citing contemporary testimonies, see D. Shub, *Lenin* (Madrid, 1977), vol. 1, pp. 213ff.

28. V. Grinevich, *Die Gewerkschaftsbewegung in Russland I (1905-14)* (Berlin, 1927), p. 289.

29. *Rabochee Dvizhenie v Petrograde v 1912-17 gg* (Leningrado, 1958), n. 102, p. 209.

30. On Russia's role in World War I, see: General A. Denikin, *The Russian Turmoil* (London, 1922); Lieutenant Colonel N. N. Golovin, *The Russian Army in the World War* (London, 1931); General B. Gourko, *Memories and Impressions of War and Revolution in Russia*, (London, 1918); General Sir Alfred Knox, *With the Russian Army 1914-1917* (London, 1921); B. Pares, *Day by Day with the Russian Army* (Lonon, 1915); W. Rutherford, *The Russian Army in World War I*, (London, 1975).

World War I was a huge bloodbath for Russia. During 1915, the Russians suffered two million casualties among the dead and wounded and no less than 1.3 million prisoners. By the end of the year, the Russians had lost Libau, Galicia, Warsaw, Lithuania, and, to top it off, the German fleet had entered Riga. In addition, the total number of Russian casualties caused by the war until then was already a frightening four million three hundred and sixty thousand people.[31] In 1915, social conflicts also reappeared, which the Germans saw as a magnificent opportunity to destroy their adversary from within. Thus, through the Jew Parvus[32] they began to subsidize some of the Russian revolutionaries, including Lenin.[33]

The situation became even worse after the failure of the Russian offensive in 1916. It is true that, thanks to it, the Russians, who were being used as cannon fodder, managed to save Italy from an Austrian invasion and absorbed a considerable number of German forces that, otherwise, would have clashed with the British and French armies. However, during that year the Russians suffered two million casualties among the dead and wounded, in addition to 350,000 prisoners.

On February 13, 1917, some demonstrations began to take place in Petrograd during which people broke windows to steal food and shouted slogans against the war, the police, and extortion. Considering what the years 1915 and 1916 had been like, the phenomenon almost seemed the least that could be expected. On February 22 and 23, hunger catapulted striking workers into the streets. On several occasions, the soldiers not only refused to repress them but also joined them. On February 25, the troops mutinied. On the 29th, the entire Petrograd garrison, one hundred and seventy thousand men, had declared themselves in open rebellion.

31. J. S. Curtiss, *Oc*, p. 24.

32. The biography on Parvus is yet to be written despite its enormous importance in the revolutionary process. It can be consulted in the work of Z. A. B. Zeman and W. B. Scharlau, *The Merchant of Revolution. The Life of Alexander Israel Helphand (Parvus)* (New York, 1965).

33. Naturally this aspect was radically denied by the Bolsheviks, who once in power even sought to make disappear documents referring to payments received by them from Germany. Only the recent declassification of the documents has made it possible to settle this question definitively. Of particular interest on the subject, see: Z. A. B. Zeman, *Germany and the Revolution in Russia and Idem and W. Scharlau, The Merchant of Revolution* (Oxford, 1965).

In a final attempt to save the dynasty, the deputies of the Duma pleaded with Grand Duke Michael Alexandrovich, the brother of the Tsar, to assume dictatorial powers, overthrow the government, and force Nicholas II to appoint responsible ministers. The tsar, against the law, gave up the crown for himself and his successors. He also did so to avoid bloodshed and civil war. It was this factor, together with the passivity of the monarchists, that gave the revolutionaries victory[34] Certainly, the results could not have been worse. The alternative did not work. In fact, Michael would only reign one day, and like his brother, the tsar, he would be killed by the Bolsheviks. At midnight on February 27, the various party leaders formed a provisional committee in the Duma. After much hesitation, three days later the committee appointed a provisional government. The monarchy had collapsed, not because of the strength of its enemies, but because of the lack of firmness of its defenders.

From the Bolshevik Coup to the Collapse of the Soviet Union

Russia had become a democratic republic—the freest country in the world, one would say—but the new regime did not manage to survive. Its insistence on continuing the war alongside her allies rather than withdrawing from the conflict, the failure of a new military offensive, and Lenin's return from exile—due to the conditions agreed between Parvus and the German empire, and determined to establish a socialist dictatorship—sealed the fate of the new regime that had emerged from the collapse of tsarism. After months of deterioration of the provisional government, in October 1917, the Bolsheviks staged a coup d'état that would lead to a socialist revolution, a terrible civil war and the establishment of the first totalitarian state in history.

34. In this same vein, see: A. Solzhenitsyn, *Raznyshlenya o fevralskoi rievoliutsii* (1995), end of chapter 1 and the beginning of chapter 2.

It goes far beyond the scope of this book to describe the historical evolution of the Soviet Union. However, it is necessary to point out that, a little more than a century later, the Bolshevik Revolution has provided lessons of undeniable relevance related to historical analysis, the development of social engineering, and geopolitics. In the former USSR, with political guidelines dictated by the government and closed archives, it was not difficult to impose an official—and false—view of what had happened. Among the gross simplifications of propaganda was that of the inevitability of a revolution or the consideration of the period between the February and October revolution as a pause. Likewise, the Bolshevik coup d'état of October 1917 was transformed into mass action. The climax was that the Bolsheviks would have laid the foundations of a true worker and peasant State in which terror had only been a response to counterrevolutionary provocations and the dictatorship of Stalin a dramatic accident. What is certain, however, is that the February revolution was initially peaceful and bloodless, and if Tsar Nicholas II had decided to remain on the throne by fire and sword, neither the first revolutionaries nor the Bolsheviks would have come to power. Even with the abdication of the tsar, if the revolutionary regime of February had been able to stabilize, the result would have been a Russia governed by the most modern, democratic, and socialized system up until then. However, the provisional government presided over by Kérensky did not know how to handle the war situation, respected the law in an exaggerated manner, and feared more the possibility of a military coup more than the Bolsheviks. Lenin had none of these scruples and knew how to face all challenges with a ruthless tactical talent.

When the elections to the Constituent Assembly, held in November and December of 1917, ended in a Bolshevik defeat, Lenin dissolved with military force the Assembly that had been voted in at the ballot boxes, and began to arrest his opponents en masse. Lenin never believed that he could stay in power except by terror, and he told his comrades this time and time again. The declassified documents following the collapse of the Soviet Union[35] contain precise instructions ordering mass killings, the internment of whole sections of society in concentration camps, and the unleashing of reprisals against the relatives of unfortunate suspects. Lenin even ceded huge portions of the Russian empire to his enemies simply to buy time.

The Bolshevik victory was a direct result of a combination of material superiority, ruthless terror (Lenin's term), pragmatism, indifference to Russia as a nation (the vast majority of the Bolshevik leaders were not Russians, including Lenin himself, who was only one eighth Russian), and the interests of an active clientele (the Communists, whose party reached nearly three quarters of a million people during the war). The end of the civil war did not bring about the end of terror, but it became, as Lenin had made clear on many occasions, a substantial and inseparable element of the regime. Thus, Stalin, who ruled the Soviet Union from 1922 until his death in 1953, was not a dangerous mutation, but a direct and legitimate son of Lenin and his ideas.

Between 1929 and 1953 alone, twenty-three and a half million citizens of the USSR were imprisoned, and one-third of them lost their lives before a firing squad. However, Russia was not the only one who paid a high price. The Western powers certainly did not take steps to bring about the end of Leninist rule. In addition, there was no shortage of businessmen and financiers who saw the Bolsheviks as a direct and safe way to access the immense raw materials lying beneath Russian soil. What was important for these people was neither the suffering nor the freedom of the Russian people, but their own economic benefits. Stalin's triumph prevented this in the end, but not before immense fortunes were amassed and conclusions were drawn so that a very similar situation could be repeated more successfully when the USSR collapsed.

The second set of lessons from the Bolshevik Revolution relates to the social engineering project. Religion, music, poetry, the press... everything could be controlled by the State's political power while reducing the rebels to nothing. In the course of a few years, there was

35. The translation, for the first time, of some of these documents into Spanish can be found in César Vidal, *La revolución rusa: Un balance a cien años de distancia* (Buenos Aires, 2017), pp. 250ff.

no moral reference to even look at, and any cultural manifestation became a propaganda act. The Bolsheviks controlled private life to the most intimate extremes. Thus, they proceeded to legalize abortion, for the first time in history, and to introduce State control over children. In addition, they deprived the citizens of their property, while the number of officials and patrons in power increased dramatically. This new class born out of the growth of the State would be key to Stalin's rise to absolute power. Finally, education was remodeled to become an instrument of indoctrination, of shaping souls and hearts, and of consolidating a new society. However, once again, Stalin realized the damage that such a scheme could cause to the nation. The literary, musical, artistic talents, in short, of his time were not matched later, and include such great names as Prokofiev, Shostakovich, Khachaturian, Pasternak, Sholokhov, Eisenstein, and many others that have found no parallel after the fall of the Soviet Union.

The results of this set of social experiments were mixed. The fact that art collapsed amidst apathy and even ridicule mattered little to those who viewed it only as propaganda. However, Lenin himself soon realized the negative impact of not having capable scientists, and Stalin understood the damage that a collapse of the family institution could cause to the USSR. Thus, within a few years, the view of the family ended up centered around a socialist conservatism, and abortion was once again banned. Even art acquired moral tones known canonically as socialist realism, which extolled work, love of country, sacrifice, and selflessness. A certain degree of destruction of the social fabric was unacceptable, because it implied, in the end, the destruction of the nation.

This system of social engineering would be used in the following decades, even after the collapse of the USSR, in different parts of the world. In the end, its use was seen as an advance in the history of the human race, although, in truth, it was only a way of imposing ideological totalitarianism. The parallels in this respect with the imposition of gender ideology and the agenda of the LGTB lobby present notable similarities. Both have already resulted in the approval of inquisitorial laws in several countries, but it is precisely those who were censored, persecuted, and retaliated against by these norms who appear before the forum of public opinion as antiquated enemies of progress. More than a hundred years after the Bolshevik victory, there is no doubt that some of the most important lessons have not been learned.

What happened in Russia appeared to be an internal Russian affair, waged by Russians and resolved by Russians. In reality, it was very different. To begin with, both the German Empire and Wall Street played an extraordinary role in the development of the revolution.[36] It is more than doubtful that the outcome would have been what it was without those foreign interventions. The State Department's collection of documents known as the State Department Decimal File (861.00/5339) is a veritable gold mine for the researcher who wishes to know who engineered the revolution in Russia. In a document dated November 13, 1918, it is stated that the revolution was planned in February 1916, and that the persons and firms that supported it from abroad were Jacob Schiff; Kuhn, Loeb and Company; Felix Warburg; Otto H. Kahn; Mortimer L. Schiff; Jerome J. Hanauer; Guggenheim; Max Breitung; and Isaac Seligman. The report notes, for example, that banker Jacob Schiff was already financing Trotsky in the spring of 1917. The reality is that Lenin and Trotsky would certainly not have set foot on Russian soil without such direct and conscious support. Added to this is a terrible factor that is always overlooked. The repression would not have been so brutal either—seven hundred and fifty thousand people to whom Putin[37] would pay homage—if it were not for the fact that the executioners were not part of them. The whole process of social engineering was carried out in a totally ruthless way precisely because it was executed with "other" people who were not Russian. The facts, in this respect, are quite revealing. Lenin had only an

36. A. C. Sutton's *Wall Street and the Bolshevik Revolution* (Forest Row, 2011) is still a must-read, but the bibliography has become more extensive over time. Of particular interest are Mikhail Heller and Aleksandr M. Nekrich, *Utopia in Power. The History of the Soviet Union from 1917 to the Present* (New York, 1986), pp. 213ff., which describes the business of American companies with the Soviet Union at a time that was economically very sensitive for the Bolsheviks.

37. https://www.bbc.com/news/world-europe-41809659.

eighth of Russian blood, and had more Jewish and German blood than Russian; Trotsky, Zinoviev, Kameniev, Radek, Kagan, Yagoda, and Molotov were Jewish; Dzerzhinsky, creator of the ChKa, predecessor of the KGB, was Polish; Stalin, forever associated with the communist horror, was Georgian, as was Beria; his successor Khrushchev was Ukrainian, as were Brezhnev, Chernenko, and Gorbachev. Of all the general secretaries of the Communist Party, only Andropov was born in Russia, although he was raised by a Jewish family. Certainly, Russia paid a very high tribute under a government of communists who, generally speaking, were not Russians and did not regard Russia as their own, but as the clay that could be molded. Unfortunately, that clay was not made of clay, but of the blood, flesh, and bones of Russians.

The creation of the Soviet Union had different results. Terrible were those related to the totalitarian and repressive nature of the system based from the beginning, as Lenin pointed out, on mass terror. However, it cannot be denied that, as Churchill himself acknowledged: "The Red Army decided the fate of German militarism."[38] Undoubtedly, the nation that paid by far the greatest tribute in human lives was the Soviet Union. Its more than twenty-six million dead[39] fighting Nazism certainly explains a lot. In the course of the so-called Great Patriotic War, the Soviet Army had 8,668,400 dead and a total of 23,326,905 casualties.[40] Stalin had exercised absolute and cruel power, but it was no less true that he defeated Hitler and that, at the end of that colossal confrontation, he had turned the Soviet Union into the second world power, a power that had agreed with the United States and Great Britain to form a hegemony over Eastern Europe. For the Left, the Soviet Union became a focus for attention for years. It was the first socialist State in history, it had added half a continent

38. *Correspondence of the Council of Ministers of the USSR with the U.S. Presidents and Prime Ministers of Great Britain during the Great Patriotic War of 1941–1945.*, V. 2. M. (1976), p. 204.

39. E. M., Andreev, L. E. Darski, T. L. Kharkova, TL (September 2002). "Population dynamics: consequences of regular and irregular changes" in W. Lutz; S. Scherbov; A. Volkov, (eds.), *Demographic Trends and Patterns in the Soviet Union Before* (1991).

40. G. F. Krivosheev, *Soviet Casualties and Combat Losses in the Twentieth Century* (London, 1997), p. 290.

to its name, and stirred up hopes that socialism would be extended throughout the globe. The big problem was that the system, apart from repression, was far from working.

In 1985, Mikhail Gorbachev became Secretary General of the Communist Party of the Soviet Union. Aware that the system had to be reformed in order to survive, Gorbachev made two terms fashionable. The first was *perestroika,* or reconstruction, and the second, *glasnost,* or transparency. In the Soviet Union, freedom of expression was not introduced, but a multitude of information was published that would have been impossible to know publicly only a short time before. In 1991, the Soviet publishing house Novosti published a book entitled *URSS: Crónica de un decenio* (URRS: Chronicle of a Decade) in which data related to the situation in the country was collected year by year. Much of the data presented in the book was truly disturbing. In 1988, for example, the poverty line was established. In the Soviet Union, after more than seventy years of the Bolshevik coup d'état, 41 million people, or 14.5% of the population, were poor. Some specialists pointed out that, in reality, the figure was between 20 and 25, and the worst thing was that there was no tendency for it to decrease.[41] The year 1989 was declared the "Year of Charity" by the Soviet government. By January 1, 17.1% of the population, or 58.6 million people, were elderly. Sixty percent of them suffered from poor home care services, and three million disabled people needed prosthetics.[42] Likewise, four hundred thousand people lived in nursing homes, but there were another one hundred thousand who could not afford it due to lack of space. They must not have had a particularly efficient service because half of the people who were admitted died in the first two months for psychological reasons. They simply could not cope with this new environment.[43] That same year, there were nearly 1.2 million homeless children in the Soviet Union. 2,194 of them committed suicide and 1,500

41. *URSS. Crónica de un decenio*, p. 207.
42. *Idem*, p. 238.
43. *Idem*, p. 239.

disappeared, possibly becoming homeless.[44] Infant mortality was also disturbing. Fifty-seven out of every thousand children did not reach the age of fifteen. In some republics, such as Turkmenistan, one in 20 died before the age of one.[45] The alleged legitimization of the system of repression on the basis of social progress was not being sustained. Certainly, it could be argued that in the Soviet Union people lived better than in much of the planet, but the system certainly did not produce encouraging results.

In addition, 20% of the GDP went on the defense budget, yet the Soviet Union could not even remotely compete with the United States.[46] Every day, the Soviet army requested two dozen coffins. The deficiency of its structures had caused the death of twenty thousand Soviet soldiers from 1987 to 1990. This was more than the number of soldiers killed in the war in Afghanistan.[47] In spite of everything, the Soviet Union could have kept its head above water, as dictatorships in much worse conditions have managed to do so and are still doing so to this day. Not surprisingly, almost no one expected its downfall to take place, but the downfall did happen and with it came chaos.

From the "Rape of Russia" to Putin

In 1990, the Soviet Union disappeared, but what came after was not a paradise. While the West sold the idea that Russia was moving steadily towards democracy and material prosperity, the process that followed can only be described as truly frightening for the majority of the nation. In 1993, a prestigious New York publishing house signed a contract with American journalist Anne Williamson to describe what had happened in Russia. The book was delivered in 1997 and was very critical of the Clinton administration, but also of George Soros. It was

44. *Idem*, p. 269.
45. *Idem*, p. 316.
46. *Idem*, p. 290.
47. *Idem*, p. 368.

never published. The author, in fact, attributed this to what could be called the Soros factor.[48] Nevertheless, a private version of the text was widely circulated exactly as were the works of dissidents in the former Soviet Union, and Anne Williamson even testified before Congress in 1999. Certainly, what happened in that decade more than explains Vladimir Putin's rise to power, his politics, and his popularity. This is because what took place was not the democratization of the nation, but what has been called the "rape of Russia."

Admittedly, the West, led by the United States, spent 325 million dollars on the process of supposedly modernizing Russia, but the results were dreadful, indeed, those that, surely, no one would wish for their nation.

First of all, and with a remarkable collaboration of the intelligence services and George Soros' foundations, Russia was dismembered. In some cases, such as Estonia or Latvia, one can argue that these were nationalities that deserved to gain independence. In others, such as the Ukraine or Belarus, there was no historical justification for this because they have always been part of Russia. That reality, by the way, was always known to experts in the United States. A document entitled *U.S. Objectives with Respect to Russia* and classified as top secret, dated August 18, 1948, was drawn up following a request dated July 10, 1948, from James V. Forrestal, United States Secretary of Defense. Its purpose was to articulate measures to weaken the USSR. The document contained radical statements. For example, the Ukrainians had never shown any signs of being a "nation." For example, there was no clear dividing line between Russia and Ukraine. Or, that the cities on Ukrainian territory had been predominantly Russian and Jewish. For example, Ukrainian was no more than a peasant dialect. Or, that trying to separate Ukraine from Russia would be as artificial and destructive as trying to separate the Corn Belt, including the Great Lakes industrial zone, from the economy of the United States. The diagnosis of the US intelligence services was obvious: Ukraine is

48. https://www.unz.com/isteve/the-rape-of-russia-explained-by-anne/.

Russia, it is not a nation, and it only speaks a peasant dialect. To forget such elementary data constitutes an immoral and dangerous action. Nevertheless, in any case, Russia lost 30% of its territory, a frightening result that has only occurred after terrible military defeats.

Secondly, Russia's wealth was divided between American and British multinationals, for the most part, and corrupt politicians and officials from a very large number of the former KGB. If there was one thing that Westerners in Russia did not spread during those years, it was honesty, respect for the law, and transparency. On the contrary, they systematically plundered Russia's natural resources, leading to the emergence of the corrupt caste of oligarchs.

Thirdly, the commitments made to the former Soviet Union[49] were breached in such a way that, contrary to the promises made by the United States and some Western nations, NATO was extended to the very borders of Russia and incorporated former Warsaw Pact nations under the promise that they would in turn join the European Union. Far from being nations that ran to place themselves under the protection of the NATO, what happened is that they entered, mostly, in order to enjoy the economic prosperity of the EU.

Fourthly, the collapse of the welfare system, despite its shortcomings, had a frightening effect on the population. It is estimated that the deaths caused by the collapse of social services reached eight million people, far more than those suffered by the United States not only in the two World Wars, but in all the warlike conflicts in its history. With Yeltsin, millions more left Russia than because of the Bolshevik revolution and the civil war, which should give us pause for thought.

When Boris Yeltsin—who had won the elections thanks to the direct interference of the Clinton administration[50]—announced his with-

49. https://www.latimes.com/opinion/op-ed/la-oe-shifrinson-russia-us-nato-deal--20160530-snap-story.html;https://nsarchive.gwu.edu/briefing-book/russia-programs/2017-12-12/nato-expansion-what-gorbachev-heard-western-leaders-early; https://nationalinterest.org/blog/the-buzz/newly-declassified-documents-gorbachev-told-nato-wouldnt-23629.

50. The 2003 film *Spinning Boris* addressed the issue. It was certainly uncomfortable and provoked some discussion in the press. https://www.theguardian.com/world/2003/sep/07/film.russi; https://www.nytimes.com/1996/07/09/world/moscow-journal-the-americans-who-saved-yeltsin-or-did-they.html.

drawal in 1999 from politics that were wrapped up in cases of corruption that benefited even his family, most Russians were ready to vote for the Communist Party in the next electoral process. Such a prospect was awful, to be sure, but it should not come as a surprise after a decade of dismemberment of the national territory, appalling impoverishment, absolute social neglect, violence and corruption, and repeated humiliation on the international level. The era of the Soviet Union might have been dreadful in terms of freedom of expression, but it had undoubtedly been more prosperous, more peaceful, and more internationally respected. If the return of the Communist Party to power through the ballot box did not take place, it was due to Vladimir Putin.

It will surely be discussed for a long time to come whether, when Putin became President of Russia on December 31, 1999, he had won the elections fairly or whether there was fraud in some constituency. What is impossible to argue is that, had he not won, the new president of Russia would have been a communist. On his arrival in power, Putin found a nation that was at risk of further territorial disintegration and was economically bankrupt. Drastic measures such as lowering taxes and persecuting the mafias had the direct effect of increasing Russia's purchasing power by 72% over the next eight years. Not only that. After Rusia's application to join the West through her entry into NATO was rejected—one of the greatest strategic mistakes of the last decades—and after it became clear that neighboring countries would continue to be used against Russia, Putin opted for a policy of response rather than cooperation. The policy of using Ukrainian nationalists as a battering ram against Russia also contributed to this. In 2004, the electoral defeat of the Ukrainian nationalists was reversed by a coup d'état disguised as a colorful revolution. Propaganda could say what it wanted in the West, but, as Diana Johnstone has written, "The trouble with Putin is that he understood this, considered it unacceptable, and dared to say so."[51] In 2012, Putin won the election again with 64% of the votes.

51. Diana Johnstone, *Queen of Chaos. The Misadventures of Hillary Clinton* (Petrolia, 2016), p. 129.

In 2010, the rise to power in Ukraine of a president who was not anti-Russian and who viewed Western politics with some skepticism ended in a nationalist coup d'état supported, among others, by George Soros' organizations and neo-Nazi groups.[52] This time, Putin responded by entering the Crimea—which was never part of the Ukraine—and calling for a referendum in which the overwhelming majority of voters voted to return to Russia. For the West, this was Russian aggression; Russia, however, experienced it as a response to a Western coup d'état in Ukraine that threatened its national security. In 2015, the Ukrainian crisis and the sanctions imposed on Russia caused a recession, but by 2016, the nation had managed to emerge from it. In 2018, Putin understandably won the presidential election again with 76% of the vote. His popular support is certainly unparalleled by any Western politician.

For most Russians, Putin has been a providential politician. When he came to power, the nation was bankrupt, and there was a real risk that the process of dismemberment would continue. In a more than literal sense, Putin saved Russia from disaster, and yet he has not managed to restore the international influence that the Soviet Union formally had. He has returned it to the status of a power to be reckoned with on the world stage. In the West, on the contrary, Putin is presented as a character similar to the villains of the James Bond films and is credited with participating in conspiracies that are not infrequently nonsensical. That he might have been essential to Donald Trump's victory in 2016 is just one of them.

However, all these approaches that seek, quite wrongly, to equate today's Russia with the former Soviet Union and Putin with Stalin are, to say the least, serious errors of judgment. They are often negative propaganda exercises against someone who has clearly defined himself as being against the globalist agenda.

Of course, Putin is not prepared to have the international bodies intervene in the Russian economy, because the Russian experience in

52. D. Johnstone, *Queen of Chaos*, pp. 152ff.

this respect has been very bitter. In fact, the fact that on September 20, 2006, the foreign ministers of Brazil, Russia, India, and China met in New York for the general debate of the UN General Assembly and formed the so-called BRICS group is just one of the attempts to avoid this. Russia's economy may work better or worse, but it is not going to submit itself to international bodies for development. Economically, Russia is not going to be a protectorate.

Similarly, Putin—like Orbán—has not hesitated to point out the allegedly subversive content of George Soros' organizations.[53] It is not surprising that Soros accused Putin—without any proof—of financing Salvini, the Italian Minister of the Interior who is against the open-door policy on immigration,[54] nor that Putin pointed out that Soros "gets into everything," although he made it clear that this is not the position of the United States, but only that of the magnate.[55] For the globalists, Putin is an enemy to be beaten.

Moreover, Putin is one of the few politicians in the world who has spoken out against gender ideology and who has not bowed to international pressure to impose it on Russia. In a series of interviews with film director Oliver Stone,[56] Putin made it clear that no one in Russia was persecuted for being gay, and that there were even celebrities in different areas who were gay. However, he stated categorically that he would not allow homosexual proselytism in schools because the basis of Russian society was the family. The fact that the LGTBI collectives called for a boycott of the winter games in Russia[57] or that the Pussy Riot desecrated a religious service in Russia does not seem to have led Putin to give up. He probably even felt deep contempt when he learned that at the Women in the World Summit held in New York

53. To be honest, it must be said that Soros himself has been quite transparent about some of his intentions in Ukraine. https://www.theguardian.com/business/2014/may/29/how-eu-can-save-ukraine-political-risk-insurance; https://www.ft.com/content/4ddfb410-9664-11e4-a40b-00144feabdc0.

54. https://www.zerohedge.com/news/2018-06-03/war-erupts-between-italys-government-and-soros-you-profited-death-hundreds-people.

55. https://mundo.sputniknews.com/politica/201807171080473377-magnate-soros-injerencia-mundo/.

56. Oliver Stone, *The Putin Interviews* (New York, 2017), p. 96ff.

57. https://www.bbc.com/news/world-europe-26043872; https://www.theguardian.com/sport/2013/aug/09/russia-gay-world-athletics-sochi.

on April 4, 2014, Hillary Clinton posed for a photograph with two of the defilers while defining them as a group of "strong and brave young women" who "refuse to let their voices be silenced." Respect for the beliefs of citizens did not seem to matter particularly to Hillary Clinton.[58]

Nor does it look as if Putin is going to let himself be influenced by the advocates for global warming on the basis of his statements concerning Greta Thunberg that we quoted earlier. In each and every case, Putin has opted for a patriotic line that, precisely for this reason, is in direct opposition to the globalist agenda. His authoritarian government—it is excessive to call it a dictatorship—is not a desideratum for a person who believes in democratic purity, but if democracies do not decide to defend themselves against the assault of the globalist agenda, there can be little doubt that millions of inhabitants of this planet would like to see someone like Vladimir Putin appear in their nation. If that were to happen, it would at least guarantee that their nation would not become a protectorate subject to the globalist agenda. On the other hand, as we will see in the next chapter, the alternative to that submission to the globalist agenda may be even more disturbing.

58. "Clinton praises Pussy Riot as 'strong and brave,'" *Associated Press*, April 8, 2014.

CHAPTER XXI

RESISTANCE TO THE GLOBALIST AGENDA (II): China

China Was Always There

It was the year 1925 when a colonel in the United States Army named Billy Mitchell was subjected to a military trial. The reason was the strong and forceful way in which he had expressed himself against the alleged negligence of the United States Navy and Air Force in planning for the future. In the course of the proceedings, Mitchell demonstrated not only that he was a patriot, but also that he was remarkably accurate in predicting what would happen. Thus, in front of his colleagues who looked down arrogantly on Japan, Mitchell warned that Japan was an enemy that could not be ignored, and that she could bomb Pearl Harbor from the air at any time, endangering America's control of the Pacific. Mitchell was convicted and stripped of his command by a court that included, for example, General McArthur, but history proved him right. Instead of his opponents' stupid, ignorant, and arrogant predictions, Mitchell had learned to read the signs of the times. Unfortunately for everyone, they did not want to listen to him, and on December 7, 1941, the Japanese air force bombed Pearl Harbor, precipitating America's entry into World War II.

The case of Billy Mitchell has had an important parallel in recent years. The military-industrial complex has managed to extract billions of dollars from the pockets of American taxpayers by talking about a Russian threat that is ridiculous, even though Russia's GDP is the size of Spain's. Meanwhile, China, supposedly an Asian country devoid of talent and only equipped to copy what others do, has been looked down upon for years. Such an image of China may satisfy those who are prey to intellectual laziness, those who look down on Asians or the ignorant, but it does not correspond in the least with reality. As one young author recently pointed out, the United States can learn a lot from China.[1]

China has the oldest language spoken in history, older even than Hebrew. It is also the oldest nation today, an antiquity that in political terms gives it an age of no less than four thousand years. If we take into account that the United States and the Spanish American republics are barely two centuries old, and that even the oldest European nations, such as Spain, are barely a millennium and a half old, there can be little doubt that China's perspective on time is necessarily very different from ours. Throughout these millennia, the history of China has been one of an uninterrupted succession of peaks and valleys, of periods of height in which it became the first world power, surpassing even the Roman Empire, and of falls linked, as a rule, to foreign invasions. However, as with the much younger Russia, China has always managed to successfully shake off its foreign domination by assimilating or expelling it.

Some of its dynasties, such as the Han (206 B.C.-A.D. 220), enjoyed the greatest technological developments of the time, making continual advances that would take centuries to appear in other cultures, such as papermaking, the compass, and a considerable number of agricultural and medical achievements. While Europe was

1. Ann Lee, *What the U.S. Can Learn from China. An Open-Minded Guide to Treating Our Greatest Competitor as Our Greatest Teacher* (San Francisco, 2012).

struggling with the attacks of Islam and the invasions of the East (7th-9th centuries), China was not only a great empire, but also made regular use of gunpowder and printing. At that time, China's economic influence extended from the Far East to the Horn of Africa and the Middle East along the Silk Road. Until the nineteenth century, with one dynasty or another, alternating periods of invasion and decline with others of extraordinary and even enviable splendor, China did not cease to be a great power and, very possibly, had the highest GDP on the planet.

The Century of Humiliations

The situation changed radically in the first half of the nineteenth century. Britain had ambitions for Chinese silk, tea, brass ,and porcelain, but discovered, not without surprise, that China was not interested in any British products in exchange for its own. The result was that Britain decided to introduce drug trafficking, and more specifically opium, into China as a way of getting hold of the coveted Chinese goods. When China tried to prevent opium trafficking, Britain attacked it militarily. The first opium war (1839-1842) was so successful that the second (1856-1860) was joined by France. In the end, China not only had to tolerate the entry of opium into its territory with frightening consequences, but she also had to endure the unequal treaties that included the annexation of Hong Kong by Great Britain. Portugal, which had maintained a colony in the Chinese territory of Macao since the sixteenth century, took advantage of the situation to extend its domination.

As a result of these abuses, China would suffer the Taiping Rebellion (1850-1864), the Nationalist Boxer Rebellion (1899-1901), and the revolution that would lead to the fall of the monarchy (1911-1912). Time and again, successive Chinese governments attempted to push through the reforms needed to bring China out of its powerlessness and free it from intolerable foreign interference. However, these attempts were unsuccessful. China had already been attacked by Japan in the first Sino-Japanese War (1894-5), which resulted in the loss of Taiwan to the Japanese empire. It was only the prelude to some of the worst disasters suffered by China in the twentieth century.

In 1916, China was being ripped apart politically. The Guomindang founded by Sun Yatsen in an attempt to modernize China did not control anywhere near the whole territory that suffered from the existence of the so-called warrior generals. To make matters worse, in 1927, the Chinese civil war broke out between the Guomindang and the Soviet-inspired Chinese Communist Party. The Guomindang forces under the command of Chiang Kai-shek inflicted defeat after defeat on the communists to the point of forcing them to flee in the incident known as the Long March. It would be an external interference that would truncate, as so many times in the past, the historical evolution of China. In 1936, the Xi'an incident took place that opened the way for Japan to attack China.

The Second Sino-Japanese War was a succession of horrors that ended up in the Second World War. Although unknown in the West, the truth is that China suffered the death of more than twenty million civilians—a loss, however, inferior to that suffered by the Soviet Union—and that in the city of Nanjing alone more than a quarter of a million civilians were killed by Japanese troops. Japanese brutalities went to the extreme of killing Chinese civilians in gas chambers and conducting chemical experiments on them. This is the case with Unit 731, which put to shame the horror of the Nazi death camps.[2] It is not surprising that in the face of such a threat, the Guomintang and the Chinese Communist Party agreed to a truce to fight together against the Japanese invader.

At the end of the war, China was recognized as one of the Big Four in the United Nations Declaration, and Taiwan was returned to it along with fishermen who had been captured by Japan. In 1947, a constitution was even enacted that, theoretically, was to lay the

2. https://www.nytimes.com/1995/03/17/world/unmasking-horror-a-special-report-japan-confronting-gruesome-war-atrocity.html.

foundations of a democratic China. However, neither the nationalist Chiang Kai-shek nor the communist Mao Zedong was willing to give in to their desire to become leaders of all of China. Not surprisingly, civil war broke out.

The Triumph of the Revolution

The Chinese civil war was an extraordinarily harsh conflict.[3] The corruption of the Guomindang, the social measures carried out by the Communist Party, the aid from the Soviet Union, and the remarkable military talent of Mao's generals all culminated in the triumph of the Communist army. On September 21, 1949, Mao proclaimed the establishment of the People's Republic of China. In 1950, the Chinese government recovered Hainan, which was still in the hands of the Guomindang, and Tibet, which all Chinese parties, including the Guomindang, claimed as part of their national territory. Retired to Taiwan, where he established a harsh rule unknown to the West,[4] Chiang Kai-shek had to settle for establishing a personal dictatorship that would last until his death.

The communist regime was ruthlessly consolidated. The land reform involved the execution of a number of landowners, which is estimated at between one and two million. Meanwhile, the Chinese population increased from 550 million to 900 million in 1974. In the 1950s, the Chinese government intervened in the Korean War, preventing an American victory and consolidating the division of the nation into two. In addition, China became a nuclear power. However, the return to great power status enjoyed in other times was accompanied by indescribable tragedies. In 1958, Mao launched the so-called Great Leap Forward with the intention of turning China from a peasant nation into a communist society. The result—as had happened before

3. The literature on the Chinese civil war is very extensive and, on many occasions, biased. Of particular interest is Frank Dikötter, *The Tragedy of Liberation. A History of the Chinese Revolution 1945-1957* (New York, 2013).

4. Of great interest is the book by George H. Kerr, *Formosa Betrayed* (Irvine, 1992).

in the Soviet Union—was a colossal famine that was not caused by the evil of the Communist leaders, as is often repeated, but by their economic incompetence. Between 1958 and 1961, an estimated fifteen and thirty-five million Chinese died, mostly from hunger. The terrible economic stagnation resulted in a loss of Mao's position within the party. In 1966, Mao bypassed the party elites and appealed to the youth, in particular, to start the Cultural Revolution. It is true that during this period communist China replaced Guomindang China in the United Nations Security Council (1971), but it is no less true that the nation suffered a veritable hurricane of death and repression that lasted until Mao's death in 1976.

China's Resurgence

In 1978, Deng Xiao Ping, who had been removed during the Cultural Revolution, took power and proceeded to prosecute the Gang of Four as responsible for the Cultural Revolution unleashed by Mao. At that point, China's economic situation was dire. Between 1958 and 1978, annual income in the cities had increased by an average of less than 4 RMB a year. Moreover, China had only one bank, no insurance companies or financial institutions, and total reserves amounted to 108 billion RMB. This unfortunate situation changed radically with the appearance of Deng Xiao Ping, who convened a national science conference where it was recognized that the nation was fifteen to twenty years behind the rest of the world and warned that it was suffering from "extreme left-wing thinking." On May 11, the *Guangming Daily* published an editorial stating that "experience based on facts is the only measure of truth." That same summer in 1978, the university was opened and received over six million applicants, and four hundred thousand were admitted.

From December 18 to 22, 1978, the Third Plenary Session of the 11th Central Committee of the CCP set a new course for the Chinese economy under the slogan "Shifting the Focus of All Party Work to

Socialist Modernization and Construction." The consequences would be spectacular. If in 1978 the national reserves amounted to 167 million dollars, in 2008 China had multiplied them by more than ten thousand times, an economic feat without parallel in history. In that same year of 1978, the government set a ten-year plan to capture sixty billion dollars in foreign investment. In 1978, agreements for nearly eight billion had been signed.

In August 1978, the Chinese government invited multinationals such as Toyota, Mercedes, and GM to invest in China. GM was the first to go, and the next year, Coke followed it. The multinationals' demand for transparency led to the creation of special economic zones like Shenzhen, where resale (*dao-ye*) was allowed, laying the foundations for a trading system. One would not speak of "private property" until the year 2000, but the truth is that it has existed since the 1980s.

In 1979, in Wuhu, Anhui Province, a man named Sha-zi (the fool) started growing melons and needed more than eight employees, which, in theory, made him an exploiter of the masses. When Deng Xiao Ping learned that he was producing nine tons of sunflower seeds a day, he decided to "wait and see." Thus, the first *ge ti hu*, or entrepreneurs, appeared. Many of them were uneducated, unemployed, and even delinquent, but they had a prodigious ability to adapt. For example, Wu Renbao, secretary of the Communist Party in the village of Huaxi, opened a clandestine workshop to manufacture hardware. In 1999, that village was the first to raise money in the capital markets. Communist China had more than decisively entered capitalism.

In 1984, China set up its first big companies. The first step was Deng Xiao Ping's visit to Guangdong and Zhang Ruimin, discovering all that was wrong with the factories. The introduction of strict discipline—the ban on going to the bathroom, for example—and quality control had extraordinary effects. In Beijing, Liu Chuanzhi—who visited the workshops on his bicycle—created Lenovo, which eventually bought the laptop business from IBM, while Pan Ning, who had started manufacturing refrigerators from soda cans, created an appliance industry.

For his part, Deng Xiao Ping announced at the Communist Party Central Committee "the opening of fourteen coastal cities to foreign investment as well as the island of Hainan." This was the recognition of the *zou-si*, or business for personal gain. Significantly, despite the desire of the communist leaders to maintain state-owned enterprises, public bidding began to be won by private ones.

In 1988, Milton Friedman arrived in China and recommended the liberalization of "commodity" prices. The Chinese government deregulated prices in Shanghai, and growth became so feverish that inflation was compounded by a lack of raw materials to sustain it. The following year, it was concluded that following Friedman's advice had been a mistake, as the growth rate fell to the lowest level since 1978. However, China did not collapse.

Despite the sanctions unleashed against China by the Tiananmen Square crackdown in 1989, the growth process continued. In February 1990, Deng Xiao Ping decided to make Shanghai the "dragon's head" of economic growth. That same year, the city already had an extremely important stock exchange. Deng Xiao Ping had announced that he was retiring, but before doing so, he made a tour of the south from January 18 to February 21, formulating slogans such as "avoid leftism" or "achieve common prosperity." Two years later, the fourteenth Congress of the CCP set the goal of "establishing a socialist market economy system." Three years later, China had ceased to be a planned economy and had become the cheapest nation on the world market, the most attractive for investment, and the leading producer of manufactured goods in the world. Significantly, GM discovered that it could not compete in the world marketplace with China.

In 1997, Deng Xiao Ping died; Hong Kong was reintegrated into China by Britain, and within months, George Soros unleashed an economic attack on Far Eastern currencies. The Thai currency lost 20% of its value; the Philippine lost 61%; the Indonesian lost 37%; and the South Korean lost 50%. In 1998, Soros decided to attack the Hong Kong dollar to which the Chinese currency was attached. Unlike other nations, China managed to resist Soros' aggression. It was Soros' first, and perhaps the only, defeat, which explains, even in part, the millionaire's aversion to the Far Eastern country ever since. In 1999, the China that had defeated Soros managed to enter the World Trade Organization. At that point, while Southeast Asia was suffering from Soros' actions, and Russia and Brazil were going through considerable difficulties, in China the *zhuang-jin* (speculator) was triumphing. In 2001, the Beijing Olympics were announced for 2008.

Deng's successors continued the reforms initiated by the late president without hesitation. In an impressive way, China was a Communist Party dictatorship that, at least in theory, did not renounce Marxism, but at the same time its economic system was capitalist and presented many advantages that were not found in capitalist countries.

In 2012, Xi Jinping became the general secretary of the CCP. Xi has managed to gain control over the party that is superior even to that exercised by Mao, and has been carrying out reforms related to the economy, the prison system, and the one-child policy while nipping in the bud the possibility of jihadist outbreaks or subversive actions. In 2013, China announced its Belt and Road Initiative, that was recovering the millennial perspective of the Silk Road by expanding it, which would probably end with China's world hegemony in 2049 without the need to extend its political system or fire a single shot. In 2014, China managed to surpass the United States in terms of GDP and has been in a clear battle with the American power for that first place ever since.

In 2019, while Taiwan continued to lose diplomatic ground—except for the United States, it is recognized by only a dozen small countries, and some broke off diplomatic relations with it—China is the first holder of U.S. debt and has lent more than twice the money it has borrowed from the World Bank and the IMF.[5] This circumstance

5. https://bigthink.com/politics-current-affairs/china-loans.

has given it immense power over these nations, and it must be said that Chinese progress in Africa and Latin America is truly spectacular.

The keys to China's unparalleled success are due to a number of factors that are, in no small measure, overlooked by the West. These include a pragmatism that is not weighed down by ideological prejudices; the importance that continues to be given to the family, which can even be considered as a guarantee of credit; spending on education; work; a friendly policy towards all nations; the refusal to pursue an imperial policy; the rejection of foreign intervention, and knowledge of one's adversary. The clash of these behaviors with the globalist agenda is more than evident.

In 2019, faced with China's resistance to accept the globalist agenda, Soros publicly placed China on his list of targets to defeat.[6] At the same time, a democratic revolt broke out in Hong Kong, which exists inside the system of "One country, two systems", and Trump was supposedly confronting China in the trade arena. Both claims would be widely aired in the media, but they require further explanation. Let's start with Hong Kong.

The current crisis began when, in February 2019, a young Hong Kong man named Chan Tang-kai murdered pregnant girlfriend while they were on vacation in Taiwan. Chan immediately fled to Hong Kong and, according to the 1997 statute, the Hong Kong authorities refused to extradite him. Since the crime had not been committed in the United States, it went unnoticed in the West, but in the Far East it was such a spectacular scandal that Lam, the prime minister of Hong Kong, decided to push for an extradition law that would prevent similar situations. The Hong Kong system is not a democracy, as it is so wrongly called, but it is remarkably similar to the so-called organic democracy of General Franco's regime. Thus, in a legislative system that is very reminiscent of the courts of Franco's regime, which were not democratic, but which were somewhat representative, demonstrations against the law began to take place, supposedly to prevent

6. https://www.cnbc.com/2019/01/24/davos-soros-says-chinas-xi-most-dangerous-opponent-of-open-society.html.

anyone from being extradited to China, but very possibly so that no one could be extradited and their status as a place of refuge for criminals would be maintained. As happens with these cases, the Hong Kong authorities—which operate autonomously from China—tried to make a deal, the foreign powers intervened more or less openly, and everyone else was waiting for a reaction from the Chinese government. However, Beijing has been much more subtle. Over the course of the following months, the protesters have launched an escalation of violence that is already taking its toll on Hong Kong's economy. At this point, hotels, businessmen, bankers, professionals, in short, all those who have turned the island into an economic power have been disassociating themselves from the demonstrators and insisting that the situation must end because it is painfully damaging to Hong Kong's image and economy. At some point, the protesters even took the air routes in and out of Hong Kong out of business, tragically isolating the country. As these lines are written, the Chinese government has not intervened violently, possibly in the belief that the riots in Hong Kong, a territory usurped by Britain and returned to China, will disappear once a trade agreement is reached with the United States that favors President Trump.

The conflict in Hong Kong—which China could militarily suppress in a few hours—and the trade war conceal a much more disturbing reality. To study it, we must go back to 1956. Back then, an intelligence alliance known in English as the Five Eyes was created. Formed by the United States, Great Britain, Canada, Australia, and New Zealand, this alliance exists today and is above any other alliance such as NATO. The member nations of the Five Eyes not only share intelligence with one another at a level that is unthinkable for other allies, but they also spy on their own allies and install doors in their systems and territories that allow them access to all kinds of political, economic, and social secrets and influence the outcome of elections or the performance of economies. In 2009, France had the opportunity to join the Five Eyes, but the fact that it was not granted an equal status with the other members and, above all, the fact that it was not guaranteed that it would not be spied on by them led her to reject it. In 2013, Germany expressed an interest in joining the big spy club, but her application fell on deaf ears. Today, the Five Eyes is the most powerful intelligence agency in the world, and its surveillance extends, thanks to technological superiority, to enemies and friends alike, guaranteeing a clear hegemony of the Anglo-Saxon world. That guarantee has been challenged by China.

In 1987, a former Chinese People's Army officer and Communist Party member named Ren Zhengfei founded a company with an initial capital of a few thousand dollars in Shenzhen, a city in southeast China that was the first special economic zone created in the country and is known as the city of 50,000 millionaires. The company known as Huawei is, three decades later, the largest manufacturer of telecommunications equipment in the world and may become the first to implement 5G mobile technology worldwide. In addition, Huawei is the second largest mobile phone manufacturer in the world by market share, 15%, only behind Samsung. In addition, Huawei has overtaken Apple from its hegemonic position and has annual revenues of more than $92 billion and a workforce of about 180,000.

In addition to being a serious competitor with the United States in the technology market, Huawei has recently offered to sell sophisticated equipment to various Western governments that would prevent Five Eyes ability to spy. In other words, China would be offering to make it difficult for the United States to spy on its allies or enemies.

This threat to the Five Eyes was responded to by Australia and New Zealand prohibiting Huawei from building 5G networks. Meanwhile, Britain began removing Huawei's equipment from its telephone network. Finally, in August 2018, Donald Trump banned the Chinese company's hardware from US government networks, citing national security concerns, particularly in relation to the deployment of 5G networks. In the midst of this wave of measures against Huawei that could dismantle the Five Eye surveillance system, the U.S. Attorney's Office demanded the extradition of the CFO of the Chinese technology company Huawei, Meng Wanzhou. Thus, on December 1, 2018,

Meng, the forty-six-year-old daughter of the founder and president of Huawei, was arrested in Canada on charges of attempting to circumvent financial sanctions against Iran.

The reality is that Canada does not have the legal power to arrest Meng and extradite her to the United States, but, as a member of the Five Eyes, the possibility existed. As expected, China's Foreign Ministry spokesman, Geng Shuang, said neither Canada nor the United States had provided evidence that Meng had broken the law in either country and demanded her immediate release. For its part, the Chinese press accused the United States of attacking Huawei to stop the global expansion of Chinese companies.

The arrest, apparently for criminal reasons, of the daughter of the founder and CEO of the Chinese company Huawei is undoubtedly one of the episodes in the struggle between the United States and China for world hegemony. The thesis that the Chinese company would have provided material to Iran can work well as official propaganda, since it turns China into a collaborator of the great world villain in the eyes of public opinion. The United States would simply be preventing Huawei from helping a repugnant regime and would defend the free world from the threat by proceeding to the arrest the founder's daughter and future heiress of the technological empire. However, it is not certain that that version corresponds to reality, and even more so that it can be supported judicially, since the United States has no right to request a third party to proceed with the arrest of someone who has allegedly violated sanctioning rules that are not universal but particular in nature. Something closer to reality is the Chinese thesis that the United States is acting against the technological rivalry represented by Chinese companies.

However, both governments have hidden the truth, which is none other than the struggle for world hegemony and the role of the intelligence media in that struggle. If the United States has the very powerful instrument of the Five Eyes that allows it to have a solid core of allies and to monitor even friendly nations, then China is willing to weaken the United States' power network by unraveling its devices.

The possible sale to nations allied to the United States of devices for intercepting the intelligence resources used by the Five Eyes would be fatal for the United States not only because it would loosen the control it has over its allies, but also because it would give China an extraordinary capacity for blocking American intelligence operations.

This situation, which could be reduced to a confrontation between two great powers for world hegemony, acquires a much deeper and more transcendent dimension when one considers that China is a fierce opponent of the globalist agenda. Not only is it unwilling to have its economy determined by supranational bodies, but it is also totally contrary to the theses of the global warming advocates and to the gender ideology that they even perceive as opium no less harmful than that which the British introduced into Chinese territory in the mid-nineteenth century. Even more so, China is convinced that it can assert itself as the first hegemonic power without firing a single shot by only taking advantage of economy—especially high technology—and diplomacy.

Certainly, China does not intend to export its system as the Soviet Union once did or as the United States currently claims. On the contrary, it believes that its system is only possible in China, which may include a certain feeling of historical and cultural superiority. However, its resistance to the globalist agenda and its undeniable success make it, perhaps unwittingly, a model for patriots.

Unlike those who have continued to claim that America's main rival is Russia, the reality is that that adversary is China now and has been for a long time. The eastern nation has become an extraordinary colossus that has begun to outgrow the United States in areas such as manufacturing or high technology while extending its influence across the globe in an extraordinary way.

In the face of this real threat, it is deplorable to listen to the judgments of the ignorant, the arrogant, and the foolish. The ignorant who believe that the China of today is the China of the Cultural Revolution, and insist on denying its astronomical economic growth, repeating cliché after cliché that only shows their deplorable ignorance on the subject and who, to top it all, think that ignoring it and pontificating or closing educational centers is somehow a virtue. The arrogant ones who despise the Chinese and attribute their success only to their ability to copy or to attract foreign investments without realizing that China has for millennia had an enviable inventiveness, an unparalleled capacity for recovery, and an undeniable talent that makes a difference with other nations that have had equal or superior opportunities and have not taken advantage of them. The fools who, instead of facing reality and studying how to change it in the most favorable way, believe that they are facing the obsolete apparatus of the Soviet Union or the starving dictatorship of Cuba, when the reality is that China has pulled more than a billion people out of poverty in the last few decades, drastically and unequivocally reducing the number of hungry people on the planet. To tell the truth, no one has ever managed to accomplish such a feat. To all these circumstances, China adds that it is fiercely opposed to the globalist agenda, convinced that it is harmful to any nation.

In 2020, China is a huge challenge because of its immense flexibility, because of its undeniable talent, and because, paradoxically, it is following principles of the Founding Fathers that the United States seems to have forgotten, which is the desire to trade with everyone regardless of their regime or ideas, or the refusal to engage in perpetual military alliances. Its resistance to gender ideology also provides it with an enormous social force from which nation after nation in Europe and America is breaking away. Each and every one of these factors must be taken into account.

Whether the confrontation will be sealed with a victory or with a failure will depend largely on whether we listen to the ignorant, the arrogant, and the foolish, or to those who analyze the Chinese reality in a documented way. On top of that, in the face of the political patronage policies followed in the United States, China has shut down any national political movements; in the face of tax increases, she maintains a very low taxation, and in the face of a cultural isolation that barely sees beyond her own borders, she demonstrates an enormous interest in learning and knowing what is culturally foreign to her. This is not a scenario that makes one feel calm. After all, the United States is the largest democracy on the planet, and China is a communist dictatorship. That American democracy is collapsing and that the world is looking to China's example for the survival of nations is certainly disturbing.

CONCLUSION

In the previous chapters, we have dealt with an overview of the world that most likely has been striking to some of the readers. Far from supporting the thesis that we are still living through the Cold War and that its paradigms are useful today, the text claims that, fundamentally, we are facing two problems of enormous relevance today. The first is whether democracies will be able to survive beyond certain formal aspects—in most nations, if they actually were implemented—and the second is the ruthless advance of the globalist agenda. The reality is that on these two questions depends whether the human race will be subjected to a totalitarian dictatorship or, perhaps, to national dictatorships, or whether it will manage to live in freedom.

The possibilities have been clearly set out in the preceding pages. Democracy existed in ancient times, but it disappeared and did so for the same reasons that threaten it today. The lack of moral fiber in societies; the adulation of the masses to gain power and keep it; the creation of immense electoral clienteles that are moved by incentives, but not by critical reflection; the migratory processes that inject entire social segments into a country culturally different from their own; an aggressive international policy...each and every one of these factors is contributing to the end of democracy in those places where it exists and to the impossibility of implanting solid democracies where they have rarely or never existed.

Added to this undeniable risk are the objectives of a globalist agenda that lacks the slightest democratic legitimacy and is cooked up and served from obscure organizations with real power. Of course, the globalist agenda can end up imposing its objectives and even achieve them in 2030 when, it is assumed, it will have managed to consummate its plans thanks to the support of, among others, the United Nations. This Agenda 2030 is certainly one of the most interesting designs of the globalist agenda.

On September 25, 2015, the UN General Assembly adopted the Agenda 2030 for Sustainable Development. The Agenda—which was not submitted to a referendum in a single country—proposes 17 objectives with 169 goals of an integrated and indivisible nature that cover economic, social, and environmental fields. This agenda subjects the legislation, economy, and development of the different nations to its criteria and also commits the different nations not only to obey it, but to finance it. In other words, although theoretically Agenda 2030 does not affect the independence of the different countries, the reality is that it scandalously limits national sovereignty. Defended even by observer States at the UN such as the Vatican, its goals include gender ideology, drastic birth control, and the assumption of the theses of the global warming advocates as true. In other words, it constitutes a historically unprecedented mechanism of global control. Significantly, in Spain, one of the nations of the European Union, the communist Pablo Iglesias is in charge of leading the government's Agenda 2030. In 2019, Futuro en común ("Common Future"), a confederation of secular and Catholic NGOs, expressed its support for Agenda 2030 in Spain, stating that it was necessary to "make effective a multilevel coordination and follow-up from the Executive and the Legislative branches with the participation of all members, including civil society." This system of government, according to Futuro en común, must be carried out by a Command Panel "through a public and participatory work plan" in order "not to leave anyone behind." In a document entitled "Key elements for a transformative development of Agenda 2030," Futuro en común pointed out that the six key elements for advancing Agenda 2030 would be, first, a new economic model that would affect even purchasing habits, especially related to food; secondly, a new public pension system that takes into account gender bias; thirdly, a tax increase aimed at reducing inequalities and, fourthly, advancing gender ideology by improving the quality of the democratic sphere. The interventionist nature of Agenda 2030 could hardly be expressed more clearly.

Agenda 2030 will, first, empty governments of executive power by subjecting them to global action that, in many cases, would be absolutely detrimental to them, as it interferes with their economy and institutions. Secondly, it assigns the development or the falling behind of the different nations by always following, of course, the theses of the global warming advocates turned into gods, who will decide which nations advance and which will fall behind. Thirdly, this process does not work democratically, but implies the submission of the government and its institutions and the increasing action of oligarchic NGOs that also live off public budgets. Fourthly, they imply the strengthening of powerful oligarchies that will be maintained on the basis of tax increases in each nation. Finally, in fifth place, the impoverishment of hundreds of millions of human beings will be dealt with as an advance in the fight for equality, equality that will be achieved from below, and that will even include food.

The project, which we insist is masked by elegant words, constitutes a real threat to the freedom and prosperity of the world and will mean the end of real democracy and freedoms for the benefit of national oligarchies subject to a single global government. It cannot be the least bit surprising that in Spain a totalitarian communist like Pablo Iglesias has now become its leader.

In the end, as Rockefeller once pointed out, the world will be controlled by a small elite number of financiers and intellectuals that no one has elected, devoid of the slightest democratic legitimacy. The nations will retain, perhaps, their formal existence, but they will be like empty shells. Their economy, their foreign policy, their family laws, their education, even their constitutions will depend on that small supranational elite that will act through the national parties, the unions, the NGOs, and the media. Of course, the same freedoms of worship and conscience, the first foundation of democracy, will disappear because the great religious powers will either agree with the globalist agenda—the case of the Holy See is obvious, not to say scandalous—or they will be outlawed. In this regard, it is significant that the evangelicals have become the main obstacle to the advancement of the globalist agenda in the American continent. Whether the world will also be divided into large blocs—as Orwell pointed out—or into one is hard to say, but what is certain is that national sovereignty and freedom will disappear.

Such a situation will be easy to achieve, insofar as democracy will have been decisively eroded during the previous years and disappeared—a democracy impossible to sustain without the conditions pointed out by the Founding Fathers—and only three options will remain for the human race: a globalist dictatorship, a patriotic authoritarian dictatorship, or the Chinese style of dictatorship. In either case, freedom will have become a thing of the past.

That is precisely why the only way out is to defend freedom for us and for the generations to come. In that sense, every step taken against the globalist agenda will be a step towards preserving freedom, and every step towards living democracy in accordance with the principles that emerged from the Reformation and were embodied by the Founding Fathers will be a step towards a future in freedom. There is no other option for us to act otherwise. Let me even add an observation: no person who loves God, his nation, and freedom can act otherwise.

In that resistance, there are many fronts from which to fight, and fight with success and hope of victory: those who defend the freedom of their children in schools so as not to be indoctrinated in gender ideology; those who broadcast materials related to the truth of the globalist agenda on social networks; those who support and finance those radio and television programs that resist the imposition of that agenda; those who demand accountability in myriad ways of politicians who are determined to surrender to globalist objectives; those who take to the streets in defense of freedom of conscience, life, and education without indoctrination; to support projects to take in single mothers or children who might be aborted; to provide courses and seminars to prevent children and teenagers from being cut off from their natural development; those who create alternative means to tell the truth that many silence, hide, and even persecute; those who, alone or in the company of others, bow their heads before God asking Him for light and strength to face this fight. All these people and many more are decisive in the fight for their country and freedom, and you can be part of them.

The year was 1781, when Thomas Jefferson, a brilliant politician from the newborn nation of the United States of America, wrote the following about slavery in his notes on the state of Virginia: "Indeed I tremble for my country when I reflect that God is just: that his justice cannot sleep for ever: that considering numbers, nature and natural means only, a revolution of the wheel of fortune, an exchange of situation, is among possible events: that it may become probable by supernatural interference!"

The words written by Jefferson contained a truly chilling reflection. For many of his contemporaries, and especially for people in his own state, slavery posed no moral problem. It was an accepted custom and even an avenue of economic gain that related to a tiny but certainly influential and powerful minority. Jefferson was aware, however, that in politics not everything comes down to economic, social, or institutional analysis. In fact, he firmly believed that there is a supernatural factor in a nation's existence that is often overlooked, but no less present. That factor is God's justice, a justice that may seem dormant, but ends up making its presence felt under human forms such as revolution or change, due, in fact, to a supernatural drive. Reflecting on this question, this politician could only tremble because, sooner or later, God's justice would be unleashed against an institution like slavery.

Like it or not, our world—a world that is changing even though millions do not realize it—is facing a similar situation to that which

Moses presented to the children of Israel before they entered the Promised Land (Deuteronomy 30:15-19). Before him lay a path of good and a path of evil; a path of freedom and a path of slavery; a path of prosperity and a path of misery; a path of life and a path of death. The future will be a direct result of the path he takes, and we can be sure that if the path is the wrong one, as happened with Jefferson's unheeded warming, it will lead to blood, suffering, pain, and death. But more important than that is that anyone who has read this book, if they understand what is at stake, even in part, and choose to defend freedom and their country, they can be an instrument of change. That instrument of change has in itself enormous potential to bring about positive transformation in our societies, to ensure that their nation will live in freedom and be endowed with the self-evident and God-given rights that Jefferson referred to, and to stop a monstrous but not invincible totalitarian offensive against national independence and individual rights. You can join that resistance. *You have to join that resistance* as hundreds of thousands of people have done in the world, knowing that we take risks by taking a stand in this confrontation. Do not hesitate any longer, and do it for your freedom and that of your children and for your country and for your children's country. This is the time to take on a personal responsibility that no one else can assume for you and no one can replace you. If, finally, you do so, may the God who grants victory in these battles bless you!

APPENDIX

The Middle East Is Not What It Used to Be

Many readers may have been struck by the fact that, instead of focusing the description of the world in the Middle East, the book's thesis focuses on other points. Without doubt, the Middle East has played a radical importance in the history of the last century. In fact, the last wars initiated by the United States in the area owe a lot to that understanding. From those wars, apart from the reasons given to justify them in the arena of public opinion, we expected to secure the security of the oil supply, the security of Israel, and the security derived from democratic governments. Let us briefly consider these three aspects, albeit in reverse order.

First, it should be noted that in none of the cases has the result of military interventions—interventions which, as a whole, have cost hundreds of thousands of deaths—led to the establishment of democracies. It is, of course, debatable whether there is a right for a third country to invade another that has not previously attacked it in order to transform it into a democracy. But if such a case does exist, it must be acknowledged that the failure has been glaring. Neither Afghanistan, nor Iraq, nor Libya, nor Syria, nor the other nations where interventions have taken place are a democracy today, nor do they look like one. Not only that. Certainly, terrible dictators such as Saddam Hussein or Colonel Qadhafi have disappeared, but it is doubtful whether the current situation in Iraq or Libya is any better. To tell the truth, they are much worse. It must be emphasized loud and clear: wherever direct intervention has taken place, or intermediary agents have been in involved, not a single nation has improved its situation. On the contrary, that nation has seen the drama lead to an appalling tragedy that, in turn, has had repercussions in other nations.

To this factor we must add the immense cost of these operations. Turning Iraq into a ruin nation that can no longer fulfill its balancing role in the Middle East, in which more than three trillion dollars of American taxpayers' money was spent in 2008, should call for serious reflection. In fact, that is the title of Nobel Prize winner Joseph Stiglitz's book, and, since then, more than a decade of excessive and useless expenditure has occurred.[1] It is excessive for two wars like Afghanistan and Iraq, which the United States has not won, that remain unfinished,[2] and from which we do not know how to get out of. Among other reasons, with what was spent in Iraq until 2010, the United States would have been able to pay for the health of its citizens for half a century. And that is only the figure for Iraq. By 2018, it was already obvious that since 2001, the United States has spent nearly six trillion dollars on its Asian wars. In addition, nearly half a million people have died as a direct result of the fighting. Nearly a quarter of a million civilians have perished in these wars, and ten million people have been displaced, creating enormous problems not only for neighboring nations, but also for European ones.[3] Has it really been worth it?

In the end, none of these interventions has made the world safer. In fact, security has decreased. In the Middle East, the disappearance of Iraq as a power has been able to satisfy Netanyahu

1. J. E. Stiglitz and L. J. Bilmes, *The Three Trillion Dollar War. The True Cost of the Iraq Conflict* (New York, 2008).

2. Regarding Iraq, see: T. E. Ricks, *Fiasco.The American Military Adventure in Iraq* (New York, 2006).

3. https://www.cnbc.com/2018/11/14/us-has-spent-5point9-trillion-on-middle-east-asia-wars-since-2001-study.html;https://watson.brown.edu/costsofwar/files/cow/imce/papers/2018/Crawford_Costs%20of%20War%20Estimates%20Through%20FY2019%20.pdf.

and other Israeli leaders, but the truth is that it has led to a direct confrontation between Saudi Arabia and Iran, both nations governed by Islamic theocratic systems, with no respect for human rights and with ambitions for expansion. The weakening of either and the victory of either would plunge the area into a real disaster. In that sense, Obama's policy of balance was the lesser evil, and, on the contrary, support for Saudi Arabia—a nation which is capable of murdering and chopping up dissidents[4]—against Iran is a move of enormous recklessness.

If one looks impartially at the situation, there can be little doubt that in relation to cost and result, the path followed to date must be abandoned.

Secondly, despite the enormous media attention, Israel is in no danger from opponents much weaker than itself. Indeed, Israeli historians themselves acknowledge that Israel was never threatened in its existence by the surrounding nations for the simple reason that it always had enormous military superiority. In this respect, works such as those of Simha Flapan, who was national secretary of the Israeli party Mapam and director of its department of Arab affairs, are very enlightening,[5] as is that of Nathan Weinstock.[6] The same could be said of the magnificent studies by Avi Shlaim[7] or Ilan Pappe.[8] It is true that Israel can suffer terrorist attacks—although, fortunately, it has never suffered from one like 9/11—but its dissimilarity with the surrounding countries is immense. Israel can even lose local wars against forces other than armies as happened in Lebanon with Hizbullah—an incident that has deeply wounded Israeli pride—but no nation in the entire area can dream of being its rival. First, Israel possesses an army far superior to that of all nearby countries combined; second,

4. https://www.bbc.com/mundo/noticias-internacional-49892850.

5. Simha Flapan, *The Birth of Israel. Myths and Realities* (New York, 1987). In a very similar, but broader, sense, see: Benjamin Beit-Hallahmi, *Original Sins. Reflections on the History of Zionism and Israel* (New York, 1993).

6. N. Weinstock, *El sionismo contra Israel. Una historia crítica del sionismo* (Barcelona, 1970).

7. A. Shlaim, *The Iron World. Israel and the Arab World* (New York, 2000).

8. I. Pappe, *The Modern Middle East* (London, 2010) and *Ten Myths about Israel* (London and New York, 2017).

Israel possesses nuclear weapons,[9] a circumstance that does not exist in any nation around it;[10] third, despite the fact that for two decades we have heard that Iran was working on a nuclear weapon and could have it the following year, the reality is that has not been and is not the case. In fact, Iran abandoned such plans at the beginning of the century, and even Ayatollah Ali Khamenei publicly condemned by means of a *fatwa* the use of nuclear weapons.[11] In fact, Netanyahu himself has not been able to provide the slightest proof that Iran tried to manufacture nuclear weapons after 2002,[12] and, quite significantly, the US intelligence agencies have rejected that possibility,[13] which cannot be confused with the peaceful use of nuclear energy to which Iran is entitled, because it belongs to the organization for the nonproliferation of nuclear weapons; and fourthly, the United States, under the presidency of Obama, decided to hand over to Israel the sum of thirty-eight billion dollars,[14] which is more than the Marshall Plan for nearly thirty countries after the Second World War. This is an astronomical amount that shows the extent to which the United States is committed to Israel's interests more than any other nation in the world. In fact, contrary to the claims of some propaganda, the truth is that Obama may not have agreed with Netanyahu and rejected his insistence that he go to war with Iran, but he helped Israel extraordinarily.[15]

We must also accept other undeniable realities in order to fully understand the situation. In 1947, with Britain impoverished by World War II and eager to break away from its empire, the UN

9. There are different estimates of the size of Israel's nuclear arsenal, which could amount to several hundred atomic bombs. See: Avner Cohen, *The Worst-Kept Secret: Israel's bargain with the Bomb* (Columbia, 2010), Table 1, p. xxvii and p. 82.

10. L. Toscano, Triple Cross. *Israel, the Atomic Bomb and the Man Who Spilled the Secrets*, (New York, 1990).

11. https://www.sfgate.com/news/article/Nuclear-weapons-unholy-Iran-says-Islam-forbids-2580018.php.

12. https://www.washingtonpost.com/world/israel-says-it-holds-a-trove-of-documents-from-irans-secret-nuclear-weapons-archive/2018/04/30/16865450-4c8d-11e8-85c1-9326c4511033_story.html?noredirect=on.

13. https://www.latimes.com/archives/la-xpm-2012-feb-23-la-fg-iran-intel-20120224-story.html.

14. https://www.reuters.com/article/us-usa-israel-statement/u-s-israel-sign-38-billion-military-aid-package-idUSKCN11K2CI.

15. https://foreignpolicy.com/2012/08/16/obama-has-been-great-for-israel/.

decided to divide the Palestinian Mandate into an Arab and a Jewish State. The Arabs had 69% of the population and ownership of 92% of the land, but they would receive only 43% of the land. In contrast, the Jews being 31% of the population and having less than 8% of the land were to receive 56% of the territory. In addition, the most fertile land would pass into the hands of the Jews. This land distribution, which is clearly debatable, was the result of the guilty conscience of the Western nations because of the Holocaust. However, it is striking that this guilty conscience tried to sooth itself with territory and peoples outside Europe. On the other hand, it should not be surprising to anyone that this distribution led the Arab population of the Palestinian Mandate to believe that they had been subjected to an immense injustice.

To further aggravate the situation, after attacking the neighboring Arab nations in 1967, Israel occupied a number of territories. Sinai was returned to Egypt, but President Netanyahu's intention to annex the Golan Heights from Syria and to do the same with almost the entire West Bank is obvious. Such actions are contrary to international law and will not go unnoticed by the vast majority of the international community—not just the Arab nations—simply because the White House decides to support them. We cannot expect a total peace as long as such conduct persists, but it is also doubtful that a conventional war will break out because of them, or that Israel's existence will be threatened. It cannot come by Palestinians without an army or by Syria being annihilated in a terrible war as a result of foreign intervention. Simply—and sad to say—the presumption of having occupied territories and total peace is a pipe dream, and the retention of these territories since 1967 will always imply a negative view that goes far beyond the Middle East even if it is not understood by much of the media in the United States or Canada.

Such facts are occasionally countered with references to the alleged curse of criticizing the policies of the State of Israel on the basis of Genesis 17 and 22. Such an interpretation of the Bible is, to say the least, debatable. If, in fact, criticism of Israel's actions were subject to a curse, it would follow that all of Israel's prophets were cursed, and so was Jesus, who announced the destruction of Jerusalem and its temple (cf. Matt. 24, Mark 13, and Luke 21). On top of that, interpreting this passage clashes with the very exegesis of the New Testament, where the descendants of Abraham are not identified with a Jewish State, but with the Messiah (Galatians 3:16). In fact, it is revealing that the same text (Galatians 3:29) states that the descendants of Abraham are those who believe in Jesus as the Messiah. As so often happens in history, bad exegesis translates into bad politics.

Finally, it should be noted that the United States does not need the oil from the Middle East. Unlike what happened in the 1970s, it is self-sufficient in oil and even a net exporter. The United States is the largest in the world, by the way, and ahead of Saudi Arabia.[16]

All this is coupled with other considerations, such as the fact that the United States spends more than six hundred and ninety-eight billion dollars on military spending, which is more than ten times the amount spent by Russia. The United States spends 53% of its budget on military spending.[17] This is certainly great news for the arms manufacturers who profit from this situation, but it is terrible for the citizens of the United States who pay for it with their taxes, and, above all, it is unnecessary. The fact that such situations exist and that, at the same time, the United States cannot have a public health service like Canada or Western Europe alongside the private one is once again a matter for reflection.

At the same time, it has become clear in recent decades that it is possible to increase international influence dramatically through diplomatic and financial means rather than through military ones. China is the best example. Just as the Founding Fathers taught, China rejects perpetual military alliances and seeks above all to strengthen trade. The method is much cheaper, and one should ask whether it has not been more successful. Meanwhile, the United States risks recklessly

16. https://money.cnn.com/2018/09/12/investing/us-oil-production-russia-saudi-arabia/index.html.
17. https://comptroller.defense.gov/Portals/45/Documents/defbudget/fy2019/fy2019_Press_Release.pdf; https://www.charleskochinstitute.org/issue-areas/foreign-policy/the-military-spending-debate/.

spending its resources, like the old Athens, on military interventions abroad. There are those who benefit from them, of course, but, like Athens, it should be aware of the extent to which such action runs counter to its national interests, weakens its international position, and erodes democracy. All this could have been avoided if the traditional policy of the Founding Fathers had been maintained.

This set of reflections is mandatory because the great battle for the future of this changing world is not and will not be fought in the Middle East, but from the comfortable offices of the designers of the globalist agenda.

EPILOGUE: IN THE MIDDLE OF THE CORONAVIRUS

Between the writing of this book and its going to press, the world has been hit by the coronavirus pandemic, a pandemic that, to date, has not ended and whose final outcome cannot be fully known. However, what we have learned so far confirms, in a certainly striking way, the theses contained in the pages of this book.

In the first place, it is obvious that the globalist agenda does NOT offer better alternatives than those derived from sovereign and independent nations. If anything has become evident in the midst of this crisis, it is the distressing ineffectiveness of international entities. The European Union, NATO, the Organization of American States, the United Nations, and even the Vatican have shown themselves to be seriously incapable of taking steps to help deal with the pandemic. They may try to impose their worldview on the whole globe, they may continually advocate bringing more and more nations under their umbrella, and they may claim to have solutions for everything. Reality has shown that they are enormous and incompetent dinosaurs capable only of referring to problems that are often far from reality and of spending immense amounts of money that could be better spent on other causes. As for the silence of the globalist icons, such as Soros or Pope Francis, in the midst of the crisis, that in itself has enormous relevance. They can launch slogans that have nothing to do with the realities of human beings, but when faced with reality, they remain silent.

All this must be taken into account because when the crisis is finally over, despite their total impotence, these same entities will hammer us politically and with the media in order to push us towards a world government, a government with despotic security, but also a security unable to cope with major crises.

Secondly, the absence of real interest in the pillars of globalism for humanity as a whole has been exposed. It has taken having to face the real threat of the coronavirus to almost make us forget the issues of inclusive language, references to the climate crisis emergency, or gender laws. There is no doubt that all these aspects related to the globalist agenda are nothing more than agitation and propaganda, and because that is the reality about them, they have been forgotten by people and even by the media, because the coronavirus reality—which is undeniable—has come onto the scene. In other words, without the massive brainwashing driven by the media, NGOs, and governments, the globalist agenda would be paralyzed indefinitely.

Third, the lack of moral scruples of the promoters of the globalist agenda has been exposed. Despite the gravity of the situation, the globalist agenda has not stopped pursuing its goals without caring in the least about people's lives. Cases abound. In January 2020, the Spanish government had more than enough data from international and national entities to know that the coronavirus epidemic would be serious. However, it preferred to continue supporting gender ideology through the feminist protests on March 8. These demonstrations were held with an extremely dangerous attendance amid an epidemic, knowing that they could translate into tens of thousands of infections. In other words, its political sectarianism led the Spanish government to create immense sources of contagion because promoting gender ideology was more important than preventing the spread of the disease. Hundreds of thousands of people attended these demonstrations in Spain, who later would spread the plague. Among those infected were two vice presidents of the government—Carmen Calvo and Irene Montero—a government minister and the president's own wife, as well as countless other people. In some regions of Spain, such as Catalonia, the situation had additional aggravating elements. Thus, the attendance at a rally by the coup leader Puigdemont became another focus of contagion that would turn Catalonia into the Spanish region most affected by the coronavirus.

It was not only about the spreading of the virus. Although the Spanish government was faced with an acute shortage of funds due to high debt and economic depression caused by high taxes, it created new positions in the State administration to spread gender ideology, and while there was a shortage of health care facilities to deal with the pandemic, it declared the practice of abortions as an essential service. Instead of thinking about the common good, the globalist dogma was once again imposed.

Examples of this truly criminal behavior have had their parallels in other parts of the globe. For example, in Mexico, attempts were made to take advantage of the pandemic to promote the legalization of abortion; in Chile, by appealing to the coronavirus, legislation related to gender ideology was promoted; and in the Spanish region of Catalonia, the government promoted a health protocol that excluded entire sectors of the population from treatment and even urged its barely concealed execution. Taking advantage of the situation because of the increasing number of deaths, the globalist agenda tried to gain positions in anti-life and anti-family areas. The first priority was far from trying to save human lives. Instead they had, curiously, other priorities, such as destroying lives by abortions or applying euthanasia protocols in hospitals.

Fourthly, it has become clear which countries are the weakest to deal with the coronavirus and which are the strongest. Those that for decades opted for a path of increasing State interventionism, higher taxes, and uncontrolled debt have been the worst responders to the coronavirus. The terrible role played by Spain in the midst of this tragedy is significant because for decades it has been the protagonist in these vices that contribute to eroding the democratic system to the most dangerous extremes. In the end, fleecing the population through taxes destined to support patrons and bureaucracies and indebting the nation to maintain an ineffective system has NOT been a guarantee against a national crisis. On the contrary, it has been a death sentence for the health system, the economy, and social peace. What many—not just globalists—have considered as the path to social justice is only the path to major catastrophes and to utter helplessness in preventing and avoiding them.

When the data to date is examined, the conclusions provided by this book appear even more obvious. Democracies are in danger, and that danger can grow to appalling levels if they have engaged in perverse behavior such as increased State control, increased taxes, or increased debt. Those democracies have become ineffective, but also very close to economic and political collapse. Only systems that learn the lessons of history, exposed in the previous pages, have the possibility of navigating an ocean of life where storms like the coronavirus occasionally appear.

In addition, the manipulative, morally devoid, and damaging nature of the globalist agenda has been exposed as rarely before. Globalism—and small nationalisms like the Catalonian one—has been ineffective, while governments with a strong patriotic base have provided much more effective responses. Without a doubt, the coronavirus crisis has served, among many other things, to bring to light realities that, in a very risky way, are hidden, denied, or replaced by lies of a universal dimension. Hopefully this time mankind will learn the lesson.

Miami, in confinement, April 2020.